AF644382

ĀRYA SAYYAMBHAVA'S

DAŚAVAIKĀLIKA SŪTRA

(Dasaveyalia Sutta)

Translation and notes
By
KASTUR CHAND LALWANI

MOTILAL BANARSIDASS
DELHI : : VARANASI : : PATNA

©MOTILAL BANARSIDASS

Indological Publishers and Booksellers
Head Office : BUNGALOW ROAD, JAWAHARNAGAR, DELHI-7
Branches : 1. CHOWK, VARANASI (U.P)
2. ASHOK RAJ PATH (OPP. PATNA COLLEGE), PATNA-4 (BIHAR)

First Edition : Delhi 1973

Printed in India

BY SHANTILAL JAIN, AT SHRI JAINENDRA PRESS BUNGALOW ROAD, JAWAHARNAGAR, DELHI-7, AND PUBLISHED BY SUNDARLAL JAIN FOR MOTILAL BANARSIDASS, BUNGALOW ROAD, JAWAHARNAGAR, DELHI-7

Dedicated
to
the sacred memory
of
my beloved parents

CONTENTS

FOREWORD

1. In a religion where right conduct is as important as right faith and right knowledge, it is but expected that there should exist some authoritative texts prescribing in detail what is expected to be the content of that conduct. In fact, there are a number of Jaina *Sūtras* dealing with this subject and *Dasaveyālia* or *Daśavaikālika Sūtra* is one, and perhaps now the foremost one, among them. It lays down in a very concise, yet complete, form the code of conduct that a monk of the *śramaṇa* order, who is covetous of perfection, enlightenment and liberation, is expected to follow, and, at the same time, it gives in a precise and competent manner the fundamental tenets of Jainism.

2. Compiled around B.C. 429, the text of *Daśavaikālika Sūtra* is divided into ten chapters called *adhyayanas* or prescriptions (for details, see Summary) and has two appendices called *cūlikās*. If the prescriptions are just ten, no more, no less, it is a sheer accident, and if anyone from among the western readers of this translation derives a notion about the comparability of these ten prescriptions with other traditional things like the Ten Commandments of the Hebrews, he needs be disabused on the ground that the two have neither a comparable base nor a common end. The ten prescriptions of *Daśavaikālika* are unique and independent, and have a different motivation.

3. Keeping in view the speed at which the work was completed with a limited objective (see para 5 below), it should not be expected to be an original production. As the experts have identified, chapters IV, V and VII have been based on *Ātma-pravāda*, *Karma-pravāda* and *Sutya-pravāda* respectively, and the remaining chapters on *Pratyākhyāna-pūrva*. Chapters I through III, V through VIII and X are written in verse, one of the few Jaina canonical texts in verse form, and this form has been wholly retained in the English translation in order to give the reader the spirit of the original.

4. The author, Ārya Sayyambhava (Sejjambhava, Śreyambhava), was in direct spiritual line of descent from Śramaṇa Bhagavān Mahāvīra and was the fifth in the line. To trace this spiritual line upwards, Sejjambhava was the disciple of Ārya Prabhava, who in turn was the disciple of Ārya Jambu. Ārya Jambu was the disciple of the great Suddharman, the most accredited author of the *Jaina Āgamas*, and immediate disciple of Śramaṇa Bhagavān Mahāvīra. There is, therefore, reason to believe that Sayyambhava lived at a time when the tradition created by the great master was still a living force, and this has been transmitted to posterity through his work.

5. Although the *Jaina Āgamas* are the works of the *gaṇadhara (s)*, who were the direct disciples of the *tīrthaṅkara*, in consequence of which the *Āgamas* are believed to have preserved and transmitted the exact words of the master, *Daśavaikālika Sūtra* is one of the few exceptions, which, though not the work of a *gaṇadhara*, enjoys the dignified status of a canon and is one of the four *mūla-sūtras* or fundamental canonical texts of the Svetāmbara Jainas. As to the immediate impetus to its writing, so goes the story that Sayyambhava was inspired by the vision of a *Jina* (victor) and renounced his life as a householder. At the time of this incident, his wife was pregnant. After he had left, she gave birth to a male child, who was named Māṇaka. When the boy was eight, he enquired about his father, and when he was told that he had become a monk and *ācārya* of the *śramaṇa* order, he set out at once in search of him, found him out and joined the holy order under him. But the father knew that the boy had only a short span of six months to live on this earth, and so to help him within the time at his disposal, he prepared the short course of *Daśavaikālika* to teach his son. The story goes further that this served its purprse, and Māṇaka, on completion of his short life on earth, was assigned to a celestial abode in the upper sphere. The importance of *Daśavaikālika* can be understood from the fact that soon after its production, it replaced the *Ācārāṅga Sūtra* in the curriculum of study by the monks, and has been a constant source of inspiration and guidance for them during the past 2300 years.

6. Scholars have differed as to the meaning of the title. To the translator, who holds that the producer of a work is free to call it by whatever name he pleases, the whole thing appears like a puerile issue; but since the point has been made, he must state that he does not agree with the interpretation which sees in the title a reading assignment of the whole *Sūtra* in ten afternoon sessions, nor does he consider it palatable to conceive with other scholars who are of opinion that the father so named the work, because it was meant for the use of the son at the afternoon-hour of his short life. Taking a clue from the *Sūtra-kṛtāṅga*, it would be more appropriate to conceive the ten prescriptions as ten 'piercers' (*vaidārika*) which help to pierce through the obstruction created by anger, pride, attachment, greed, etc. A less convincing suggestion would be that '*veyālia*' is the name of the meter in which the verses are written; but the whole *Sūtra* is not in the verse form. Beyond this, the translator would take the stand—'what's there in a name ?' and resolve the controversy.

7. As to the literary style of the *Sūtra*, it has already been stated that barring Chapters IV and IX, all others are in verse form—not a very usual thing for the Jaina *Sūtras*. The literary standard of the Jaina *Sūtras* has often been a victim of adverse comment even by authorities like Winternitz, who have found it less readable and more prosaic and repetitive than the Buddhist canons. But on this some explanation is possible. The scope for literary elegance and flight of imagination is created in a work which is purely literary, and not scientific, and has its root in the sentiment of the writer. But it is questionable if any of the Jaina *Sūtras* has been inspired by literary need or sentiment or any other comparable thing. For most of them, the subject-matter has been the hard code of conduct for the monks, as in the case of *Ācārāṅga* or *Daśavaikālika*, or purely 'scientific' topics as in the case of *Bhagavatī Sūtra Prajñāpaṇā Sūtra* and many others. The discussion, therefore, does not cater to the hunger of a lover of literature and the reading of the Jaina *Sūtras* even by the monks is permitted only on the attainment of necessary

maturity by them. This is no fault of the Jaina *Sūtras*. For, how much readable to a layman is a modern work on Calculus or Cosmic Ray? But then it must be conceded that being in verse form, *Daśavaikālika* at least provides a very wholesome relief to the reader, and some of its verses, particularly those pertaining to religion and religious life, have attained a high level of elegance and literary beauty. Though a later work, *Daśavaikālika* upholds the dignity and tradition of the Jaina canonical texts.

8. When conduct is considered, the almost exclusive focus of a Jaina *Sūtra* is on the conduct of the monks, and there is very sound reason behind it. The spiritual end of human life—which is very rarely attained—is to earn liberation from the bondage of *karma* through rigorous practices, precautions and penances, and in this exertion on the road to liberation, monkhood is the most essential first-step. This is perfectly consistent with the Jaina stand on determinism, which is anti-deterministic, and which enjoins that perfection, enlightenment and liberation do not come as gift, grace or favour from any superior quarter but have to be acquired by personal exertions. Now, in the Jaina order, a place has been given to lay followers, male as well as female, and for these, too, there are rigorous prescriptions to regulate life; but the lay followers work under severe limitations, and even if they be true to religion, and very near to perfection as householders, they cannot be wholly perfected and liberated till they join the holy order. The prescriptions for the lay followers are, therefore, more in the nature of inducement to join the holy order rather than 'piercers' themselves, which are only available to the monks.

9. This being so, it should logically follow that the sole aim of the monk's life is to attain perfection, enlightenment and liberation, and such an austere life as that of a monk could not have been used for a lesser purpose. There are indeed items like social service, social reform, literary productions, even scholarship, in which monks of certain religious orders are involved, but, for a Jaina monk, these are not ends in themselves, but mere deviations from the goal, and these do not strictly fall in his curriculum. There are people in the society,

outside the holy order, who can take care of these, and as for social service and social reform, the whole agency of the 'welfare state' is now directed to that end. But, well, where the issue is the liberation of the soul from the bondage of *karma*, this is an exclusive privilege of the monk and none else. The monk alone can strive for it, and if his exertions are sincere and well directed, the goal is his.

10. It may be asked why conduct is so very important for the monk who has already renounced worldly life and has taken the vow to conform strictly to the holy words. The reason is apparent. To conform strictly to the code of conduct requires a long discipline under suitable guidance and only when this is done, a monk is fixed in right conduct. To explain this difference between a beginner-monk and a veteran, the Jainas have two words, *chadmasta* and *sthavira*, the former being one who is in the process of being fixed in right conduct, though not yet wholly free from lapse, while the latter is one who is fixed in right conduct. Things were perhaps a little easier at the time of Śramaṇa Bhagavān Mahāvīra, when the monks led a wholly detached life, wandered over long distances and regions, and halted outside a city in some park or *yakṣa*'s abode. They visited the city only to beg, and as soon as this was done, they withdrew. It was even then considered necessary to lay down elaborate prescriptions for the monks so that their outward journey and return journey, the mode of begging and acceptance and the mode of giving, the post-begging behaviour of the monks, etc.,—all these could be rendered free from lapses incurred due to omission and commission. If conduct was necessary then when the monks usually kept at a distance from the society, it is all the more so now when the majority of the monks are planted in the very midst of society and are all the time exposed to influences emanating from it.

11. Some may even ask if the goal of monkhood, viz., liberation from the bondage of *karma*, is still available in this age. These may go the whole length to quote from the *Kalpa Sūtra* the following lines, with Hermann Jacobi's footnote as follows :

> "The Venerable Ascetic Mahāvīra instituted two epochs in his capacity as a Maker of an end; the epoch relating to generations, and the epoch relating to psychical condition; in the third generation ended the former epoch and in the fourth year of his *Kevali-ship* the latter." (*Sūtra* 146)

In the course of his footnote, Jacobi writes,

> "The meaning of this rather dark passage is, according to the commentary, that after three generations of disciples (Vīra*, Sudharma, Jambu) nobody reached *nirvāṇa*; and after the fourth year of Mahāvīra's *Kevali-ship*, nobody entered the path which ends in final liberation, so that all persons who before that moment had not advanced in the way to final liberation, will not reach that state, though they may obtain the *Kevalam* by their austerities and exemplary conduct."

12. Thus if the attainment of liberation is no longer the goal now, the major attraction for monkhood evaporates. This would, however, be taking too pessimistic a view of the situation In the humble opinion of the translator, even though it may be conceded that there are more limitations on the physical and spiritual capacity of man now than in the past, these have been more than adequately compensated by a steady rise in the intelligence quotient (IQ), so that if one is really serious, there is nothing in the *Daśavaikālika* prescriptions which one may not be able to practice. If limitations are there, there are facilities too,--facilities that were unthinkable 2300, even 200, years back—facilities of the entire treasure of canonical texts and holy words being at our disposal, from which we can freely drink, and derive inspiration.

13. During the past 200 years or so, life has changed so much that the traditional culture is virtually on the defensive against the onslaught of the technological culture. What C. P. N. Snow has written about 'two cultures' in the context of the western society is now fast becoming a reality even in

*Vīra was not a disciple.

this country. Technology has created complications for life, the simple care-free life of the traditional people having been replaced by one whose very basis is care, tension, competitive ostentation, externalism and the sleeping pill. When life is such, to many, any religious prescription has become meaningless, incongruous and anachronistic in this age. The socialists have gone to the length of denouncing religion as opium. This may, in a sense, be correct. But then a moment comes in life when man becomes conscious of the hollowness of the materialistic culture, when he is caught up in a stagnation of his own making and is a prey of his own machines. At such a moment, he turns from the technological to the traditional culture to seek solace and peace. This is why the prescriptions of religion, though old, are not yet too old to be discarded as impotent and worthless. They are still a living word, not replaced by anything more enchanting and more noble, so that they are still a beacon-light to show the way, sure, unfailing and infallible. Religion is opium indeed, but it is opium put to a good end by millions over millennia.

14. The ideal upheld by *Daśavaikālika Sūtra* is that of free monkhood, an *aṇagara* (homeless), a *nirgrantha* (tie-free), wherein a monk lives freely like the air and blows freely like the wind. The ideal is so admirably introduced in the opening chapter of the *Sūtra* which uses the analogy of the bee that collects honey without either molesting the flower or even leaving a trace of its touch on it. The analogy is carried further in a later chapter when the monk's search for food is compared with the cow's grazing, which is free from care or discrimination, from one end of the field to the other end, at paces slow and gentle, without care or concern. These indeed are very noble analogies which one cannot read without a feeling of ecstasy. At the same time, one may be left conjecturing how far the ideal is upheld by the monks in contemporary life.

15. This translation of *Daśavaikālika Sūtra* has been the outcome of a flight of fancy on the part of the translator, and has had no serious contemplation behind. It was in 1968, just before the summer vacation in May-June, that the voluminous work by Muni Nāgarāja and his team of Terapanth (a

sect of Śvetāmbara Jainas) monks fell in his hands, and he decided to try a hand at its translation during the holidays. The work started in the second week of May, and by intensive labour, was completed on June 19. Looking back on this brief period of six weeks, the translator has the gratification to record that the period has been most stimulating and rewarding for him. Muni Nāgarāja's has been a work of great industry and patience, in which the learned monks have amassed the vast treasure of commentaries by way of footnotes, and, exhaustive notes by the monks themselves. The work will surely save a lot of time and trouble for the future researchers. The present work is, however, no verbatim translation of the Terapanth version, nor was it ever intended to be so. Since the translator set for himself the maxim, '*strictly according to the text*', from the very start, he kept clear of the wilderness of the conflicting commentaries, though he consulted them all, and adhered strictly to the text of the *Sūtra*, and he has striven to give what has appeared to him to be the most convincing and the most logical. Such a single interpretation helps a large majority of readers, particulary readers through English medium, for whom it becomes a trying job to make a selection from conflicting commentaries. At many places, again, he has been obliged to differ from the interpretations given by the Terapanth monks. But then it is always the advantage of the democratic way of life that even when we differ, we do not lose appreciation for each other's work. For the rest, the translator owes a great debt of gratitude to the team of aforesaid monks whose work provided him with the inspiration to enter into an arena which, by his professional specialisation, he could not claim to be his own. But for this inspiration, this work would never have seen the light of the day. The task has not been very difficult, since, unlike the *Sūtras* of Pāṇini and Patañjali and many other Hindu scholars, which are invariably in the form of terse formulae, the Jaina *Sūtras*, by and large, are very elaborate texts, which it is not very difficult to follow even independent of the commentaries. The works of the commentators help at places, but one has to be carefully selective in using them.

16. If the decision to translate the work was the outcome of a flight of fancy, it was no less so when it was decided to put it to the press. Writing is an agreeable pastime for one who writes, but not everything scribbled can be put in print, the more so when the writing on a *Sūtra* has been done by one who is neither a professional Jainologist nor a Jaina monk. But as luck would have it, the work of publication is now in the most competent hands. For the benefit of the readers, particularly for those who are hard-pressed for time and patience, a summary of the ten prescriptions is given at the beginning in the words of the late Dr. B. C. Law.

12 Duff Street, Calcutta 6
May 1, 1973.

K. C. Lalwani

DAŚAVAIKĀLIKA SŪTRA—A SUMMARY

Dr. B. C. Law*

Prescription One entitled 'The Blossoms of the Tree' states that religion which is the highest bliss is made up of non-injury, self-restraint and penance.

Prescription Two deals with monkhood which is the first effective step on the road to liberation. This is attained on the renunciation of the mundane life, followed by faith in, and practice of restraint which is the central theme of this Prescription. A person can be said to have renounced the world when he casts away enjoyments and gives up pleasures. A monk should control his passions regarding a woman; he should mortify himself, abandon all idea of delicacy, overcome desires, remove the feeling of hatred, and control all passions. Above all, he should be steadfast in his goal. It is interesting that the need for steadfastness in a monk comes from the mouth of a worthy woman, Rajimati, herself a nun of the Order, to fix her own brother-in-law, a monk, who had been somewhat shaken by her sight in a lonely cave.

Prescription Three deals with the behaviour or conduct of a monk, and is specific and categorical as to what he is to discard in order to remain fixed in right conduct. The following list gives an idea of the things that are to be discarded by a monk :

(1) a thing done knowingly and purposely for the monk;
(2) a thing bought knowingly and purposely for the monk;
(3) a thing brought knowingly and purposely for the monk from a distant place;
(4) food collection, accumulation and intake at night hours;
(5) using scents, flowers, fan and cosmetics;
(6) playing at counters;
(7) playing at dice;

* Adapted from B. C. Law, *Some Jaina Canonical Sūtras*, Royal Asiatic Society, Bombay, 1949.

(8) bearing umbrella except in permitted situations;
(9) wearing shoes;
(10) kindling fire;
(11) washing body parts or the whole body;
(12) accepting service from the householders;
(13) remembering past pleasures when ill;
(14) using ginger, sugar-cane which is unripe, sea-salt, purgative, collyrium painting the teeth, decorating the body, etc.

A monk who is free from worldly ties, is well-acquainted with the ways of *karma* influx, is well-restrained towards all classes of living beings, and has a complete command over his sense-organs. He has courage and contentment, and exposes himself to the hot and cold blasts of weather to harden his physical frame.

Prescription Four which deals with non-violence or non-injury prescribes a through examination of the presence of life in various living things of the world. Life exists wherever there is growth with or without movement (since Jaina biology contains elaborate account of living beings in inferior category which have no movement). A monk ought to see that no violence of any kind, by mind, speech or body, is done to any living being, howsoever small, insignificant, even invisible. The six Great Vows, including the one that prescribes the avoidance of food intake at night, are enunciated at length. The following are of special interest :

(1) knowledge of life and non-life, on which depends the chain of successive higher steps to spiritual progress, made up of the knowledge of various resulting future conditions;
(2) knowledge of freedom and bondage;
(3) disgust with worldly life;
(4) abandonment of pleasure;
(5) state of homelessness;
(6) practice of restraint;
(7) removal of *karma* dirt;
(8) right knowledge and faith;
(9) knowledge of world and non-world;
(10) rock-like motionless state of the body;

(11) annihilation of *karma*;
(12) state of perfection.

Prescription Five deals with selection of right food, including search for it, the mode of acceptance, of bringing, and of sharing, with the fellow monks. The monk is required to move out for food at the proper time and return at the proper time. When out to beg food, he should not sit anywhere, nor begin to narrate any religious story; he should not recline anywhere against anything, but move at normal pace, perfectly undejected, and wholly unconcerned. In this connection, the analogy of the cow is particularly appropriate which should suggest a total lack of selectiveness in a monk about the household from which to accept, and also about the food, provided it fulfils the criterion of being of right type, and is rightly served. Other details in the Prescription are that a monk moving for this purpose in a village or a town should be completely free from mental agitation as to the outcome of the quest. He should carefully walk, avoiding all living beings, water, pits, and uneven surfaces. He should not go near brothels, avoid a dog or a recently-delivered cow on the road. Moving for food in all families without distinction, he should not walk fast, nor indulge in gossip or laughter. He should not look at windows and baths, and avoid from a safe distance private chambers of kings, householders and policemen. He should stand within an area permissible for strangers. Then follow elaborate prescriptions about the manner of offering, which makes right food acceptable for a monk, about the mode of carrying food to the monk's abode, and then about the mode of eating it.

Prescription Six entitled 'On Determining Conduct' is a brilliant exposition on *dharma*. A monk should not tell a lie,, nor indulge in sex behaviour. He does not take anything howsoever insignificant, without begging. In other words, begging is an important ingredient of mendicancy. The earthly possessions of a monk consist of a pot, a blanket and a duster, and even for these, he is free from attachment. He never injures anyone himself, nor orders another to do so, nor approves it in others. He should observe rigorous restraint avoiding four things which are unfit for him, viz., food, residence, garment and utensils. Unfit is food, drink or water prepared, bought or brought from a distance. Bringing food from a distance may cause pain to the householder, and so it is prohibited. He should not take food, drink or water in a metallic vessel, or an earthen jug. He should not use chair, cot, stool or arm-chair. While begging, he is not allowed to sit, except under very exceptional circumstances. Self-introspection and regular confession to a superior monk or the head of the order is a regular part of his life.

Prescription Seven is entitled 'Purifying Speech'. A monk should not speak what is not true, what is only partly true, what is false, and what is not fit to be said by the enlightened monks. He should avoid harsh or harmful words. He should not speak with definiteness about a thing he does not know. He should not address a woman improperly, not talk of cows fit to be milked, and similar other things. He should not address a house-holder in any one of the following ways : 'sit down', 'come', 'go', etc. A wise monk should always speak what is conducive to greater good.

Prescription Eight entitled 'Conduct' gives further details on restraint, which is all important. For, a monk by definition is one who is endowed with right knowledge and right conduct, and who is fixed in restraint and penance. He should not use a seat full of dust. He should not take cold water, ice or hail-stone. He should only take hot water which is made life-free by boiling, or water which is made life-free by any other means. He should never kindle, stir or extinguish fire. He should not trample under his feet seeds which may germinate, fungus or moss, nor should he cut grass. Particular care on his part is necessary for eight subtle forms of life : water-life, flour-life, subtle germs, subtle insects, subtle moss-life, subtle seed-life, subtle plant-life and subtle egg-life. A self-restrained monk, vigilant and well-composed in all his sense-organs, should exert himself with all his mental powers. He should keep clean his begging bowl, blanket, place of residence, place of depositing excreta, etc.

Prescription Nine deals with 'Humility' which is very important for the monk's conduct. It is stated that just as the root is the first important thing in a tree which helps to give it trunk, branches, twigs, leaves, flowers, fruits and ultimately juice, so humility is the very root of a monk's conduct whose ultimate juice is liberation. The prescription is that a monk should not despise others, nor should he be puffed up. Anger ends love, conceit destroys humility, deceit destroys friendship, and avarice destroys everything. Anger is to be destroyed by calmness, conceit by softness, deceit by straightforwardness, and avarice by contentment. A monk should behave modestly before other monks of superior merit. He should not sleep too much, nor show delight in secret talks, but devote all his activities to the practice of monkhood. In case of doubt, he should seek clarification from his learned preceptor. He should sit near him by keeping in proper position his hands, feet and body, with senses well under control. He should speak in a language which is perfect, distinct and unambiguous. He should not laugh at a sage, not talk to a householder about astrology, meaning of a dream, etc. He should not narrate any story to a woman in a lonely place, nor should he gaze at a woman who is well-adorned. To a monk seeking liberation of the soul, decoration, contact with women and dainty food are all like deadly poison. He should not feel attachment for lovely things. A monk who is devoted to religious study and to good meditation, who is engaged in penance, and is not sinful gets rid of sins committed in previous births. He should not show disrespect to his preceptor on any ground; for, the displeasure of the preceptor leads to the mental delusion of the pupil. Sense of dishonour, campassion, self-restraint and celibacy lead to the purification of the soul. It is by obedience that one quickly gets fame and learning. An ignorant man who is proud, deceitful and bad-tongued is driven down the currrent of worldly life like a log of wood in a stream. A monk should have a lower bed than that of his preceptor, sit lower and walk behind him. He should adore the preceptor's feet with humility. If perchance he touches the preceptor's body or garment, he should say, "Forgive me, sir; I shall not repeat it again." A monk should not blame anyone in his absence, nor use harsh words at any time. A monk who neither blames nor disdains anyone, who has conquered conceit and anger, is really a worthy person. A wise monk, on hearing the excellent precepts of a worthy preceptor, roams, as rooted in the Great Vows, guarded in protections, and freed from passions.

Prescription Ten deals with four items of spiritual ecstasy, viz., humility, study of scriptures, penance and conduct. Included under modesty are : listening attentively to instructions, understanding them thoroughly, conforming strictly to spiritual learning, and being totally free from conceit. A monk should not practise penance for securing an interest in this world, but he should do so for solely one end, viz., the destruction of *karma* bondage, past as well as potential. Besides, he must have right faith. There is prescription for the monk to take up a motionless position, rock-like, not to be afraid of any dreadful sight and to be perfectly unconcerned about the body in the practice of penance. A real monk is he who recognises birth and death to be the real dangers, who exercises control over his limbs and sense-organs, who cares not for his life, and who is always steady and above deceit. He is neither proud of caste nor of form, gain or earning, but is wholly devoted to spiritual meditation.

पढमं अज्झयणं (प्रथममध्ययनम्)
PRESCRIPTION ONE

दुमपुप्फिया (द्रुमपुष्पिका)
The Blossoms of the Tree

(On the nature and distinctiveness of spirituality and the greatness of holy men)

धम्मो मंगलमुक्किट्ठं अहिंसा संजमो तवो ।
देवा वि तं नमंसंति जस्स धम्मे सया मणो ॥१॥

धर्मः मङ्गलमुत्कृष्टम् अहिंसा संयमः तपः ।
देवा अपि तं नमस्यन्ति यस्य धर्मे सदा मनः ॥१॥

Spirituality is the highest weal—
Non-violence, Restraint and Penance
Even the gods revere a mind
Always set on the Spiritual Path. 1

Note : *Dhammo (dharma)* is spirituality whose object is ultimate liberation. *Maṅgala* or weal is of two types, *dravya-maṅgala* and *bhāva-maṅgala*. The former is transcient but the latter is real. Religion or spirituality is the only real weal and hence the highest weal, since it liberates. The term 'non-violence' has to be understood in a very comprehensive sense as it has been conceived by the Jainas. *Saṁjamo (saṁyamaḥ)* or restraint is a state of equanimity and freedom from malice or attachment. *Tavo (tapas)* or penance stands for a religious practice that ends the eight types of *karma*-bondage.

(On alms-taking or mādhukarī—the habit of the bee)

जहा दुमस्स पुप्फेसु भमरो आवियइ रसं ।
न य पुप्फं किलामेइ सो य पीणेइ अप्पयं ॥२॥

यथा द्रुमस्य पुष्पेषु भ्रमर आपिबति रसम् ।
न च पुष्पं क्लामयति स च प्रीणाति आत्मकम् ॥२॥

एमेए समणा मुत्ता जे लाए संति साहुणो ।
विहंगमा व पुप्फेसु दाणभत्तेसणे रया ॥३॥

एवमेते श्रमणा मुक्ता ये लोके सन्ति साधवः ।
विहंगमा इव पुष्पेषु दानभक्तैषणे रताः ॥३॥

As the black bee drinks gently
Of the blossoms of the tree
Hurting not the flowers
And yet drinks deep
To its heart's content, 2

So on earth, bee-like,
śramaṇa, **liberated, recluse**
Seeks food pure, with caution due
Offered wilfully by a devotee-donor 3

Note : Just as a bee gathers honey from many flowers, not leaning heavily on any, so does a *śramaṇa* accept a morsel out of food prepared by the devotee-donor for his domestic use. Aptly it is called *mādhukarī* or habit of the bee. A *dāṇa-bhatta (dāna-bhakta)* or devotee-donor is one who gives a portion of his own food to the *sādhu*. The idea is that the flower contains honey, nomatter whether the bee partakes of it or not. And even when it does, it does so gently so that the flower bears not the mark of molestation. The initiative comes from the side of the taker (the bee) and not from that of the donor (the flower). This point is emphasized in the *sūtra* in *esaṇe rayā (eṣaṇe ratā)* which means that it is the *sādhu* who is on the look-out for food, that it is he who is to find a devotee-donor with pure food and with a willingness to part with a morsel out of it and that the *sādhu* has to accept and use it with prescribed caution. Nomatter whether a *śramaṇa* approaches him for food or not, a devotee-giver prepares food for his own use and even when he wilfully gives a portion out of it, when approached, he does so without a feeling of deprivation.

वयं च वित्तिं लब्भामो न य कोई उवहम्मई ।
अहागडेसु रीयंति पुप्फेसु भमरा जहा ॥४॥

वयं च वृत्तिं लप्स्यामहे न च कोऽप्युपहन्यते ।
यथाकृतेषु रीयन्ते पुष्पेषु भ्रमरा यथा ॥४॥

Like bees from flowers
Shall we derive subsistence from alms
Out of what is readymade
Without burden on anyone. 4

Note : The word *ahāgaḍesu* (*yathākṛteṣu*) in the *sūtra* stands for 'readymade'. Since the house-holder prepares food, etc., for his own use, these are readymade so far as the *sādhu* is concerned, like honey in the flower for the bee.

महुकारसमा बुद्धा जे भवंति अणिस्सिया ।
नाणापिंडरया दंता तेण वुच्चंति साहुणो ॥५॥

त्ति बेमि

मधुकर-समा बुद्धा ये भवन्त्यनिश्रिताः ।
नाना-पिण्ड-रता दान्ताः तेन उच्यन्ते साधवः ॥५॥

इति ब्रवीमि

The enlightened, bee-like,
Leans not wholly on one source
But accepts food from householders many
Conquering self by self,
Sādhus **are they. 5**

So say I.

Note : *Aṇissiyā*—(*aniśritāḥ*) in the *sūtra* means one who leans not exclusively on one source, like the bee leaning not on a single flower. The word *nāṇāpiṇḍarayā (nānā-piṇḍa-ratā)* has several implications. First, it means that a *sādhu* accepts a morsel from each house-holder and thus collects his requisite food from many sources rather than one. Second, it means that his conduct in almstaking is regulated by many rules as to where, from whom, how and what he should accept. Third, he accepts diverse types of coarse and none-too-dainty stuff. The word *dantā (dāntāḥ)* very frequently occurs throughout the *sūtra*. The Lord very much desired that a *sādhu* should be a *dānta, i. e.,* one who controls his self by restraint and penance. According to Śīlaṅkācārya the word *dānta* stands for one who has complete control over his sense-organs.

बीयं अज्झयणं (द्वितीयमध्ययनम्)
PRESCRIPTION TWO

सामण्णपुव्वयं (श्रामण्यपूर्वकम्)
Faith in and practice of Restraint

(*On attachment and the way of the śramaṇa*)

कहं नु कुज्जा सामण्णं जो कामे न निवारए ।
पए पए विसीयंतो संकप्पस्स वसं गओ ॥१॥

कथं नु कुर्याच्छ्रामण्यं यः कामान्न निवारयेत् ।
पदे पदे विषीदन् संकल्पस्य वशं गतः ॥१॥

How indeed does he follow the way of a ***śramaṇa***
Who checks not perseverence to attachment
Is over-powered by sadness at every step
And is himself a prey of desires. 1

Note : In our worldly life, we persevere to attachment. When we have some portion of an object, we run after more of it. This is *saṁkappa (saṁkalpa)* or perseverence to attachment. Sadness is caused by a lack of taste for restraint and spirituality.

(*On the renouncer*)

वत्थगन्धमलंकारं इत्थीओ सयणाणि य ।
अच्छन्दा जे न भुंजन्ति न से चाइ त्ति वुच्चइ ॥२॥

वस्त्रं गन्धम् अलङ्कारं स्त्रियः शयनानि च ।
अच्छन्दा ये न भुञ्जन्ति न ते त्यागिन इत्युच्यते ॥२॥

He who enjoys not apparel
Nor perfume nor jewellery
Nor woman nor a cosy cushion
Because he has them not,
Renouncer is not he—
So it is said. 2

Note : *Acchandā* signifies absence—'he has them not'. Either he has not them in his possession at this moment or he has not them at all. This is wretchedness, not renunciation.

जे य कन्ते पिए भोए लद्धे विपिट्ठिकुव्वई ।
साहीणे चयइ भोए से हु चाइ त्ति वुच्चइ ॥३॥

यश्च कान्तान् प्रियान् भोगान् लब्धान् विपृष्ठीकरोति ।
स्वाधीनः त्यजति भोगान् स एव त्यागीत्युच्यते ॥३॥

A renouncer is he, so it is said
Who wilfully accepts not
Pleasures approaching, covetable and dear
But straight turns his back 3

Note : A renouncer renounces all pleasures that are available to him as a free agent acting on the basis of enlightenment. One can renounce only when one has; one who has not cannot renounce.

(On the means to restrain desire and attachment)

समाए पेहाए परिव्वयंतो सिया मणो निस्सरई बहिद्धा ।
न सा महं नोवि अहं पि तीसे इच्चेव ताओ विणएज्ज रागं ॥४॥

समया प्रेक्षया परिव्रजन् (तस्य) स्यान्मनो निःसरति बहिस्तात् ।
न सा मम नापि अहमपि तस्या इत्येवं तस्या विनयेद् रागम् ॥४॥

While wondering with detachment full
Perchance the mind goes astray
'That's not mine, nor I of this'—
So considering, one desirous of liberation
Allays momentary weakness. 4

Note : Such a thing is not usually to occur. But, despite the attachment to equanimity, if, because of the coming up of the *mohanīya karma*, such a deviation perchance forces its way, then the *sādhu* should know how to overcome this momentary weakness. 'This is not mine, nor I of this'—this is the normal line of thinking to set the mind on a differentiation which, when stretched to its logical extreme, would even differentiate the body from the soul. At this stage, the recluse realises that his body is different from his real self.

आयावयाही चय सोउमल्लं कामे कमाही कमियं खु दुक्खं ।
छिन्दाहि दोसं विणएज्ज रागं एवं सुही होहिसि संपराए ।।५।।

आतापय त्यज सौकुमार्यं कामान् क्राम क्रान्तं खलु दुःखम् ।
छिन्धि दोषं विनयेद् रागं एवं सुखी भविष्यसि सम्पराये ।।५।।

Roast thy Self in penance
Give up dainty joys
Overcome all desires and attachments
And then indeed are ye free from misery.
Tear off resistance (to penance)
Hoot out attachments (to objects)
And positive happiness is thine on earth. 5

Note : Four are the ways to overcome misery : (1) roasting oneself in penance : (2) giving up dainty joys which impart transcient pleasure; (3) conquering all desires and (4) overcoming all attachments. The earthly existence is full of misery; but by practising these exercises a recluse can attain positive happiness on earth.

(More on restraint : a simile)

पक्खन्दे जलियं जोइं धूमकेउं दुरासयं ।
नेच्छंति वन्तयं भोत्तुं कुले जाया अगन्धणे ।।६।।

प्रस्कन्दन्ति ज्वलितं ज्योतिषं धूमकेतुं दुरासदम् ।
नेच्छन्ति वान्तकं भोक्तुं कुले जाता अगन्धने ।।६।।

Serpents of *agandhana* specie
Prefer immolation in dreary flame
To swallowing back venom
They have emitted once. 6

Note : Two species of serpents have been distinguished. Of these, those belonging to the *agandhana* specie are steadfast in their habits. They never take back the venom they have emitted once, even though this may cost their life. Not so with those that belong to the *gandhana* variety who drink back their own poison when overpowered by charms or *mantras*. The *agandhana* serpent is ignorant; he has no knowledge of spiritualism. His reaction is purely instinctive. It is not so with us who know the words of knowledge uttered by the liberated souls. How do we dare then retake objects of pleasure that we discarded once ?

(Rājīmatī advises Rathanemi)

धिरत्थु ते जसोकामी जो तं जीवियकारणा ।
वन्तं इच्छसि आवेउं सेयं ते मरणं भवे ।।७।।

धिगस्तु त्वां यशस्कामिन् यस्त्वं जीवितकारणात् ।
वान्तमिच्छस्यापातुं श्रेयस्ते मरणं भवेत् ।।७।।

अहं च भोयरायस्स तं चऽसि अन्धगवण्हिणो ।
मा कुले गन्धणा होमो संजमं निहुओ चर ।।८।।

अहं च भोजराजस्य त्वं चाऽसि अन्धकवृष्णेः ।
मा कुले गन्धनौ भूव संयमं निभृतश्चर ।।८।।

'Oh ye, seeker of attachment, fie on thy fame
That ye, for earthly living, desireth,
Swallowing back things that ye discarded once.
Better give up thy life. 7

'Daughter am I of King Bhoja
And ye the son of Andhaka-Vṛṣṇi
May we not be like
Serpents of the *agandhana* **specie!**
Practise ye restraint undisturbed. 8

Note : The idea is that both are born in great houses and hence, conscious of their brilliant heredity, they cannot be less steadfast. That will not only undermine their personal stature but also the good name of the family.

जइ तं काहिसि भावं जा जा दच्छसि नारिश्रो ।
वायाइद्धो व्व हडो श्रट्ठियप्पा भविस्ससि ॥९॥

यदि त्वं करिष्यसि भावं या या द्रक्ष्यसि नारीः ।
वाताविद्ध इव हटः अस्थितात्मा भविष्यसि ॥९॥

'If on seeing a woman
Yieldeth ye to passion
Then like a '*haṭa*' plant swept by a gust
Shall ye be restless in thy soul.' 9

Note: The dialogue is occasioned by a chance meeting between the two in a cave where Rathanemi was practising penance and Rājīmatī who was battered by rain and storm and was unaware of his presence there entered into it to protect herself. Her clothes were all drenched and so she took them out to dry them when her eyes suddenly fell on a passionate Rathanemi. Hence this advice. *Haṭa* is a type of vegetation, alternatively called '*hada*'. Perhaps this was a flora growing in water with roots not very firm. Rājīmatī tenders a priceless advice here. The world is full of women. Now, if the sight of a woman evokes passion, the soul can never rest. Such a soul will be driven on earth like a water-plant in the gust of wind. There had been a sudden temptation in Rathanemi at the sight of the nude figure of Rājīmatī. So he had to be restrained.

(Rathanemi regains restraint)

तीसे सो वयणं सोच्चा संजयाए सुभासियं ।
श्रंकुसेण जहा नागो धम्मे संपडिवाइश्रो ॥१०॥

तस्याः स वचनं श्रुत्वा संयतायाः सुभाषितम् ।
श्रंकुशेन यथा नागो धर्मे सम्प्रतिपादितः ॥१०॥

On hearing these piercing words
Uttered by the restrained lady
Rathanemi became so fixed in *dharma*
Like an elephant hit by iron hook. 10

So say I

(On the duty of the enlightened)

एवं करेन्ति संबुद्धा पण्डिया पवियक्खणा ।
विणियट्टन्ति भोगेसु जहा से पुरिसोत्तमो ।।११।।

त्ति बेमि ।

एवं कुर्वन्ति सम्बुद्धाः पण्डिताः प्रविचक्षणाः ।
विनिवर्तन्ते भोगेभ्यः यथा स पुरुषोत्तमः ।।११।।

इति ब्रवीमि ।

So do behave the enlightened
Savant and recoiler from sin.
Rebound these from pleasure,
Like Rathanemi, the best among men. 11

Note : Rathanemi has been called the best among men because he not only regained restraint at the words of Rājīmatī but never thereafter deviated from his path till he acquired the highest knowledge and, restraining all influx and efflux, attained the most coveted realm of the liberated souls. This episode is also recorded at length in the *Uttarādhyayana Sūtra*.

———

तइयं अज्झयणं (तृतीयमध्ययनम्)
PRESCRIPTION THREE

खुड्डियायारकहा (क्षुल्लकाचारकथा)

Knowledge of ācāra (behaviour) and anācāra (misbehaviour)

(On the determination of what is not to be done by the nirgrantha or tie-free)

संजमे सुट्ठिअप्पाणं विप्पमुक्काण ताइणं ।
तेसिमेयमणाइण्णं निग्गंथाण महेसिणं ॥१॥

संयमे सुस्थितात्मनां विप्रमुक्तानां त्रायिणाम् ।
तेषामेतदनाचीर्णं निर्ग्रन्थानां महर्षीणाम् ॥१॥

Those who are well-set in restraint
Totally liberated, saviours of souls
To such tie-free *ṛṣis* **great,**
The *nirgranthas*
Are the following a taboo.
(To accept not, to use not, to perform not.) 1

Note: The implication is that these prohibitions have never been violated by the *nirgranthas* in the past, so they will never be violated in future. They accept not, use not and perform not the prohibited things. In other words, in the prescription, no concession or relaxation is envisaged in any sense. Those who deviate on any plea cease to be *nirgranthas*.

उद्देसियं कीयगडं नियागमभिहडाणि य ।
राइभत्ते सिणाणे य गंधमल्ले य वीयणे ॥२॥

श्रौद्देशिकं क्रीतकृतं नित्याग्रमभिहृतानि च ।
रात्रिभक्तं स्नानं च गन्धमाल्ये च वीजनम् ॥२॥

Things prepared for a *nirgrantha*
Or bought or made
Or offered with propitiation everyday
Or brought to his presence from afar
Taking food at night
Or dip (at any time)
Smelling or besmearing perfumes
Decorating self with garland
Or enjoying the use of a fan 2

Note: 'Things prepared' may include food, clothing and residence and if they are prepared for the *nirgranthas*, they are unacceptable. The word *uddesiyaṁ* (*auddeśikam*) in the *sūtra* stands for 'with the object of'. A monk is prohibited to accept a thing bought for him or a thing made for him out of purchased material. Taking food from the same household everyday with or without invitation is taboo. This practice is discouraged lest this should induce a householder to prepare extra food for the monk. Equally prohibited is the practice of encouraging a householder to prepare food in his house and bring it for the monk. It is for the monk to be on the look-out for the food and when got, to accept only a morsel out of it when all prescribed conditions about purity, etc., are duly met. Taking food at night has four implications as follows: (1) bringing food today and taking it tomorrow during the day avoiding the night; (2) bringing it during the day and taking it at night; (3) bringing it at night but taking it during the day: and (4) bringing and taking food during the night. The prohibition covers all these four modes of behaviour. Other prohibitions about bath, perfumes, etc., are intended to fix one to hard life of penance.

सन्निही गिहिमत्ते य रायपिंडे किमिच्छए ।
संबाहणा दंतपहोयणा य संपुच्छणा देहपलोयणा य ।।३।।

संनिधिर्गृह्यमत्रं च राजपिण्डः किमिच्छकः ।
सम्बाधनं दन्तप्रधावनं च संप्रच्छनं देहप्रलोकनं च ।।३।।

Collecting food for later use
Or using vessels of householder
Seeking from the monarch
Or accepting offerings from him
Rubbing the body
Or applying stick to teeth to cleanse
Towelling (or enquirying welfare)
Or viewing limbs in a looking-glass. 3

Note: Accumulation or collection of food is a total prohibition for the monk. With the Śvetāmbara monk some accumulation of food can be seen but it is reduced to a minimum and is perhaps not inconsistent with a rigorous living. Seeking food, favour or object from the king is an essential prohibition. Rubbing(pressing?) the body gives some pleasure to the bones, muscles, skin-holes and is hence prohibited. Applying stick to the teeth is prohibited, since it may involve molestation of the twigs or branches of a tree. The word *sampucchaṇā—(Sampracchanam)* has been rendered as 'towelling'; but it may as well have alternative meanings such as asking somebody about his own limbs or parts thereof which he himself cannot see, or enquiring about the householder's welfare or asking if somebody has done something or not or simply asking an ailing man if he has recovered.

अट्ठावए य नालीय छत्तस्स य धारणट्ठाए ।
तेगिच्छं पाणहा पाए समारंभं च जोइणो ।।४।।

अष्टापदश्च नालिका छत्रस्य च धारणमनर्थाय ।
चैकित्स्यमुपानहौ पादयोः समारम्भश्च ज्योतिषः ॥४॥

Playing chess or gambling for gain
Covering head with umbrella for no reason
Administering medicine to self
As an antidote or cure of illness
Using shoes or lighting a flame 4

Note: All sorts of gambling is prohibited but not the use of umbrella when there is sufficient reason for its application. Under certain circumstances of illness or physical debility the use of umbrella is permitted, but not surely for physical comfort or as a protection against the sun or rain. Not only is the taking of medicine prohibited, even the whole of medical science has been considered to be a sinful science. Shoes include both leather stuff and the wooden sandals. Fire has been ranked as a sinful instrument—more sinful than even iron-made weapons—since it burns all and in all directions.

सेज्जायरपिंडं च आसंदीपलियंकए ।
गिहंतरनिसेज्जा य गायस्सुव्वट्टणाणि य ॥५॥

शय्यातरपिण्डश्च आसन्दी-पर्यङ्कः ।
गृहान्तरनिषद्या च गात्रस्योद्वर्तनानि च ॥५॥

To accept board from one
Who provides lodging
Or to accept a seat on cot or cushion
In the abode of a house-holder
When collecting alms
Or rubbing paste on the limbs. 5

Note: Board should include food, drink, vessels, wear, etc. When accepting shelter from anyone, the monk should not take food, etc., from him. Some commentators go to the length of extending the prohibition to as many as seven adjacent houses. Accepting a seat in the house-holder's abode when the monk has gone in for collecting alms is a sinful act. He must accept food standing and retrace his steps.

गिहिणो वेयावडियं जा य आजीववित्तिया ।
तत्तानिव्वुडभोइत्तं आउरस्सरणाणि य ॥६॥

गृहिणो वैयापृत्यं या च आजीववृत्तिता ।
तप्ताऽनिर्वृतं भोजित्वं आतुरस्मरणानि च ॥६॥

Or sharing own food with a house-holder
Or serving him in a gainful way
Or accepting food on the basis of means
Enjoying food or water of mixed boil
Or browsing on things enjoyed in the past. 6

Note: Sharing his own food with the house-holder or rendering him any gainful service is each a sinful act. So is the accepting of food on the basis of means which are five, *vij*., caste, sect, industry, profession and sex. When a Brahmin seeks offering by citing that he is a Brahmin, he is using his caste for a sinful act. Likewise with sect, profession, etc. A monk seeks a morsel of food as a monk and never by citing his caste, sex, etc.,which may enkindle a sectarian compassion or be a sort of appeal to a professional brotherhood. A thing is *sacit* when it has life within; when there is no life in it, it becomes *acit*. Now, when a thing is not duly boiled, only a part of its life may go out and a part may still remain. Such a thing is half boiled or is of mixed boil, and to take it is an act of impiety. The commentators are particularly specific about the sort of water that a monk may accept. It must boil thrice on fire before it is acceptable to the monk. Even boiled water when removed from the oven starts regaining living organisms after sometime and hence becomes as bad as half-boiled water and so is not acceptable. Browsing on things enjoyed in the past is also a sinful act. For, it may generate a comparison, pleasant or painful, that is not consistent with spiritual life.

मूलए सिंगबेरे य उच्छुखंडे अनिव्वुडे ।
कंदे मूले य सच्चित्ते फले बीए य आमए ।।७।।

मूलकं श्रृंगबेरं च इक्षुखण्डमनिर्वृतम् ।
कन्दो मूलं च सचित्तं फलं बीजं चामकम् ।।७।।

सोवच्चले सिंधवे लोणे रोमालोणे य आमए ।
सामुद्दे पंसुखारे य कालालोणे य आमए ।।८।।

सौवर्चलं सैन्धवं लवणं रुमालवणं चामकम् ।
सामुद्रं पांशुक्षारश्च काललवणं चामकम् ।।८।।

धूव-णेत्ति वमणे य वत्थीकम्मविरेयणे ।
अंजणे दंतवणे य गायाभंगविभूसणे ।।९।।

धूमनेत्रं वमनञ्च वस्तिकर्मविरेचने ।
अंजनं दन्तवणं च गात्राभ्यङ्गविभूषणे ।।९।।

Eating or accepting raddish
Tender and fresh
Ginger or sugar-cane
Or trunk or root which is green
Fruit unripe or half-ripe corn. 7

And salt of six types
Sovaccale (sauvarcala) **or** *sindhave (saindhava)*
From mine or from sea
Alkali coming out of earth
Or salt that is black 8

Or possession of a smoking pipe
And all devices crude
To safeguard body from illness
Or restore health
Or preserve beauty and strength
Dyeing the eyes
Or applying stick to teeth
Oiling the body
Or bedecking it with ornaments. 9

Note : Three crude devices have been envisaged in the *sūtra,* viz., *vamaṇa* or vomiting, *vatthikamma (vasti-karma)* or inhaling oil and *vireyaṇa (virecana)* or taking purgative. They may be applied as cures or antedotes or simply for preserving beauty and strength. Whatever the purpose, their use is sinful.

सव्वमेयमणाइण्णं निग्गंथाण महेसिणं ।
संजमम्मि य जुत्ताणं लहुभूयविहारिणं ॥१०॥

सर्वमेतदनाचीर्णं निर्ग्रन्थानां महर्षीणाम् ।
संयमे च युक्तानां लघुभूतविहारिणाम् ॥१०॥

For great sages of *nirgrantha* order
Who are rooted in restraint
And are free like the wind
Are all these a taboo. 10

(On the Traits of a Nirgrantha)

पंचासवपरिन्नाया तिगुत्ता छसु संजया ।
पंचनिग्गहणा धीरा निग्गंथा उज्जुदंसिणो ॥११॥

परिज्ञातपञ्चाश्रवाः त्रिगुप्ताः षट्सु संयताः ।
पञ्चनिग्रहणा धीरा निर्ग्रन्था ऋजुदर्शिनः ॥११॥

The restrainer of the five *āsravas*
The observer of the *guptis* three
The most vigilant about six organisms
And conqueror of senses five
Calm, untied is he
Rooted deep in equanimity. 11

Note : The *pañcāsava* or the five *āsravas* which are influx of *karma*-bondage include falsehood including wrong vision, non-restraint, indifference or lack of interest in spiritual matters, *kaṣāyas* like anger, attachment, greed, etc., and *yoga* or involvement. Mind, Body and Speech,—these three need proper control which is *gupti*, called separately as *mana-gupti*, *vak-gupti* and *kāya-gupti*. When the soul is protected against the three, it is *tri-gutta (tri-gupta)* or thrice-protected. Six types of organisms or cells discussed in the Jaina texts, some of which are yet to be traced by biological sciences, are earth-cells, water-cells, air-cells, fire-cells and vegetation-cells plus *trasa* which are organisms with two or more senses. The conqueror of five senses has been called *pañca-niggahi (pañca-nigrahī)*. Equanimity is the surest road to liberation. One who is rooted in equanimity is called *ujjudaṁsi* or *ṛju-darśī*. *Ṛju* stands for *sama* (equanimity). He who keeps equanimity in view and discriminates not self from the rest is a *ṛju-darśī*.

(On the Nirgranthas' exposure to Seasons)

आयावयंति गिम्हेसु हेमंतेसु अवाउडा ।
वासासु पडिसंलीणा संजया सुसमाहिया ।।१२।।

आतापयन्ति ग्रीष्मेषु हेमन्तेष्वप्रावृताः ।
वर्षासु प्रतिसंलीनाः संयताः सुसमाहिताः ।।१२।।

The most advanced among the *nirgranthas*
Expose in summer to the blazing sun
And unclad to chill during the fall
And stick to a place when it rains. 12

Note : The variation in spiritual practice according to seasonal change is significant. An ordinary man behaves contrary to the seasonal pattern, covering himself in woollens during the fall and seeking shelter in an air-conditioned apartment during hot months. Not so with a *nirgrantha* who exposes himself to have the full exposure of the season on his person. Thus in summer he faces the full blast of the sun standing on one leg. In winter he is totally or partially unclad.

(On Object of Spiritual Striving : Liberation from Misery)

परीसहरिऊदंता धुयमोहा जिइंदिया ।
सव्वदुक्खप्पहीणट्ठा पक्कमंति महेसिणो ॥१३॥

दान्तपरिषहरिपवः धुतमोहा जितेन्द्रियाः ।
सर्वदुःखप्रहाणार्थं प्रक्रामन्ति महर्षयः ॥१३॥

Bearing all hardships
And sweeping off binding affections
And over-powering—the *Maharṣis*
Strive heroically to end all misery. 13

Note : Twenty-two hardships have been noted in the Jaina scriptures which have to be borne by all the pilgrims on the road to spiritual progress. These are hunger, thirst, etc. Misery is caused by birth and death. The liberated souls are no longer born. So they overcome the highest of miseries.

(On the Consequences of Restraint : Direct and Indirect)

दुक्कराइं करेत्ताणं दुस्सहाइं सहेत्तु य ।
केइत्थ देवलोएसु केई सिज्झंति नीरया ॥१४॥

दुष्कराणि कृत्वा दुस्सहानि सहित्वा च ।
केचिदत्र देवलोकेषु केचित् सिध्यन्ति नीरजसः ॥१४॥

खवित्ता पुव्वकम्माइं संजमेण तवेण य ।
सिद्धिमग्गमणुप्पत्ता ताइणो परिनिव्वुडा ॥१५॥
त्ति बेमि

क्षपयित्वा पूर्वकर्माणि संयमेन तपसा च ।
सिद्धिमार्गमनुप्राप्ता त्रायिणः परिनिर्वृताः ॥१५॥
इति ब्रवीमि ।

Thus practising the most difficult
And bearing the most unbearable
Freed from influxes and effluxes
Some *nirgranthas* repair to the abode of gods
While others attain liberation
Entering the domain of the *siddhas*. 14

Saviour of self and others, the *nirgranthas*
Exhaust past sins by penance and restraint
Take road to liberation
And are liberated in the end. 15

Note : The two *sūtras* are highly significant in so far as they indicate the consequences, direct and indirect, of the practice of restraint. If by practising the most difficult and bearing the most unbearable, the *śramaṇa* can restrain both influxes and effluxes in this birth, he may attain total liberation. If, however, these practices remain incomplete before he discards his mortal frame, then he goes to the abode of gods, returns to the earth again in the midst of a favourable family climate where his further progress to liberation is facilitated. The *śramaṇa* may thus pass through several births before he is ripe for total liberation. But with extreme hardship he may be liberated in one birth. Quoted below on this theme is a parallel *sūtra* from the *Uttarādhyayana* :

khabettā pubbakammāiṁ saṁjameṇa tabeṇa ya
sabbadukkhapahiṇaṭṭha pakkamanti mahesiṇo
khabittā pubbakammāiṁ saṁjameṇa tabeṇa ya
jayaghosa-vijayaghosā siddhiṃ pattā aṇuttaram.

———

चउत्थं अज्झयणं (चतुर्थमध्ययनम्)
PRESCRIPTION FOUR

छज्जीवणिया (षड्जीवनिका)
Restraint of Self and of other Lives (*Jivas*)

Section One—On Life (Jīva) & Non-life (Ajīva)

सुयं मे आउसं ! तेणं भगवया एवमक्खायं—इह खलु छज्जीव-णिया नामज्झयणं समणेणं भगवया महावीरेणं कासवेणं पवेइया सुयक्खाया सुपन्नत्ता सेयं मे अहिज्जिउं अज्झयणं धम्मपन्नत्ती ।।१।।

श्रुतं मया आयुष्मन् ! तेन भगवता एवमाख्यातम् – इह खलु षड् जीवनिका नामाध्ययनं श्रमणेन भगवता महावीरेण काश्यपेन प्रवेदिता स्वाख्याता सुप्रज्ञप्ता श्रेयो मेऽध्येतुमध्ययनं धर्मप्रज्ञप्तिः ।।१।।

Oh Long-lived one, have I heard
The Lord having had said thus:
In the *nirgrantha* discourses
The Study entitled *chajivaṇiyā*
Is well-acquired with the knowledge of liberated
Well-said and observed well
By Lord Mahavira, of Kasyapa *gotra*,
Foremost among the *śramaṇas*.
So it behoves me for the highest weal
To undertake the study of this discourse. 1

Note: 'Long-lived one' is the usual mode of addressing the competent disciples, who are mature enough to receive a spiritual discourse from the Master. To acquire the entire spiritual discipline, a very long life-span is required. Perhaps that is the reason why the word *āusaṁ (āyuṣman)* or long-lived one is deliberately used in the *sūtra*. Mahavira has been addressed as *bhagavāna* because of his acquisition of spiritual perfection that transcends everything. *Paveiyā* (*praveditā*) is well acquired or properly acquired and this is possible with the knowledge of the liberated. But it is also *suyakkhāyā* (*su-ākhyātā*), i.e., well said or communicated since it is of highest good to all that are desirous of spiritual liberation. It is also well observed. If it is known but not observed, then it does not remain *supannattā (su-prajñaptā)*. *Dhamma-pannattī* is another name for *chajjivaṇiyā* which deals with six living bodies.

कयरा खलु सा छज्जीवणिया नामज्झयणं समणेणं भगवया महावीरेणं कासवेणं पवेइया सुयक्खाया सुपन्नत्त सेयं मे अहिज्जिउं अज्झयणं धम्मपन्नती ॥२॥

कतरा खलु सा षड्जीवनिका नामाध्ययनं श्रमणेन भगवता महावीरेण काश्यपेन प्रवेदिता स्वाख्याता सुप्रज्ञप्ता श्रेयो मेऽध्येतुमध्ययनं धर्म्मप्रज्ञप्तिः ॥२॥

इमा खलु सा छज्जीवणिया नामज्झयणं समणेणं भगवया महावीरेणं कासवेणं पवेइया सुयक्खाया सुपन्नत्ता सेयं मे अहिज्जिउं अज्झयणं धम्मपन्नत्ती तं जहा—पुढविकाइया आउकाइया तेउकाइया वाउकाइया वणस्सकाइया तसकाइया ॥३॥

इयं खलु सा षड्जीवनिका नामाध्ययनं श्रमणेन भगवता महावीरेण काश्यपेन प्रवेदिता स्वाख्याता सुप्रज्ञप्ता श्रेयो मेऽध्येतुमध्ययनं धर्मप्रज्ञप्तिः तद्यथा—पृथिविकायिकाः अप्कायिकाः तेजस्कायिकाः वायुकायिकाः वनस्पतिकायिकाः त्रसकायिकाः ॥३॥

Which one is that study entitled *Chajjivaṇiyā*
That has been acquired & communicated well
And well-observed by foremost of *śramaṇas*
Lord Mahavira, of the Kasyapa *gotra*,

The study of which paves
The way to highest weal for me ? 2

The study of *Chajjivaniyā*
Which is so well acquired and transmitted well
And well observed by the leading-most *śramaṇa*
Lord Mahavira of the Kasyapa *gotra*
And which is of highest spiritual import to me
Containing as it does
The knowledge of six living bodies—
Of earth, water, air and fire
And of vegetation and other bodies organic. 3

Note : Earth bodies or cells consist of elements like soil, sand, minerals, etc.; water bodies or cells consist of mist, dew, rain, etc.; fire bodies or cells consist of fire, lightning, etc.; air bodies or cells consist of various kinds of wind; vegetable bodies consist of all flora; and organic bodies consist of all physical organs beginning from the smallest organs like bacteria to birds, beasts, and the most developed of them like men, gods etc.

(On Six Types of Living Beings)

पुढवी चित्तमंतमक्खाया अणेगजीवा पुढोसत्ता अन्नत्थ सत्थपरिणएणं ॥४॥

पृथिवी चित्तवती आख्याता अनेकजीवा पृथक्सत्त्वा अन्यत्र शस्त्र-परिणतायाः ॥४॥

Leaving aside earth that is turned barren
And hence can shelter no living being
The rest is full of lives
That are innumerable
And have each an identity. 4

Note: *Sattha* or *śastra* in the *sūtra* should mean weapons that hurt or kill denuding a place of living being. For this we have used the word 'barren'. *Śastras* may be of three types, viz., *svakāya śastra*, *parakāya śastra* and *ubhayakāya śastra*. When one kind of soil kills the earth-bodies of another soil, the soil itself becomes an instrument of annihilation, and hence *svakāya śastra*. When water, fire or wind destroys life in the earth, they become instruments of annihilation of the second type. If the two may be combined we have weapons of the third type. The outcome in any case is that a particular sector may become devoid of life on account of the self operation of these instruments. The implication is that leaving aside these areas, the rest is full of lives and consciousness in the plural sense. The earth is conceived as *cittamanta (cittavatī)*, i.e., full of conscious organisms, innumerable and separate. Not only this : even a particle of soil, a drop of water, a gust of wind or a spark of fire contains innumerable lives. This is consistent with the basic Jaina attitude that life is not one but innumerable. Some non-Jaina schools try to strike a middle path by suggesting that lives may be innumerable like the reflections of the moon in disturbed water but all of them emerge from one transcendental being. The Jainas, however, do not accept even this. According to them, lives are not only innumerable, they are always and eternally separate.

आऊ चित्तमंतमक्खाया अणेगजीवा पुढोसत्ता अन्नत्थ सत्थपरिणएणं ॥५॥

आपश्चित्तवत्यः आख्याता अनेकजीवा पृथक्सत्त्वा अन्यत्र शस्त्रपरिणताभ्यः ॥५॥

तेऊ चित्तमंतमक्खाया अणेगजीवा पुढोसत्ता अन्नत्थ सत्थपरिणएणं ॥६॥

तेजश्चित्तवत् आख्यातम् अनेकजीवम् पृथक्सत्त्वम् अन्यत्र शस्त्रपरिणतात् ॥६॥

वाऊ चित्तमंतमक्खाया अणेगजीवा पुढोसत्ता अन्नत्थ सत्थपरिणएणं ॥७॥

वायुश्चित्तवान् आख्यातः अनेकजीवः पृथक्सत्त्वः अन्यत्र शस्त्रपरिणतात् ॥७॥

वणस्सई चित्तमंतमक्खाया अणेगजीवा पुढोसत्ता अन्नत्थ सत्थपरिणएणं तं जहा—अग्गबीया मूलबीया पोरबीया खंधबीया बीयरुहा

सम्मुच्छिमा तणलया वणस्सइकाइया सबीया चित्तमंतमक्खाया अणेगजीवा पुढोसत्ता अन्नत्थ सत्थपरिणएणं ॥८॥

वनस्पतिश्चित्तवान् आख्यातः अनेकजीवः पृथक्सत्त्वः अन्यत्र शस्त्रपरिणतात् तद्यथा—अग्रबीजाः मूलबीजाः पर्वबीजाः स्कन्धबीजाः बीजरूहा सम्मूर्च्छिमाः तृणलताः वनस्पतिकायिकाः सबीजाः चित्तवन्त आख्याताः अनेकजीवाः पृथक्सत्त्वाः अन्यत्र शस्त्रपरिणतेभ्यः ॥८॥

Leaving aside water that is turned barren
The rest is the shelter of lives innumerable
That have a separate identity for each. 5

Leaving aside fire that is turned barren
The rest is the shelter of lives innumerable
That have a separate identity for each. 6

Leaving aside air that is turned barren
The rest is the shelter of lives innumerable
That have a separate identity for each. 7

Leaving aside flora that is turned barren
The rest is the shelter of lives innumerable
That have a separate identity for each.
Given below are the species :
Seeds that are tips or roots
Twig, trunk or seed
Or just seedless
Grass or creepers.
Leaving aside vegetation that is barren
Are considered flora till the stage of seed
Sheltering consciousness
And having lives innumerable
That have a separate identity for each. 8

Note: There are some flora whose tips serve as seeds; in other cases their roots serve the same purpose, e.g., potatoes. In some cases, such as sugarcane, twigs help procreation, while in others, the trunks shoot out the roots, as in the case of a banyan tree. In some cases, such as paddy and wheat, the corn is seed while in other cases there may be no seed at all. 'Grass and creeper' is a generic expression covering all species. The expression *sabiyā* (*sabījā*) which means 'flora till the stage of seed' needs explanation. In flora, ten elements may be distinguished as follows : root, portion just above root, trunk, skin, branch, twig, leaf, flower, fruit and seed. Starting at the root, the fruition is the seed. Hence the expression *sabiyā* covers all these ten stages.

से जे पुण इमे अणेगे बहवे तसा पाणा तं जहा—अंडया पोयया जराउया रसया संसेइमा सम्मुच्छिमा उब्भिया उववाइया। जेसिं केसिंचि पाणाणं अभिक्कंतं पडिक्कंतं संकुचियं पसारियं रुयं भंतं तसियं पलाइयं आगइगइविन्नाया जे य कीडपयंगा जा य कुंथु पिवीलिया सव्वे बेइंदिया सव्वे तेइंदिया सव्वे चउरिंदिया सव्वेपंचिंदिया सव्वे तिरिक्खजोणिया सव्वे नेरइया सव्वे मणुया सव्वे देवा सव्वे पाणा परमाहम्मिया एसो खलु छट्ठो जीवनिकाओ तसकाओ त्ति पवुच्चई ॥९॥

अथ ये पुनरिमे अनेके बहवः त्रसाः प्राणिनः तद्यथा—अण्डजाः पोतजाः जरायुजाः रसजाः संस्वेदजाः सम्मूर्च्छिमाः उद्भिजाः औपपातिकाः। येषां केषाञ्चित् प्राणिनाम् अभिक्रान्तम् प्रतिक्रान्तम् सङ्कुचितम् प्रसारितम् रुतम् भ्रान्तम् त्रस्तम् पलायितम् आगतिगतिविज्ञातारः ये च कीटपतङ्गाः याश्चकुंथुपिपीलिकाः सर्वे द्वीन्द्रियाः सर्वे त्रीन्द्रियाः सर्वे चतुरिन्द्रियाः सर्वे पञ्चेन्द्रियाः सर्वे तिर्यग्योनिकाः सर्वे नैरयिकाः सर्वे मनुजाः सर्वे देवाः सर्वे प्राणाः परमधार्मिकाः एष खलु षष्ठो जीवनिकायस्त्रसकाय इति प्रोच्यते ॥९॥

And these that are many
Multifarious organic lives
That may be born of eggs or of embryo
Or are covered with ovary at the time of birth

Or born in juicy substances
Or in sweat or by the impact of environment
Or insects bursting out from the earth
Or born of themselves, parentless.
All these living beings
That can move forward or backward
Contract, expand, yell and roam to and fro
Have fear or may run—
Actions are these—
And those with of without movement
Are they all organic (*trasa*)
And all those insects with two senses
And those having senses three, four or five
All the *tiryakas* and denizens of hells
All men, gods and living beings—
All are covetous of happiness.
Tasa (Trasakāya) **is the name**
Given to the sixth category of life. 9

Note : The organisms called *trasa* in the Jaina sacred texts are of many species and each specie contains innumerable lives. But the broad categories of *trasa* are (i) those that can move of their own volition and (ii) those who move but not of their own volition. Here the reference is to the former category. Juicy substance refers to curd, butter-milk, etc., which generate bacteria. Ants, flies, etc., are the products of environment. These have been called *sam-mucchimā* (*sam-mūrcchimā*) and are the outcome of the change of weather. Literally, the word covers those that are not born from a mother's womb, who grow and expand of themselves. *Sam-mucchimā* should also cover insects and bacteria growing in sweat, by the impact of environment or those bursting out from the earth. The beings that are born suddenly of themselves cover even gods who are the denizens of heavens and the *nārakiyas* who are the denizens of hells. *Parama* in the *sūtra* means the highest, i.e., happiness. That which is less than the highest is misery. The covetousness for happiness is a universal instinct in living beings.

(*Advice not to Chastise*)

इच्चेसिं छण्हं जीवनिकायाणं नेव सयं दंडंसमारंभेज्जा नेवन्नेहिं दंडं समारंभावेज्जा दंडं समारंभंते वि अन्ने न समणुजाणेज्जा जावज्जीवाए तिविहं तिविहेणं मणेणं वायाए काएणं न करेमि न कारवेमि करंतं पि अन्नं न समणुजाणामि तस्स भंते पडिक्कमामि निंदामि गरिहामि अप्पाणं वोसिरामि ॥१०॥

इत्येषां षण्णां जीवनिकायानां नैव स्वयं दण्डं समारभेत नैवान्यैर्दण्डं समारम्भयेत् दण्ड समारभमाणानप्यन्यान् न समनुजानीयात् यावज्जीवं त्रिविधं त्रिविधेन मनसा वाचा कायेन न करोमि न कारयामि कुर्वन्तमप्यन्यं न समनुजानामि तस्य भदन्त ! प्रतिक्रामामि निन्दामि गर्हे आत्मानं व्युत्सृजामि ॥१०॥

And to these six kinds of living beings
One should not administer chastisement
Nor order it, nor approve of it—
And that for good, and by three instruments:
Mind, Word and Deed—
I shall not myself do
Nor order nor approve of others doing
Bhante ! **My master !**
Desist I from chastisement
Committed in the past
I decry, I denounce
Dedicate I my soul. 10

Note : *Daṁḍaṁ-samārambhejjā* is chastisement by mind, word and deed that generates a state of misery or repentance. Instruments of chastisement are three, viz., mind, word and deed, and acts of chastisement are also three, viz., to do, to order and to approve of. *Bhante* is an addrees to the spiritual master. The word 'desist' stands for overcoming the past acts of chastisement overpowering the present and restraining the future. 'Decry' stands for a sort of self-confession or repentance and 'denunciation' is a state of preparedness against such deeds, past, present or future. 'Dedication' is to the path of liberation. The soul as such is neither high nor low: it is high or low according as it indulges in high or low deeds. Dedication helps to regain a total liberation from all deeds, high as well as low.

(*On Right Conduct or Cāritra-dharma*)

Already the disciple has denounced, decried and desisted from universal chastisment. This causes misery to the living beings. In the following *sūtras* he desists specifically from chastisement :

पढमे भंते ! महव्वए पाणाइवायाओ वेरमणं सव्वं भंते ! पाणाइवायं पच्चक्खामि—से सुहुमं वा बायरं वा तसं वा थावरं वा नेव सयं पाणे अइवाएज्जा नेवन्नेहिं पाणे अइवायावेज्जा पाणे अइवायंते वि अन्ने न समणुजाणेज्जा जावज्जीवाए तिविहं तिविहेणं मणेणं वायाए काएणं न करेमि न कारवेमि करंतं पि अन्नं न समणुजाणामि। तस्स भंते पडिक्कमामि निंदामि गरिहामि अप्पाणं वोसिरामि। पढमे भंते ! महव्वए उवट्ठिओमि सव्वाओ पाणाइवायाओ वेरमणं ॥११॥

प्रथमे भदन्त ! महाव्रते प्राणातिपाताद्विरमणम् । सर्वं भदन्त ! प्राणातिपातं प्रत्याख्यामि—अथ सूक्ष्मं वा बादरं वा त्रसं वा स्थावरं वा—नैव स्वयं प्राणानतिपातयामि नैवान्यैः प्राणानतिपातयामि प्राणानतिपातयतोप्यन्यान्न समनुजानामि । यावज्जीवं त्रिविधं त्रिविधेन मनसा वाचा कायेन न करोमि न कारयामि कुर्वन्तमप्यन्यं न समनुजानामि । तस्य भदन्त! प्रतिक्रामामि निन्दामि गर्हे आत्मानं व्युत्सृजामि ।

प्रथमे भदन्त ! महाव्रते उपस्थितोऽस्मि सर्वस्मात् प्राणातिपाताद्विरमणम् ॥११॥

Bhante !
The first Great Vow is
To desist from causing hurt to living beings
With full knowledge and devotion.

Bhante !
Desist I from all kinds of hurt
Caused to living beings
Be they minute or large
Mobile or without movement
Whoever may be living
Shall I not myself hurt
Nor order others to do so
Nor approve any so doing
And that for good—
By three instruments and modes three
—By Mind, Word and Deed
—I shall not do
Nor order nor approve.

Bhante !
I desist from hurt inflicted in the past
I decry, I denounce
Dedicate I my soul.

Bhante !
Present I my own self dedicated
Desisted from hurt to living beings
As in first Great Vow ordained. 11

Note : The word 'first' in the first Great Vow does not attribute to the vow a foremostness or leading-most-ness. All the five Great Vows are at par, none being either more or less important. But they have to be stated in some order and so first, second, etc. *Vrata* is *virati*, i.e., to desist. Hence all the *mahāvratas* are great vows to desist. This vow is total and rigorous *(mahā)* for a *śramaṇa* and partial or somewhat lenient *(aṇu)* for the laity. He who desists by three modes and three instruments does so in all in 49 combinations such as : perform not I by mind, order not I by mind, approve not I by mind, perform not I by mind and deed, order not I by mind and deed, approve not I by mind and deed, I do not approve not by mind, I do not approve not by deed, I do not approve not by word, etc., etc. These 49 multiplied by 3 i.e., past, present and future, will give 147 combinations which are called *bhaṅga* in Jaina texts. These 147 combinations cover all acts of hurt by mind, word and deed, done, ordered and approved, past, present and future. Any one practising these 147 combinations fulfils the first Great Vow.

अहावरे दोच्चे भंते ! महव्वए मुसावायाओ वेरमणं सव्वं भंते ! मुसावायं पच्चक्खामि—से कोहा वा लोहा वा भया वा हासा वा नेव सयं मुसं वएज्जा नेवन्नेहिं मुसं वायावेज्जा मुसं वयंते वि अन्ने न समणुजाणेज्जा जावज्जीवाए तिविहं तिविहेणं मणेणं वायाए काएणं न करेमि न कारवेमि करंतं पि अन्नं न समणुजाणामि। तस्सय भंते पडिक्कमामि निंदामि गरिहामि अप्पाणं वोसिरामि। दोच्चे भंते ! महव्वए उवट्ठिओमि सव्वाओ मुसावायाओ वेरमणं ॥१२॥

अथापरे द्वितीये भदन्त ! महाव्रते मृषावादाद्विरमणम्। सर्वं भदन्त ! मृषावादं प्रत्याख्यामि—अथ क्रोधाद्वा लोभाद्वा भयाद्वा हासाद्वा— नैव स्वयं मृषा वदामि नैवान्यैर्मृषा वादयामि मृषा वदतोप्यऽन्यान्न समनुजानामि यावज्जीवं त्रिविधं त्रिविधेन मनसा वाचा कायेन न करोमि न कारयामि कुर्वन्तमप्यन्यं न समनुजानामि। तस्य भदन्त ! प्रतिक्रामामि निन्दामि गर्हे आत्मानं व्युत्सृजामि।

द्वितीये भदन्त ! महाव्रते उपस्थितोऽस्मि सर्वस्माद् मृषावादाद्विरमणम् ॥१२॥

Bhante !
After this, in the second Great Vow

Desists one from uttering falsehood.

Bhante !
Desist I from all false utterances
By passion or greed
In fear or joke
Shall I not myself utter a lie
Nor cause others to do so
Nor approve of indulging in falsehood
And that for good—
By three instruments and modes three—
By Mind, Word and Deed
I shall not do nor order
Nor approve of others' doing.

Bhante !
I desist from falsehood uttered in the past
I decry, I denounce
Dedicate I my soul.
Bhante !
Restrained am I from falsehood
As in second Great Vow ordained. 12

Note : Falsehood may be of three types : (i) to deny what is, (ii) to establish what is not, and (iii) to alter the meaning.

अहावरे तच्चे भंते ! महव्वए अदिन्नादाणाओ वेरमणं सव्वं भंते अदिन्नादाणं पच्चक्खामि—से गामे वा नगरे वा रण्णे वा अप्पं वा बहुं वा अणुं वा थूलं वा चित्तमंतं वा अचित्तमंतं वा नेव सयं अदिन्नं गेण्हेज्जा नेवन्नेहिं अदिन्नं गेण्हावेज्जा अदिन्नं गेण्हंते वि अन्ने न समणुजाणेज्जा जावज्जीवाए तिविहं तिविहेणं मणेणं वायाए काएणं न करेमि न कारवेमि करंतं पि अन्नं न समणुजाणामि। तस्स भंते ! पडिक्कमामि निंदामि गरिहामि अप्पाणं वोसिरामि

तच्चे भंते ! महव्वए उवट्ठिओमि सव्वाओ अदिन्नादाणाओ वेरमणं ॥१३॥

अथापरे तृतीये भदन्त ! महाव्रते अदत्तादानाद्विरमणम् । सर्वं भदन्त ! अदत्तादानं प्रत्याख्यामि—अथ ग्रामे वा नगरे वा अरण्ये वा अल्पं वा बहुं वा अणुं वा स्थूलं वा चित्तवद्वा अचित्तवद्वा—नैव स्वयमदत्तं गृह्णामि नैवान्यैरदत्तं ग्राहयामि अदत्तं गृह्णतोऽप्यन्यान्न समनुजानामि यावज्जीवं त्रिविधं त्रिविधेन—मनसा वाचा कायेन न करोमि न कारयामि कुर्वन्तमप्यन्यं न समनुजानामि । तस्य भदन्त ! प्रतिक्रामामि निन्दामि गर्हे आत्मानं व्युत्सृजामि ।

तृतीये भदन्त ! महाव्रते उपस्थितोऽस्मि सर्वस्माददत्तादानाद्विरमणम् ॥१३॥

Bhante !
After this, in the third Great Vow
Is contained non-possession
Of a thing not wilfully bestowed.

Bhante !
Desist I from all unbestowed possessions
In forest, town or in countryside
Small or large, quantity or value
Minute or voluminous
Shall I not myslf accept
Nor order nor approve acceptance
Of objects unbestowed
And that for good—
By three instruments and modes three
By Mind, Word and Deed
I shall not take nor order
Nor approve of others taking.

Bhante !
I desist
From unbestowed gifts of the past
I decry, I denounce
Dedicate I my soul.

Bhante !
Restrained am I from gifts unbestowed
As in third Great Vow ordained. 13

अहावरे चउत्थे भंते ! महव्वए मेहुणाओ वेरमणं सव्वं भंते ! मेहुणं पच्चक्खामि—से दिव्वं वा माणुसं वा तिरिक्खजोणियं वा नेव सयं मेहुणं सेवेज्जा नेवन्नेहिं मेहुणं सेवावेज्जा मेहुणं सेवंते वि अन्ने न समणुजाणेज्जा जावज्जीवाए तिविहं तिविहेणं मणेणं वायाए काएणं न करेमि न कारवेमि करंतं पि अन्नं न समणुजाणामि । तस्स भंते ! पडिक्कमामि निंदामि गरिहामि अप्पाणं वोसिरामि ।

चउत्थे भंते ! महव्वए उवट्ठिओमि सव्वाओ मेहुणाओ वेरमणं ॥१४॥

अथापरे चतुर्थे भदन्त ! महाव्रते मैथुनाद्विरमणम् ! सर्वं भदन्त ! मैथुनं प्रत्याख्यामि—अथ दिव्यं वा मानुषं वा तिर्यग्यौनिकं वा—नैव स्वयं मैथुनं सेवे नैवान्यैर्मैथुनं सेवयामि मैथुनं सेवमानानप्यन्यान्न समनुजानामि यावज्जीवं त्रिविधं त्रिविधेन—मनसा वाचा कायेन न करोमि न कारयामि कुर्वन्तमप्यन्यं न समनुजानामि । तस्य भदन्त ! प्रतिक्रामामि निन्दामि गर्हे आत्मानं व्युत्सृजामि ।

चतुर्थे भदन्त ! महाव्रते उपस्थितोऽस्मि सर्वस्माद् मैथुनाद्विरमणम् ॥१४॥

Bhante !
After this, in the fourth Great Vow
Is contained cessation from sex.
Bhante !
Desist I from all kinds of sex
Of gods, men or beasts
Shall I not enjoy myself
Nor order nor approve
And that for good
By three instruments and modes three
By Mind, Word and Deed
I shall not enjoy nor order
Nor approve of others enjoying.
Bhante !
Desist I from sex enjoyed in the past
I decry, I denounce
Dedicate I my soul.
Bhante !
Restrained am I from all sex-pleasures
As in fourth Great Vow ordained. 14

अहावरे पंचमे भंते ! महव्वए परिग्गहाओ वेरमणं सव्वं भंते ! परिग्गहं पच्चक्खामि—से गामे वा नगरे वा रण्णे वा अप्पं वा बहुं वा अणुं वा थूलं वा चित्तमंतं वा अचित्तमंतं वा नेव सयं परिग्गहं परिगेण्हेज्जा नेवन्नेहिं परिग्गहं परिगेण्हावेज्जा परिग्गहं परिगेण्हंते वि अन्ने न समणुजाणेज्जा जावज्जीवाए तिविहं तिविहेणं मणेणं वायाए काएणं न करेमि न कारवेमि करंतं पि अन्नं न समणुजाणामि । तस्स भंते पडिक्कमामि निंदामि गरिहामि अप्पाणं वोसिरामि ।

पंचमे भंते ! महव्वए उवट्ठिओमि सव्वाओ परिग्गहाओ वेरमणं ॥१५॥

अथापरे पञ्चमे भदन्त ! महाव्रते परिग्रहाद्विरमणम् । सर्वं भदन्त ! परिग्रहं प्रत्याख्यामि—अथ ग्रामे वा नगरे वा अरण्ये वा अल्पं वा बहुं वा अणुं वा स्थूलं वा चित्तवन्तं वा अचित्तवन्तं वा—नैव स्वयं परिग्रहं परिगृह्णामि नैवान्यैः परिग्रहं परिग्राहयामि परिग्रहं परिगृह्णतोऽप्यन्यान्न समनुजानामि यावज्जीवं त्रिविधं त्रिविधेन—मनसा वाचा कायेन न करोमि न कारयामि कुर्वन्तमप्यन्यं न समनुजानामि । तस्य भदन्त ! प्रतिक्रामामि निन्दामि गर्हे आत्मानं व्युत्सृजामि ।

पञ्चमे भदन्त ! महाव्रते उपस्थितोऽस्मि सर्वस्माद् परिग्रहाद्विरमणम् ॥१५॥

Bhante !
After this, in the fifth Great Vow
Is contained renunciation of all interest
In mundane objects.
Bhante !
Desist I from all earthly objects
In forest, town or in countryside
Anywhere, little or more
Large or small
Living or non-living
Of any object shall I myself partake
Nor order nor approve of others partaking
And that for good—
By three instruments and modes three

By Mind, Word and Deed
I shall have no interest
Nor order nor approve of others having.
Bhante !
I desist from possessions past
I decry, I denounce
Dedicate I my soul.
Bhante !
Restrained am I from all possessions
As in fifth Great Vow ordained. 15

अहावरे छट्ठे भंते ! वए राईभोयणाओ वेरमणं सव्वं भंते ! राईभोयणं पच्चक्खामि—से असणं वा पाणं वा खाइमं वा साइमं वा नेव सयं राइं भुंजेज्जा नेवन्नेहिं राइं भुंजावेज्जा राइं भुंजते वि अन्ने न समणुजाणेज्जा जावज्जीवाए तिविहं तिविहेणं मणेणं वायाए काएणं न करेमि न कारवेमि करंतं पि अन्नं न समणुजाणामि। तस्स भंते ! पडिक्कमामि निंदामि गरिहामि अप्पाणं वोसिरामि।

छट्ठे भंते ! वए उवट्ठिओमि सव्वाओ राईभोयणाओ वेरमणं ॥१६॥

अथापरे षष्ठे भदन्त ! व्रते रात्रिभोजनाद्विरमणम्। सर्वं भदन्त ! रात्रिभोजनं प्रत्याख्यामि—अथ अशनं वा पानं वा खाद्यं वा स्वाद्यं वा—नैव स्वयं रात्रौ भुञ्जे नैवान्यान् रात्रौ भोजयामि रात्रौ भुञ्जानानप्यन्यान् न समनुजानामि यावज्जीवं त्रिविधं त्रिविधेन—मनसा वाचा कायेन न करोमि न कारयामि कुर्वन्तमप्यन्यं न समनुजानामि। तस्य भदन्त ! प्रतिक्रामामि निन्दामि गर्हे आत्मानं व्युत्सृजामि।

षष्ठे भदन्त ! व्रते उपस्थितोऽस्मि सर्वस्माद् रात्रिभोजनाद्विरमणम् ॥१६॥

Bhante !
After this, in the sixth Great Vow
Is contained cessation from food at night.
Bhante !
Renounce I all meal during the night
Edibles that appease hunger

Drinks or dishes heavy and tasty
Shall I not myself eat during the night
Nor order nor approve of others eating
And that for good—
By three instruments and modes three
By Mind, Word and Deed
I shall not eat,
Nor order nor approve of others so doing.
Bhante !
I desist from night-meals taken in the past
I decry, I denounce
Dedicate I my soul.
Bhante !
Refrained have I myself
From taking anything at night
As in sixth Great Vow ordained. 16

इच्चेयाइं पंच महव्वयाइं राईभोयणवेरमणछट्ठाइं अत्तहियट्ठ-याए उवसंपज्जित्ताणं विहरामि ॥१७॥

इत्येतानि पञ्च महाव्रतानि रात्रि-भोजन-विरमणषष्ठानि आत्महितार्थं उपसम्पद्य विहरामि ॥१७॥

For the welfare of my soul
Do I embrace these Great Vows five
And also the sixth
Which is denunciation of meal at night
And thus do I set out on my way. 17

Note : Welfare of the soul is the attainment of liberation from the bondage of deeds. The *śramaṇa* accepts these Great Vows in the presence of his spiritual master and then sets out on foot. This movement is an integral part of the spiritual discipline and hence of progress towards liberation. If this is not done, then, according to some authorities, there is a deviation from the Great Vows.

(On how to safeguard oneself from Violence)

से भिक्खू वा भिक्खुणी वा संजयविरयपडिहयपच्चक्खाय पावकम्मे दिया वा राओ वा एगओ वा परिसागओ वा सुत्ते वा जागरमाणे वा— से पुढविं वा भित्तिं वा सिलं वा लेलुं वा ससरक्खं वा कायं ससरक्खं वा वत्थं हत्थेण वा पाएण वा कट्ठेण वा किलिंचेण वा अंगुलियाए वा सलागाए वा सलागहत्थेण वा न आलिहेज्जा न विलिहेज्जा न घट्टेज्जा भिंदेज्जा अन्नं न आलिहावेज्जा न विलिहावेज्जा न घट्टावेज्जा न भिंदावेज्जा अन्नं आलिहंतं वा विलिहंतं वा घट्टंतं वा भिंदंतं वा न समणुजाणेज्जा जावज्जीवाए तिविहं तिविहेणं मणेणं वायाए काएणं न करेमि न कारवेमि करंतं पि अन्नं न समणुजाणामि । तस्स भंते ! पडिक्कमामि निंदामि गरिहामि अप्पाणं वोसिरामि ॥१८॥

स भिक्षुर्वा भिक्षुकी वा संयत-विरत-प्रतिहत-प्रत्याख्यातपापकर्मा दिवा वा रात्रौ वा एकको वा परिषद्गतो वा सुप्तो वा जाग्रद्वा—अथ पृथिवीं वा भित्तिं वा शिलां या लेष्टुं वा ससरक्षं वा कायं ससरक्षं वा वस्त्रं हस्तेन वा पादेन वा काष्ठेन वा कलिञ्चेन वा अङ्गुल्या वा शलाकया वा शलाका-हस्तेन वा—नालिखेत् न विलिखेत् न घट्टयेत् न भिन्द्यात् अन्येन नालेखयेत् न विलेखयेत् न घट्टयेत् न भेदयेत् अन्यमालिखन्तं वा विलिखन्तं वा घट्टयन्तं वा भिन्दन्तं वा न समनुजानीयात् यावज्जीवं त्रिविधं त्रिविधेन— मनसा वाचा कायेन न करोमि न कारयामि कुर्वन्तमप्यन्यं न समनुजानामि । तस्य भदन्त ! प्रतिक्रामामि निन्दामि गर्हे आत्मानं व्युत्सृजामि ॥१८॥

A monk or a nun
Who is well restrained
Desisted from all sinful acts
Protected against influxes and effluxes
Who neither in the day nor at night
When asleep or wide awake
Alone or in assemblage
Neither molests once nor repeats such acts
Nor moves nor divides
The earth, the mountain or the river coast
A lump of clay or a slab of stone
An object or a cloth having particles alive

By hand, leg or wood
By bamboo or finger or stick or broom
Nor orders such digging, or molesting
Moving or dividing,
Nor approves of these
And that for good—
By three instruments and modes three
By Mind, Word and Deed.
Neither shall I perform, nor order
nor approve.
Bhante !
Desist I from violence
To earth-bodies in the past
I decry, I denounce
Dedicate I my soul. 18

Note : Well-restrained is one who performs all the 17 restraints enumerated in the sacred books. There are effluxes and influxes of sinful acts which have to be checked by the monk. For, these perpetuate bondage and rebirth and thus delay liberation.

से भिक्खू वा भिक्खुणी वा संजयविरयपडिहयपच्चक्खायपावकम्मे दिया वा राम्रो वा एगम्रो वा परिसागम्रो वा सुत्ते वा जागरमाणे वा—से उदगं वा म्रोसं वा हिमं वा महियं वा करगं वा हरतणुगं वा सुद्धोदगं वा उदम्रोल्लं वा कायं उदम्रोल्लं वा वत्थं ससिणिद्धं वा कायं ससिणिद्धं वा वत्थं न म्रामुसेज्जा न संफुसेज्जा न म्रावीलेज्जा न पवीलेज्जा न म्रक्खोडेज्जा न पक्खोडेज्जा न म्रायावेज्जा न पयावेज्जा म्रन्नं न म्रामुसावेज्जा न संफुसावेज्जा न म्रावीलावेज्जा न पवीलावेज्जा न म्रक्खोडावेज्जा न पक्खोडावेज्जा न म्रायावेज्जा न पयावेज्जा म्रन्नं म्रामुसंतं वा संफुसंतं वा म्रावीलंतं वा पवीलंतं वा म्रक्खोडंतं वा पक्खोडंतं वा म्रायावंतं वा पयावंतं वा न समणुजाणेज्जा जावज्जीवाए तिविहं तिविहेणं मणेणं वायाए काएणं न करेमि न कारवेमि करंतं पि म्रन्नं न समणुजाणामि। तस्स भंते ! पडिक्कमामि निंदामि गरिहामि म्रप्पाणं वोसिरामि ॥१९॥

स भिक्षुर्वा भिक्षुकी वा संयत-विरत-प्रतिहत-प्रत्याख्यात-पापकर्मा दिवा वा रात्रौ वा एकको वा परिषद्गतो वा सुप्तो वा जाग्रद्वा—अथ उदकं वा 'ओसं' वा हिमं वा महिकां वा करकं वा 'हरतनुकं' वा शुद्धोदकं वा उदकार्द्रं वा कायं उदकार्द्रं वा वस्त्रं सस्निग्धं वा कायं सस्निग्धं वा वस्त्रं—नाऽऽमृशेत् न संस्पृशेत् नाऽऽपीडयेत् न प्रपीडयेत् नाऽऽस्फोटयेत् न प्रस्फोटयेत् नाऽऽतापयेत् न प्रतापयेत् अन्येन नाऽऽमर्शयेत् न संस्पर्शयेत् नाऽऽपीडयेत् न प्रपीडयेत् नाऽऽस्फोटयेत् न प्रस्फोटयेत् नाऽऽतापयेत् न प्रतापयेत् अन्यमामृशन्तं वा संस्पृशन्तं वा आपीडयन्तं वा प्रपीडयन्तं वा आस्फोटयन्तं वा प्रस्फोटयन्तं वा आतापयन्तं वा प्रतापयन्तं वा न समनुजानीयात् यावज्जीवं त्रिविधं त्रिविधेन—मनसा वाचा कायेन न करोमि न कारयामि कुर्वन्तमप्यन्यं न समनुजानामि । तस्य भदन्त ! प्रतिक्रामामि निन्दामि गर्हे आत्मानं व्युत्सृजामि ॥१६॥

A monk or a nun
Who is well restrained
Desisted from all sinful acts
Protected against influxes and effluxes
Who neither in the day nor at night
When asleep or wide awake
Alone or in assemblage
Touches not and presses not
Lashes not and dries not
Either once or time and again
Water (flowing on earth)
Dew or mist, snow or ice
Water in marshes or pouring from above
Objects or cloth drenched
Or body or garment wet
Nor orders
Such touching, pressing, lashing or
drying
Nor approves of such deeds by others
And that for good
By three instruments and modes three
By Mind, Word and Deed
Neither shall I do

Nor order nor approve.

Bhante !

Desist I from past violence to water-bodies

I decry, I denounce

Dedicate I my soul. 19

Note : Two types of water are distinguished, one earthly and the other heavenly. The former flows on the earth or emanates from the subterranean sources while the latter drops from the sky in some form. Pure water signifies the latter variety, Water in contact with the soil is usually impure. The idea is that the molestation of the water-bodies is not to be done either once or as a matter of habit.

से भिक्खू वा भिक्खुणी वा संजयविरयपडिहयपच्चक्खायपावकम्मे दिया वा राम्रो वा एगवो वा परिसागम्रो वा सुत्ते वा जागरमाणे वा— से ग्रगणि वा इंगालं वा मुम्मुरं वा अच्चिं वा जालं वा अलायं वा सुद्धागणि वा उक्कं वा न उंजेज्जा न घट्टेज्जा न उज्जालेज्जा न निव्वावेज्जा अन्नं न उंजावेज्जा न घट्टावेज्जा न उज्जालावेज्जा न निव्वावेज्जा अन्नं उंजतं वा घट्टंतं वा उज्जालंतं वा निव्वावंतं वा न समणुजाणेज्जा जावज्जीवाए तिविहं तिविहेणं मणेणं वायाए काएणं न करेमि न कारवेमि करंतं पि अन्नं न समणुजाणामि। तस्स भंते ! पडिक्कमामि निंदामि गरिहामि अप्पाणं वोसिरामि ॥२०॥

स भिक्षुर्वा भिक्षुकी वा संयत-विरत-प्रतिहत-प्रत्याख्यात-पापकर्मा दिवा वा रात्रौ वा एकको वा परिषद्गतो वा सुप्तो वा जाग्रद्वा—अथ अग्निं वा अङ्गारं वा मुर्मुरं वा अर्चिर्वा ज्वालां वा अलातं वा शुद्धाग्निं वा उल्कां वा— नोत्सिञ्चेत् न घट्टयेत् नोज्ज्वालयेत् न निर्वापयेत् अन्येन नोत्सेचयेत् न घट्टयेत् नोज्ज्वालयेत् न निर्वापयेत् अन्यमुत्सिञ्चन्तं वा घट्टयन्तं वा उज्ज्वालयन्तं वा निर्वापयन्तं वा न समनुजानीयात् यावज्जीवं त्रिविधं त्रिविधेन—मनसा वाचा कायेन न करोमि न कारयामि कुर्वन्तमप्यन्यं न समनुजानामि। तस्य भदन्त ! प्रतिक्रामामि निन्दामि गर्हे आत्मानं व्युत्सृजामि ॥२०॥

A monk or a nun
Who is well restrained
Desisted from all sinful acts
Protected against influxes and effluxes
Who neither in the day nor at night
When asleep or wide awake
Alone or in assemblage
Neither ignites nor fans
Nor flames nor wipes out
Fire or burning charcoal
Or husk aflame
Or the tip of a burning lamp
Or the flame, half-burning log
Fire pure, or lightning in the sky
Nor orders such acts by others
Nor approves of any one indulging in them
And that for good—
By three instruments and modes three
By Mind, Word and Deed
Neither shall I perform
Nor order nor approve.
Bhante !
Desist I from past violence to fire-bodies
I decry, I denounce
Dedicate I my soul. 20

Note : All types of fire beginning from ordinary flame to heavenly meteors are covered in the description and all these shelter fire-bodies. These are not to be molested in any way.

से भिक्खू वा भिक्खुणी वा संजयविरयपडिहयपच्चक्खायपावकम्मे दिया वा राम्रो वा एगम्रो वा परिसागम्रो वा सुत्ते वा जागरमाणे वा— से सिएण वा विहुयणेण वा तालियंटेण वा पत्तेण वा साहाए वा साहा- भंगेण वा पिहुणेण वा पिहुणहत्थेण वा चेलेण वा चेलकण्णेण वा हत्थेण वा मुहेण वा अप्पणो वा कायं बाहिरं वा वि पुग्गलं न फुमेज्जा

न वीएज्जा अन्नं न फुमावेज्जा न वीयावेज्जा अन्नं फुमंतं वा वीयंतं वा न समणुजाणेज्जा जावज्जीवाए तिविहं तिविहेणं मणेणं वायाए काएणं न करेमि न कारवेमि करंतं पि अन्नं न समणुजाणामि। तस्स भंते ! पडिक्कमामि निंदामि गरिहामि अप्पाणं वोसिरामि।

स भिक्षुर्वा भिक्षुकी वा संयत-विरत-प्रतिहत-प्रत्याख्यात-पापकर्मा दिवा वा रात्रौ वा एकको वा परिषद्गतो वा सुप्तो वा जाग्रद्वा—अथ सितेन वा विधुवनेन वा तालवृन्तेन वा पत्रेण वा शाखया वा शाखाभङ्गेन वा 'पेहुणेण' वा 'पेहुण' हस्तेन वा चेलेन वा चेलकर्णेन वा हस्तेन वा मुखेन वा आत्मनो वा कायं बाह्यं वाऽपि पुद्गलं—न फूत्कुर्यात् न व्यजेत् अन्येन न फूत्कारयेत् न व्याजयेत् अन्यं फूत्कुर्वन्तं वा व्यजन्तं वा न समनुजानीयात् यावज्जीवं त्रिविधं त्रिविधेन मनसा वाचा कायेन न करोमि न कारयामि कुर्वन्तमप्यन्यं न समनुजानामि। तस्य भदन्त ! प्रतिक्रामामि निन्दामि गर्हे आत्मानं व्युत्सृजामि ॥२१॥

A monk or a nun
Who is well restrained
Desisted from all sinful acts
Protected against influxes and effluxes
Who neither in the day nor at night
When asleep or wide awake
Alone or in assemblage
Neither puffs nor fans the *pudgala*
Existing outside or on his own person
With *camara* **or fan or palm-leaf**
Leaf, branch or twig
The feather of a peacock
Or a bunch thereof
Neither orders puffing or fanning
Nor approves of such acts
And that for good
By three instruments and modes three
By Mind, Word and Deed
Neither shall I perform
Nor order nor approve.

Bhante !
Desist I from past violence to air-bodies
I decry, I denounce
Dedicate I my soul. 21

से भिक्खू वा भिक्खुणी वा संजयविरयपडिहयपच्चक्खायपावकम्मे दिया वा राश्रो वा एगश्रो वा परिसागश्रो वा सुत्ते वा जागरमाणे वा —से बीएसु वा बीयपइट्ठिएसु वा रूढेसु वा रूढपइट्ठिएसु वा जाएसु वा जायपइट्ठिएसु वा हरिएसु वा हरियपइट्ठिएसु वा छिन्नेसु वा छिन्न-पइट्ठिएसु वा सच्चित्तकोलपडिनिस्सिएसु वा न गच्छेज्जा न चिट्ठेज्जा न निसीएज्जा न तुयट्टेज्जा श्रन्नं न गच्छावेज्जा न चिट्ठा-वेज्जा न निसीयावेज्जा न तुयट्टावेज्जा श्रन्नं गच्छंतं वा चिट्ठंतं वा निसीयंतं वा तुयट्टंतं वा न समणुजाणेज्जा जावज्जीवाए तिविहं-तिविहेणं मणेणं वायाए काएणं न करेमि न कारवेमि करंतं पि श्रन्नं न समणुजाणामि। तस्स भंते! पडिक्कमामि निंदामि गरिहामि श्रप्पाणं वोसिरामि ॥२२॥

स भिक्षुर्वा भिक्षुकी वा संयत-विरत-प्रतिहत-प्रत्याख्यात-पापकर्मा दिवा वा रात्रौ वा एकको वा परिषद्गतो वा सुप्तो वा जाग्रद्वा—श्रथ बीजेषु वा बीजप्रतिष्ठितेषु वा रूढेषु वा रूढप्रतिष्ठितेषु वा जातेषु वा जातप्रतिष्ठितेषु वा हरितेषु वा हरितप्रतिष्ठितेषु वा छिन्नेषु वा छिन्नप्रतिष्ठितेषु वा सचित्तकोल-प्रतिनिश्रितेषु वा—न गच्छेत् न तिष्ठेत् न निषीदेत् न त्वग्वर्तेत् श्रन्यं न गमयेत् न स्थापयेत् न निषादयेत् न त्वग्वर्तयेत् श्रन्यं गच्छन्तं वा तिष्ठन्तं वा निषीदन्तं वा त्वग्वर्तमानं वा—न समनुजानीयात् यावज्जीवं त्रिविधं त्रिविधेन—मनसा वाचा कायेन न करोमि न कारयामि कुर्वन्तमप्यन्यं न समनु-जानामि। तस्य भदन्त ! प्रतिक्रामामि निन्दामि गर्हे श्रात्मानं व्युत्सृजामि ॥२२॥

A monk or a nun
Who is well restrained
Desisted from all sinful acts
Protected against influxes and effluxes
Who neither in the day nor at night

Alone or in assemblage
Neither treads nor stands, sits or lies
On seeds or objects placed thereon
Or seeds germinating or objects thereon
Or on trees about to sprout
Or objects placed thereon
Broken limbs of vegetations
Or objects thereon
Or wood connected with eggs or cricket
Neither orders such treading, standing, etc.
Nor approves of such acts
On vegetations aforesaid
And that for good—
By three instruments and modes three
By Mind, Word and Deed
Neither shall I perform
Nor order nor approve.
Bhante !
Desist I from past violence to vegetable-bodies
I decry, I denounce
Dedicate I my soul. 22

से भिक्खू वा भिक्खुणी वा संजयविरयपडिहयपेच्चक्खायपावकम्मे दिया वा राओ वा एगओ वा परिसागओ वा सुत्ते वा जागरमाणे वा—से कीडं वा पयंगं वा कुंथुं वा पिवीलियं वा हत्थंसि वा पायंसि वा बाहुंसि वा ऊरुंसि वा उदरंसि वा सीसंसि वा वत्थंसि वा पडिग्गहंसि वा रयहरणंसि वा गोच्छगंसि वा उंडगंसि वा दंडगंसि वा पीढगंसि वा फलगंसि वा सेज्जंसि वा संथारगंसि वा अन्नयरंसि वा तहप्पगारे उवगरणजाए तओ संजयामेव पडिलेहिय पडिलेहिय पमज्जिय पमज्जिय एगंतमवणेज्जा नो णं संघायमावज्जेज्जा ॥२३॥

स भिक्षुर्वा भिक्षुकी वा संयत-विरत-प्रतिहत-प्रत्याख्यात-पापकर्मा दिवा वा रात्रौ वा एकको वा परिषद्गतो वा सुप्तो वा जाग्रद्वा—अथ कीटं वा पतङ्गं वा कुन्थुं वा पिपीलिकां वा हस्ते वा पादे वा बाहौ वा ऊरौ वा उदरे वा शीर्षे वा वस्त्रे वा प्रतिग्रहे वा रजोहरणे वा गुच्छके वा 'उन्दुके' वा दण्डके वा पीठके वा फलके वा शय्यायां वा संस्तारके वा अन्यतरस्मिन् वा तथा-

प्रकारे उपकरणजाते ततः संयतमेव प्रतिलिख्य प्रतिलिख्य प्रमृज्य प्रमृज्य एकान्तमपनयेत् नैनं संघातमापादयेत् ॥२३॥

A monk or a nun
Who is well restrained
Desisted from all sinful acts
Protected against influxes and effluxes
Either in the day or at night
When asleep or wide awake
Alone or in assemblage
Removes gently and carefully
With cautious sweep
Any worm, insect or ant
Seated on hand, leg or arm
On thigh, belly or head
Cloth, vessel or woollen duster
Or on cloth covering a vessel
Or a supporting stick
Or on a wooden slab
To sit or to lie on
A bed full-sized or small
And deposits it apart
But hurts it not
Nor places it in a manner
To cause inconvenience to other lives. 23

(On Spiritual Prescription)

अजयं चरमाणो उ पाणभूयाइं हिंसई ।
बंधइ पावयं कम्मं तं से होइ कडुयं-फलं ॥१॥

अयतं चरंस्तु प्राणभूतानि हिनस्ति ।
बध्नाति पापकं कर्म तत्तस्य भवति कटुक-फलम् ॥१॥

By movements careless
One who causes hurt to lives

Mobile or rooted at one place
Draws on self the bondage of evil deeds
That yield him pungent fruits. 1

अजयं चिट्ठमाणो उ पाणभूयाइं हिंसई ।
बंधई पावयं कम्मं तं से होइ कडुयं-फलम् ॥२॥

अयतं तिष्ठंस्तु प्राणभूतानि हिनस्ति ।
बध्नाति पापकं कर्म तत्तस्य भवति कटुक-फलम् ॥२॥

By standing careless
One who causes hurt to lives
Mobile or rooted at one place
Draws on self the bondage of evil deeds
That yield him pungent fruits. 2

अजयं आसमाणो उ पाणभूयाइं हिंसई ।
बंधई पावयं कम्मं तं से होइ कडुयं-फलं ॥३॥

अयतमासीनस्तु प्राणभूतानि हिनस्ति ।
बध्नाति पापकं कर्म तत्तस्य भवति कटुक-फलम् ॥३॥

By sitting careless
One who causes hurt to lives
Mobile or rooted at one place
Draws on self the bondage of evil deeds
That yield him pungent fruits. 3

अजयं सयमाणो उ पाणभूयाइं हिंसई ।
बंधई पावयं कम्मं तं से होई कडुयं-फलम् ॥४॥

अयतं शयानस्तु प्राणभूतानि हिनस्ति ।
बध्नाति पापकं कर्म तत्तस्य भवति कटुक-फलम् ॥४॥

By lying careless
One who causes hurt to lives
Mobile or rooted at one place

Draws on self the bondage of evil deeds
That yield him pungent fruits. 4

अजयं भुंजमाणो उ पाणभूयाइं हिंसई ।
बंधई पावयं कम्मं तं से होइ कडुयं-फलं ॥५॥

अयतं भुञ्जानस्तु प्राणभूतानि हिनस्ति ।
बध्नाति पापकं कर्म तत्तस्य भवति कटुक-फलम् ॥५॥

By eating careless
One who causes hurt to lives
Mobile or rooted at one place
Draws on self the bondage of evil deeds
That yield him pungent fruits. 5

अजयं भासमाणो उ पाणभूयाइं हिंसई ।
बंधई पावयं कम्मं तं से होइ कडुयं-फलं ॥६॥

अयतं भाषमाणस्तु प्राणभूतानि हिनस्ति ।
बध्नाति पापकं कर्म तत्तस्य भवति कटुक-फलम् ॥६॥

By talking careless
One who causes hurt to lives
Mobile or rooted at one place
Draws on self the bondage of evil deeds
That yield him pungent fruits. 6

कहं चरे कहं चिट्ठे कहमासे कहं सए ।
कहं भुंजंतो भासंतो पावं कम्मं न बंधई ॥७॥

कथं चरेत् कथं तिष्ठेत् कथमासीत कथं शयीत ।
कथं भुञ्जानो भाषमाणः पापं कर्म न बध्नाति ॥७॥

Then what should be the mode of movement
Of standing, sitting, lying, eating or talking
That there is no bondagc
Emanating from evil deeds. 7

जयं चरे जयं चिट्ठे जयमासे जयं सए ।
जयं भुंजंतो भासंतो पावं कम्मं न बंधई ॥८॥

यतं चरेद् यतं तिष्ठेद् यतमासीत यतं शयीत ।
यतं भुञ्जानो भाषमाणः पापं कर्म न बध्नाति ॥८॥

With movements careful and cautious,
Careful standing, sitting and lying,
And with careful eating and careful talking
One ensnares not self
In the bondage of evil deeds. 8

सव्वभूयप्पभूयस्स सम्मं भूयाइ पासओ ।
पिहियासवस्स दंतस्स पावं कम्मं न बंधई ॥९॥

सर्वभूतात्मभूतस्य सम्यग् भूतानि पश्यतः ।
पिहितास्रवस्य दान्तस्य पापं कर्म न बध्यते ॥९॥

He who treats living beings as self
And views them with equanimity
Whose influx is checked
And sense-organs in perfect command
In Mind, Word and Deed
Escapes he the bondage of evil deeds. 9

Note: This *sūtra* lays emphasis on Right Conduct, one of the *triratnas* (three jewels) of Jainism.

पढमं नाणं तओ दया एवं चिट्ठइ सव्वसंजए ।
अन्नाणी किं काही किं वा नाहिइ छेय पावगं ॥१०॥

प्रथमं ज्ञानं ततो दया एवं तिष्ठति सर्वसंयतः ।
अज्ञानी किं करिष्यति किं वा ज्ञास्यति छेक-पापकम् ॥१०॥

Knowledge first and then Compassion
In this way is the *muni* fixed.
What doeth the ignoramus
What knoweth he of weal and woe. 10

Note : This *sūtra* emphasizes the fundamental tenet of Jainism. viz., that *mokṣa* or liberation can be attained only by *jñāna* (knowledge) and *kriyā* (deeds). Even Lord Krishna ordains in the *Gītā*, "There is nothing as pure as knowledge on this earth." In the Jaina view, *jñāna* precedes *dayā* or compassion, the extent of the latter depending on the dimension of the former. The more limited the knowledge, the smaller will be the size of compassion. Knowledge gives insight about the nature of realities and shows the way to liberation. Compassion is only an instrument for practical restraint. He who has not the knowledge cannot be compassionate in true sense.

सोच्चा जाणइ कल्लाणं सोच्चा जाणइ पावगं ।
उभयं पि जाणई सोच्चा जं छेयं तं समायरे ॥११॥

श्रुत्वा जानाति कल्याणं श्रुत्वा जानाति पापकम् ।
उभयमपि जानाति श्रुत्वा यच्छेकं तत्समाचरेत् ॥११॥

On hearing *jīva* knows what is righteous
And on hearing he knows the evil deeds
Weal and woe are known from hearing
And then he practises
What is conducive to the highest weal. 11

Note: The organ of knowledge is ear, not eye. It is for this that the *Āgamas* had for long been transmitted and preserved by the word of the mouth of the *ācāryas*. Hence the emphasis on hearing. The scriptures are explicit in recognising this important role of the ear in the acquisition of knowledge. The content of knowledge, the devotion for its acquisition and the practice as per knowledge, all rank next.

(On the Outcome of Dharma)

जो जीवे वि न याणाइ अजीवे वि न याणई ।
जीवाजीवे अयाणंतो कहं सो नाहिइ संजमं ॥१२॥

यो जीवानपि न जानाति अजीवानपि न जानाति ।
जीवाऽजीवानजानन् कथं स ज्ञास्यति संयमम् ॥१२॥

How can he who knows not *jiva*
Nor *ajīva*, who is ignorant of both
Practise restraint. 12

जो जीवे वि वियाणाइ अजीवे वि वियाणई ।
जीवाजीवे वियाणंतो सो हु नाहिइ संजमं ॥१३॥

यो जीवानपि विजानाति अजीवानपि विजानाति ।
जीवाऽजीवान् विजानन् स हि ज्ञास्यति संयमम् ॥१३॥

He who knows *jīva* and *ajīva*
And is thus equipped with knowledge of both
May well know what restraint is. 13

Note: The implication is that without the knowledge of *jīva* and *ajīva*, one cannot practise restraint or non-violence. Knowledge is fundamental. The ignorant who is unaware of the distinction between *jīva* and *ajīva* is equally ignorant of restraint.

जया जीवे अजीवे य दो वि एए वियाणई ।
तया गइं बहुविहं सव्वजीवाण जाणई ॥१४॥

यदा जीवानजीवांश्च द्वावप्येतौ विजानाति ।
तदा गतिं बहुविधां सर्वजीवानां जानाति ॥१४॥

When man knows *jīva* and *ajīva*
And so equipped with knowledge of both
He further knows their different species 14

जया गइं बहुविहं सव्वजीवाण जाणई ।
तया पुण्णं च पावं च बंधं मोक्खं च जाणई ॥१५॥

यदा गतिं बहुविधां सर्वजीवानां जानाति ।
तदा पुण्यं च पापं च बन्धं मोक्षं च जानाति ॥१५॥

And when he knows *jīva* in diverse species.
Then knows he virtue and vice
And bondage and liberation. 15

जया पुण्णं च पावं च बंधं मोक्खं च जाणई ।
तया निव्विंदए भोए जे दिव्वे जे य माणुसे ॥१६॥

यदा पुण्यं च पापं च बन्धं मोक्षं च जानाति ।
तदा निर्विन्दते भोगान् यान् दिव्यान् यांश्च मानुषान् ॥१६॥

When man knows virtue and vice
And bondage and liberation
Then acquires he the indifference
To sufferings of men as well as of gods. 16

Note: 'Suffering' here stands for what is suffered, good as well as bad, pleasure as well as pain, to which both men and gods are subject. Perhaps the word 'suffering' conveys well even earthly and heavenly pleasures whose ultimate consequence is not full liberation but further bondage and suffering. A man with full knowledge becomes indifferent to all *bhogas* or sufferings, good as well as bad.

जया निर्व्विदए भोए जे दिव्वे जे य माणुसे ।
तया चयइ संजोगं सब्भिंतरबाहिरं ॥१७॥

यदा निर्विन्दते भोगान् यान् दिव्यान् यांश्च मानुषान् ।
तदा त्यजति संयोगं साभ्यन्तरबाह्यम् ॥१७॥

When man is contented
Of sufferings of men and gods
Then discards he all contact
Either within or from outside. 17

Note: External contact is with earthly objects, *dravya-sambandha*. But internal contact is correlated with *bhāva* like anger, greed, etc. A man with full knowledge of suffering, earthly as well as heavenly, overcomes all contacts. For he knows well that even though these generate momentary pleasure, really they tighten the snares of bondage.

जया चयइ संजोगं सब्भिंतरबाहिरं ।
तया मुंडे भवित्ताणं पव्वइए अणगारियं ॥१८॥

यदा त्यजति संयोगं साभ्यन्तर-बाह्यम् ।
तदा मुण्डो भूत्वा प्रव्रजत्यनगारताम् ॥१८॥

When man discards contact
External as well as internal
Then he with hairs uprooted
Accepts the life of a mendicant. 18

Note: The uprooting of hair is symbolical of the uprooting of all passions and attachments, in all ten in number as per the *Sthānāṅga*, such as anger, pride, attachment, greed, hairs, organs of vision, hearing, smell, taste and touch.

जया मुंडे भवित्ताणं पव्वइए अणगारियं ।
तया संवरमुक्किट्ठं धम्मं फासे अणुत्तरं ॥१९॥

यदा मुण्डो भूत्वा प्रव्रजत्यनगारताम् ।
तदा संवरमुत्कृष्टं धर्मं स्पृशत्यनुत्तरम् ॥१९॥

When man has his hair uprooted
And embraces the state of homelessness
Then he touches the *anuttara dhamma*
Centred round the magnificent *sambara*
(which is stoppage of all influx.) 19

जया संवरमुक्किट्ठं धम्मं फासे अणुत्तरं ।
तया धुणइ कम्मरयं अबोहिकलुसं कडं ॥२०॥

यदा संवरमुत्कृष्टं धर्मं स्पृशत्यनुत्तरम् ।
तदा धुनाति कर्मरजः अबोधि-कलुष-कृतम् ॥२०॥

When man touches *anuttara dhamma*
And the magnificent *sambara*
Then he shakes to the root
The dust of *karma*
Accumulated by the vice of ignorance. 20

जया धुणइ कम्मरयं अबोहिकलुसं कडं ।
तया सव्वत्तगं नाणं दंसणं चाभिगच्छई ॥२१॥

यदा धुनाति कर्मरजः अबोधि-कलुष-कृतम् ।
तदा सर्वत्रगं ज्ञानं दर्शनं चाभिगच्छति ॥२१॥

When he shakes to the root
The dust of *karma*
Accumulated by the vice of ignorance
Then he acquires knowledge and vision
All-penetrating, all-pervading
The knowledge of the liberated
The vision of the free. 21

जया सव्वत्तगं नाणं दंसणं चाभिगच्छई ।
तया लोगमलोगं च जिणो जाणइ केवली ॥२२॥

यदा सर्वत्रगं ज्ञानं दर्शनं चाभिगच्छति ।
तदा लोकमलोकं च जिनो जानाति केवली ॥२२॥

When he acquires such knowledge and vision
Knowledge all-pervading and vision all penetrating
(*Kevala-jñāna and Kevala-darśana*)
Then becoming a *jina* **and** *kevali*
He acquires knowledge of *loga* **and** *aloga.* 22

जया लोगमलोगं च जिणो जाणइ केवली ।
तया जोगे निरुंभित्ता सेलेसिं पडिवज्जई ॥२३॥

यदा लोकमलोकं च जिनो जानाति केवली ।
तदा योगान् निरुध्य शैलेशीं प्रतिपद्यते ॥२३॥

When by becoming a *jina* **and** *kevali*
He acquires the knowledge of *loga* **and** *aloga*

Then by checking the *yogas*
Established is he
In a state of perfect rest. 23

Note: The word *yoga* is used here in the usual Jaina sense implying the state of perfect restlessness that is the outcome of the coming together of the physical body and the soul. The soul by its very nature is perfectly calm, but when lodged in body it becomes restless by the traits of mind, word and body. But when the *jīva* is again ripe for ultimate liberation, in the penultimate state, the soul reacquires its original and inherent calm, thus first subduing the mind, then the word and lastly the body. Thus by totally checking *yoga*, the soul becomes in all respects perfectly calm, a state that is compared with the restful Mount Meru. It is in this state that the soul has been called *selesi* (*śaileśi*). In this state, even the pious deeds can cause no more bondage to the soul. In fact, nothing can now prevent his final liberation.

जया जोगे निरु'भित्ता सेलेसिं पडिवज्जई ।
तया कम्मं खवित्ताणं सिद्धिं गच्छइ नीरओ ॥२४॥

यदा योगान् निरुध्य शैलेशीं प्रतिपद्यते ।
तदा कर्म क्षपयित्वा सिद्धिं गच्छति नीरजाः ॥२४॥

When by checking *yoga*
He acquires the state of restfulness
Then, by exhausting the fund of *karma*
He is totally clean of *karma* particles
A *siddha*, truly liberated indeed. 24

जया कम्मं खवित्ताणं सिद्धिं गच्छइ नीरओ ।
तया लोगमत्थयत्थो सिद्धो हवइ सासओ ॥२५॥

यदा कर्म क्षपयित्वा सिद्धिं गच्छति नीरजाः ।
तदा लोकमस्तकस्थः सिद्धो भवति शाश्वतः ॥२५॥

When by exhausting *karma*
Totally clear of *karma* particles
He acquires the state of liberation

Attains he the highest region in *loga*
And is permanently liberated. 25

Note: After the attainment of the *loga-matthaya (loka-mastaka)* or the crest of the *loga*, he no longer acquires the mortal frame. He is now permanently liberated without any possibility of a slip. And if still he is encased in a body, he will in due course discard it and ascend straight to the abode of the liberated souls.

सुहसायगस्स समणस्स सायाउलगस्स निगामसाइस्स ।
उच्छोलणापहोइस्स दुलहा सुग्गइ तारिसगस्स ॥२६॥

सुखस्वादकस्य श्रमणस्य साताकुलकस्य निकामशायिनः ।
उत्क्षालनाप्रधाविनः दुर्लभा सुगतिस्तादृशकस्य ॥२६॥

A *śramaṇa* testing pleasures
Ever keen after them
Sleeping beyond prescription
And washing limbs too often
Finds it difficult to take the best way. 26

Note: The word *sāyāyulagassa (sātākulakasya)* in the sūtra has evoked a lot of controversy as to its meaning. This has been sought to be resolved here by translating it as "keen after pleasure". Pleasure may be of two types, viz., acquired and yet to be acquired. When they are yet to be acquired one remains keen after them. *Suggai (sugati)* is the 'best way', the way to spiritual growth and ultimate liberation.

तवोगुणपहाणस्स उज्जुमइ खंतिसंजमरयस्स ।
परीसहे जिणंतस्स सुलहा सुग्गइ तारिसगस्स ॥२७॥
[पच्छा वि ते पयाया खिप्पं गच्छंति अमर-भवणाइं ।
जेसिं पिओ तवो संजमो य खन्ती य बम्भचेरं च ॥]

तपोगुणप्रधानस्य ऋजुमति क्षान्तिसंयमरतस्य ।
परीषहान् जयतः सुलभा सुगतिस्तादृशकस्य ॥२७॥
[पश्चादपि ते प्रयाताः क्षिप्रं गच्छन्ति अमरभवनानि ।
येषां प्रियं तपः संयमश्च क्षान्तिश्च ब्रह्मचर्यं च ॥]

Suggai **is attainable by a** *śramaṇa*
Who is hard-penanced
Whose mind is directed to *mokṣa*
Who is fixed in forgiveness and restraint
And who has overpowered the bodily urges. 27
[Those to whom is dear
Penance, restraint, forgiveness and celibacy
Will soon attain heaven
By being *prabrajita.*

Note : These bodily urges have been called the *pariṣahas* and are 24 in number.

इच्चेयं छज्जीवणियं सम्मद्दिट्ठी सया जए ।
दुलहं लभित्तु सामण्णं कम्मुणा न विराहेज्जासि ॥२८॥
त्ति बेमि ।

इत्येतां षड्जीवनिकां सम्यग्-दृष्टिः सदा यतः ।
दुर्लभं लब्ध्वा श्रामण्यं कर्मणा न विराधयेत् ॥२८॥
इति ब्रवीमि ।

By attaining the rarely attainable
Life of a *śramaṇa*
By remaining ever cautious
And with Right Vision
A *śramaṇa* **causes no hurt**
To the six types of living beings
By Mind, Word and Deed. 28

Note : The word "hurt" is used here to convey the sense contained in *virāhejjāsi, (virādhayet)* which may be any kind of hurt, from a minor injury to total slaughter.

पंचमं अज्झयणं (पञ्चममध्ययनम्)

PRESCRIPTION FIVE

पिण्डेसणा (पिण्डैषणा)

Selection of Right Food

First Part (*Uddesa* or *Uddeśaka*) :

(On the Mode of Search)

संपत्ते भिक्खकालम्मि असंभंतो अमुच्छिओ ।
इमेण कमजोगेण भत्तपाणं गवेसए ।।१।।

संप्राप्ते भिक्षाकाले असंभ्रान्तोऽमूर्च्छितः ।
अनेन क्रमयोगेन भक्तपानं गवेषयेत् ।।१।।

On the arrival of right time for food
A *muni*, unconcerned and without preference,
Moves out to get food and drink
As per prescription that is given below. 1

Note : The attainment of the right time is important, since the *muni* cannot be out in search of food throughout the day. According to one text, a *muni* spends first three hours of the day in studying spiritual texts and devote the next three to get food and to take it and then be absorbed in study again for the rest of the day. In the course of the search, he must remain unconcerned as to the availability or otherwise. For, during the allotted hour, many other monks will similarly be out in search of food. A muni must remain unperturbed and should not feel that since there may be so many seekers, he may not get adequate food. He must not make haste either to reach the donor first so that he may have his share before the food is distributed. He should go at normal pace and perfectly unconcerned about its availability. There is another requirement, viz., that he must be without preference for any specific type of food and remain unaffected by the sights and sounds on the way. Such a *muni* has been called *a-mucchio (amūrcchita)* i. e., one who is not without sense. The word *bhatta-pānam (bhakta-pānam)* is significant. *Pānam* is apparently a drink but if *bhatta* or *bhāt* stands for rice, then rice must have been the staple food in the region where the *sūtra* was written.

से गामे वा नगरे वा गोयरग्गगग्रो मुणी ।
चरे मंदमणुव्विग्गो अव्वक्खित्तेण चेयसा ॥२॥

स ग्रामे वा नगरे वा गोचराग्रगतो मुनिः ।
चरेन्मन्दमनुद्विग्नः अव्याक्षिप्तेन चेतसा ॥२॥

In a village or in a town
A *muni* when out for collecting food
Moves at easy pace
Calm and with mind unperturbed. 2

Note : The word *goyaraggagao (gocarāgragata)* is significant, the simile being with a cow grazing in the field. The cow grazes from one end of the field to the other without discrimination; so does a *muni* perfectly unconcerned by the wealth or status of the donor. The simile may be extended to the pace of the cow which is slow. The *muni* should be calm, i. e., unbothered as to the availability or otherwise of food or of favourite food. The mind of the *muni* must remain unperturbed by the sight and sound during the course of food collection, the only concern being the getting of food.

पुरओ जुगमायाए पेहमाणो महिं चरे ।
वज्जंतो बीयहरियाइं पाणेय दगमट्टियं ॥३॥

पुरतो युगमात्रया प्रेक्षमाणो महीं चरेत् ।
वर्जयन् बीजहरितानि प्राणांश्च दक-मृत्तिकाम् ॥३॥

He moves viewing closely
Earth of the size of the human length

And avoiding carefully
Seed, greenery or life
Water or earth with living cells. 3

Note : Earth of the size of the human length comes within the immediate visibility of the *muni* who must make sure that nothing living is trampled in this zone on which he puts his steps.

ओवायं विसमं खाणुं विज्जलं परिवज्जए ।
संकमेण न गच्छेज्जा विज्जमाणे परक्कमे ॥४॥

अवपातं विषमं स्थाणुं 'विज्जलं' परिवर्जयेत् ।
संक्रमेण न गच्छेत् विद्यमाने पराक्रमे ॥४॥

The other way with holes deep
Uneven or with piles of dry wood
Or of grains or full of mud
He avoids, and uses not
A link of wood or of stone
To cross water or a crevice. 4

पवडंते व से तत्थ पक्खलंते व संजए ।
हिंसेज्ज पाणभूयाइं तसे अदुव थावरे ॥५॥

प्रपतन् वा स तत्र प्रस्खलन् वा संयतः ।
हिंस्यात् प्राणभूतानि त्रसानथवा स्थावरान् ॥५॥

तम्हा तेण न गच्छेज्जा संजए सुसमाहिए ।
सइ अन्नेण मग्गेण जयमेव परक्कमे ॥६॥

तस्मात्तेन न गच्छेत् संयतः सुसमाहितः ।
सत्यन्यस्मिन् मार्गे यतमेव पराक्रमेत् ॥६॥

From a fall in such a way
Or even from uneven steps
The restraint may cause an unwilling hurt
To living beings rooted or mobile.
So he avoids this other way
Or if it be so unavoidable
(For want of an alternative route)
He paces through it with caution due. 5-6

इंगालं छारियं रासिं तुसरासिं च गोमयं ।
ससरक्खेहिं पाएहिं संजओ तं न अक्कमे ।।७।।

आङ्गारं क्षारिकं राशिं तुषराशिं च गोमयम् ।
ससरक्षाभ्यां पादाभ्यां संयतस्तं नाक्रामेत् ।।७।।

A restrained *muni* places not
His feet contacted with living particles of clay
On coal or ash or husk
Or even a pile of cowdung. 7

न चरेज्ज वासे वासंते महियाए व पडंतीए ।
महावाए व वायंते तिरिच्छसंपाइमेसु वा ।।८।।

न चरेद्वर्षे वर्षति महिकायां वा पतन्त्याम् ।
महावाते वा वाति तिर्यक्संपातेषु वा ।।८।।

He goes not out for food
In the midst of a shower
Dew drops or a sharp gale
Or when the road is infested with flying insects. 8

न चरेज्ज वेससामंते बंभचेरवसाणुए ।
बंभयारिस्स दंतस्स होज्जा तत्थ विसोत्तिया ।।९।।

न चरेद् वेशसामन्ते ब्रह्मचर्यवशानुगः ।
ब्रह्मचारिणो दान्तस्य भवेत्तत्र विस्रोतसिका ।।९।।

A *muni* practising *brahmacarya*
Must not repair near a brothel
For here even a veteran *brahmacāri*
May slip from the spiritual path
And find his practice reversed. 9

अणायणे चरंतस्स संसग्गीए अभिक्खणं ।
होज्ज वयाणं पीला सामण्णम्मि य संसओ ।।१०।।

अनायतने चरतः संसर्गेणाऽभीक्ष्णम् ।
भवेद् व्रतानां पीडा श्रामण्ये च संशयः ।।१०।।

For frequenting undesirable spots
And because of contacts (with harlots)
Ailments may creep into the practices
And doubts crop up in mendicancy. 10

तम्हा एयं वियाणित्ता दोसं दुग्गइवड्ढणं ।
वज्जए वेससामंतं मुणी एगंतमस्सिए ॥११॥

तस्मादेतद् विज्ञाय दोषं दुर्गति-वर्द्धनम् ।
वर्जयेद्वेशसामन्तं मुनिरेकान्तमाश्रितः ॥११॥

So spotting it as a vice
That helps a fall
A *muni* who is after liberation
Goes not near the harlot's enclosure. 11

साणं सुइयं गाविं दित्तं गोणं हयं गयं ।
संडिब्भं कलहं जुद्धं दुरओ परिवज्जए ॥१२॥

श्वानं सूतिकां गां दृप्तं गां हयं गजम् ।
"संडिब्भं' कलहं युद्धं दूरतः परिवर्जयेत् ॥१२॥

And in his wanderings he avoids
A dog, a cow who has just calved,
An excited ox, horse or an elephant
A children's playground
An arena of quarrel or of war. 12

अणुन्नए नावणए अप्पहिट्ठे अणाउले ।
इंदियाणि जहाभागं दमयित्ता मुणी चरे ॥१३॥

अनुन्नतो नावनतः अप्रहृष्टोऽनाकुलः ।
इन्द्रियाणि यथाभागं दमयित्ता मुनिश्चरेत् ॥१३॥

A *muni* in his wanderings
Shall not turn his face skyward
Nor bend it low (earthward)
Is neither elated nor sullen
But represses senses from their objects. 13

दवदवस्स न गच्छेज्जा भासमाणोय गोयरे ।
हंसतो नाभिगच्छेज्जा कुलं उच्चावयं सया ।।१४।।

द्रवं द्रवं न गच्छेत् भाषमाणश्च गोचरे ।
हसन् नाभिगच्छेत् कुलमुच्चावचं सदा ।।१४।।

A *muni* wandering cow-like for food
In palaces or in common huts
Neither goes running
Nor chatting nor laughing. 14

आलोयं थिग्गलं दारं संधि दगभवणाणि य ।
चरंतो न विणिज्झाए संकट्ठाणं विवज्जए ।।१५।।

आलोकं 'थिग्गलं' द्वारं सन्धिं दकभवनानि च ।
चरन् न विनिध्यायेत् शङ्कास्थानं विवर्जयेत् ।।१५।।

A *muni* while wandering
Casts not a glance through openings
Or at a door set afresh
Or even at a door or gap between houses
Or a room with water in. 15

Note: A room with water in is diversely interpreted by commentators. It may be a bath-room or a room where water is stored. A public bath on the way may be an alternative interpretation, and perhaps a more appropriate one. For, it cannot be a water-store in a house or a room having a well inside, since these cannot be on the way.

रन्नो गिहवईणं च रहस्सारक्खियाण य ।
संकिलेसकरं ठाणं दूरओ परिवज्जए ।।१६।।

राज्ञा गृहपतीनां च रहस्यारक्षिकाणाञ्च ।
संक्लेशकरं स्थानं दूरतः परिवर्जयेत् ।।१६।।

He enters not, but keeps away
From the secret chambers
Of the king or the *kartā* of a house
Or of the king's counsels
For these are places
(Where decisions are taken)
That may cause pain, separation or hurt. 16

पडिकुट्ठकुलं न पविसे मामगं परिवज्जए ।
अचियत्तकुलं न पविसे चियत्तं पविसे कुलं ॥१७॥

प्रतिक्रुष्ट-कुलं न प्रविशेत् मामकं परिवर्जयेत् ।
'अचियत्त' कुलं न प्रविशेत् 'चियत्तं' प्रविशेत् कुलम् ॥१७॥

A *muni* goes not to a forbidden house
Nor to one with prohibited entry
Or where reception is unpleasant
Goes he to a house wherein welcome is he. 17

साणीपावारपिहियं अप्पणा नावपंगुरे ।
कवाडं नो पणोल्लेज्जा ओग्गहंसि अजाइया ॥१८॥

शाणी-प्रावार-पिहितं आत्मना नापवृणुयात् ।
कपाटं न प्रणोदयेत् अवग्रहे अयाचित्वा ॥१८॥

A *muni* without the permission of the house-holder
Opens not a door
Nor removes a screen
Made of *śan* or of animal fur. 18

Note: The prohibitions here are of two types—one regarding the opening of the door which is shut and the other regarding the removal of the screen at the door. The former may cause hurt to the worms and insects and is therefore an act of sin; the latter is more a matter of etiquette. It appears from this that even at this early period, the practice of screening the doors and windows was in vogue and, as now, even at that date, taking previous permission before removing the screen and entering a chamber was a part of general decorum, more particularly so for a *mvni* who was expected to avoid causing even the smallest embarrassment by such unexpected entry.

गोयरग्गपविट्ठो उ वच्चमुत्तं न धारए ।
ओगासं फासुयं नच्चा अणुन्नविय वोसिरे ॥१९॥

गोचराग्रप्रविष्टस्तु वर्चोमूत्रं न धारयेत् ।
अवकाशं प्रासुकं ज्ञात्वा अनुज्ञाप्य व्युत्सृजेत् ॥१९॥

A *muni* out in search of food
Should not check nature's call
But take out excreta
In a place free from living beings
With the permission of the landlord. **19**

Note: This is obviously a prescription on grounds of health. Normally a *muni* (this should apply to anyone) should take out his excreta before he goes out in search of food. But if by chance he forgets to do so and if he has a fresh call unanticipated at the commencement of the journey, it is prescribed that it should not be suppressed. For, apart from causing inconvenience and ultimately ill-health, it may even create an awkward situation for him. So it is better that he gets rid of it. But he must be selective about the place which should be *phāsuya (prāsuka-sthāna)* which etymologically means "free from living beings", from which it follows that the place must be clean beyond flaw.

नीयदुवारं तमसं कोट्ठगं परिवज्जए ।
अचक्खुविसओ जत्थ पाणा दुप्पडिलेहगा ॥२०॥

नीचद्वारं तमोमयं कोष्ठकं परिवर्जयेत् ।
अचक्षुर्विषयो यत्र प्राणाः दुष्प्रतिलेख्यकाः ॥२०॥

A *muni* need avoid a room
Whose door is low
And which is dark
For, barred to visibility
Insects in it may remain unseen. 2

जत्थ पुप्फाइ बीयाइं विप्पइण्णाइं कोट्ठए ।
अहुणोवलित्तं उल्लं दट्ठूणं परिवज्जए ॥२१॥

यत्र पुष्पाणि बीजानि विप्रकीर्णानि कोष्ठके ।
अधुनोपलिप्तमार्द्रं दृष्ट्वा परिवर्जयेत् ॥२१॥

A *muni* need avoid a room
Where are scattered flowers and seeds
Or which has just been smeared
With a coat of mud
And is still wet. 21

एलगं दारगं साणं वच्छगं वावि कोट्ठए ।
उल्लंघिया न पविसे विऊहित्ताण व संजए ॥२२॥

एडकं दारकं श्वानं वत्सकं वाऽपि कोष्ठके ।
उल्लंघ्य न प्रविशेत व्यूह्य वा संयतः ॥२२॥

To enter a room, a *muni*
Removes not nor crosses
A child, a ram, a pup or a calf. 22

असंसत्तं पलोएज्जा नाइदूरावलोयए ।
उप्फुल्लं न विणिज्झाए नियट्टेज्ज अयंपिरो ॥२३॥

असंसक्तं प्रलोकेत नातिदूरमवलोकेत ।
उत्फुल्लं न विनिध्यायेत् निवर्त्तेताऽजल्पिता ॥२३॥

A *muni* casts not a glance of attachment
Nor stretches far his gaze
Nor throws a look full of ecstacy
When refused, he need turn his step
Without exchanging a single word. 23

Note: Attachment here means attachment to women. To cast a wistful look at a woman is prohibited, since this may not only entail a loss of celibacy but may cause depression and disease, even loss of reputation. A *muni's* look should be concentrated only on nearby edible objects of which he seeks a morsel and should not extend to distant objects. For, the latter behaviour may rouse suspicion in the mind of the house-holder about the motive of the *muni*. Besides, if an object is to be brought from a distance to be given to the *muni*, it may lead to unconscious and unintentional molestation of living beings leading to *hiṁsā* or violence. A *muni* should not look with ecstacy which may give the impression that the *muni* is not yet free from the demands of senses and is still very light-hearted and frivolous.

अइभूमिं न गच्छेज्जा गोयरग्गगओ मुणी ।
कुलस्स भूमिं जाणित्ता मियं भूमिं परक्कमे ॥२४॥

अतिभूमिं न गच्छेत् गोचराग्रगतो मुनिः ।
कुलस्य भूमिं ज्ञात्वा मितां भूमिं पराक्रमेत् ॥२४॥

A *muni* on entering a house
For begging food
Traverses not a sector of the house
That is usually left untraversed
But knowing the house-holder's status
Goes as far as is usual. 24

Note : This is a prescription as to how far a *muni* should go on entering a house for begging food. Obviously he should not roam all over the house. Since he has come with a definite object, his steps need be directed only that far where his object is fulfilled. This again will vary depending on local custom and status of the householder. In other words, he should neither totally avoid a house nor be too much intimate with it. In each house he may go only that far as is permitted to others like him and causes no displeasure or irritation by such movement to other sectors of the house. This sector of the house in which or upto which a *muni* may go has been called *miya bhūmi* (*mitā bhūmi*) or permitted sector as distinguished from *ai-bhūmi* (*atibhūmi*) or prohibited sector, the prohibition being mostly implied or customary.

तत्थेव पडिलेहेज्जा भूमिभागं वियक्खणो ।
सिणाणस्स य वच्चस्स संलोगं परिवज्जए ॥२५॥

तत्रैव प्रतिलिखेत् भूमि-भागं विचक्षणः ।
स्नानस्य च वर्चसः संलोकं परिवर्जयेत् ॥२५॥

A *muni* acquainted with *śāstric* prescription
Stands at right place in permitted sector
And avoids a place wherefrom
He can have a view of latrine
Or a room where bath is taken. 25

Note : Apart from the fact that a latrine or bathroom is not a very pleasant object for the eye, men and women may be visible there in uncouth posture and very improperly dressed. Such a sight is not congenial for a *muni*. Not to speak of going to these sectors, he should even avoid a place wherefrom these may be within visibility.

दगमट्टियग्रायाणं बीयाणि हरियाणि य ।
परिवज्जंतो चिट्ठेज्जा सव्विंदियसमाहिए ॥२६॥

दकमृत्तिकाऽऽदानं बीजानि हरितानि च ।
परिवर्जयंस्तिष्ठेत् सर्वेन्द्रिय-समाहितः ॥२६॥

A *muni* whose senses are at rest
While he is on his legs
Avoids a way
Through which are carried
Earth or water
Or even a plot strewn with seeds
Or covered with moss. 26

(On the Mode of Acceptance)

तत्थ से चिट्ठमाणस्स ग्राहरे पाणभोयणं ।
ग्रकप्पियं न इच्छेज्जा पडिगाहेज्ज कप्पियं ॥२७॥

तत्र तस्य तिष्ठतः ग्राहरेत् पान-भोजनम् ।
ग्रकल्पिकं न इच्छेत् प्रतिगृह्णीयात् कल्पिकम् ॥२७॥

When a *muni* stands thus
And someone fetches food and drink to give
He accepts food that is permitted
And accepts not what is prohibited. 27

Note : Here the *sūtra* has two words, viz., *kappiya (kalpika)* and *a-kappiya (a-kalpika)*, the former meaning permitted and the latter not permitted. The use is highly significant, the real determinant of permission or prohibition being the congeniality of a particular deed with the attainment of equanimity. To be so, the deed need be consistent with the *śāstric* prescriptions. Since seeking food is an important activity, it must strictly conform with what is *kappiya.*

आहरंती सिया तत्थ परिसाडेज्ज भोयणं ।
देंतियं पडियाइक्खे न मे कप्पइ तारिसं ॥२८॥

आहरन्ती स्यात् तत्र परिशाटयेद् भोजनम् ।
ददतीं प्रत्याचक्षीत न मे कल्पते तादृशम् ॥२८॥

If an item of food drops
From the hands of the lady carrying them
Then the *muni* tells the donor-lady—
"Such food is not acceptable to me." 28

Note **:** The sudden change-over to a donor-lady in this *sūtra* should cause no surprise, since the act of giving food to any seeker is the prime duty of the lady of the house. But the lady must observe necessary care in carrying food for the *muni.* If any item drops from her hands, the entire food becomes *a-kappiya.* Needless to add, the practice is well-known to the ladies who exercise a profound care in carrying food for the *muni.*

सम्मद्दमाणी पाणाणि बीयाणि हरियाणि य ।
असंजमकरिं नच्चा तारिसं परिवज्जए ॥२९॥

सम्मर्दयन्ती प्राणान् बीजानि हरितानि च ।
असंयमकरीं ज्ञात्वा तादृशं परिवर्जयेत् ॥२९॥

And knowing a lady to be devoid of restraint
When she tramples under foot
Living beings or seeds or moss
From such one a *muni*
Accepts neither food nor drink. 29

Note : This prohibition is worthy of note, since lurking behind it is the emphasis on *ahiṁsā*. When a lady tramples the aforesaid objects, lives or prospective lives, she indulges in an act of violence. In consequence, she becomes devoid of restraint.

साहट्टु निक्खिवित्ताणं सच्चितं घट्टियाण य ।
तहेव समणट्ठाए उदगं संपणोल्लिया ॥३०॥

संहृत्य निक्षिप्य सचित्तं घट्टयित्वा च ।
तथैव श्रमणार्थं उदकं सप्रणुद्य ॥३०॥

आगाहइत्ता चलइत्ता आहरे पाणभोयणं ।
देंतियं पडियाइक्खे न मे कप्पइ तारिसं ॥३१॥

अवगाह्य चालयित्वा आहरेत्पानभोजनम् ।
ददतीं प्रत्याचक्षीत न मे कल्पते तादृशम् ॥३१॥

When food is transferred from one vessel
Or carried on a living object
Or when a living object is shaken
Or live water moved in a pot
Or when food is carried after bath
Or when water on the floor is swept
Before carrying food for a *muni's* use
Then the *muni* prohibits the donor-lady—
"Such food is not acceptable to me." 30-31

Note : These are very elaborate provisions regarding the handling of food which makes it acceptable or non-acceptable for a *muni*. Simultaneously the lapses are named. If some undesirable object has fallen in the food, the act of its removal is called *saṁharaṇa* and the food thus contaminated becomes *sāhaṭṭu* (*saṁhṛtya*) and hence non-acceptable. If a pot is placed on a living object, it cannot be used for carrying food. Likewise, extra food may be removed from a small cup into a bigger one or food may have been placed in a vessel too heavy to be removed. In all these three cases the food becomes *sāhaṭṭu* or contaminated. If the portion of food that is to be offered is placed on a living object, then such food becomes *nikṣipta*. Water is considered to be a living object. The stir of water, taking bath and sweeping it are all acts that affect living objects but still their specific mention has been considered necessary here. The act of taking bath before giving food to a *muni* as also the practice of shaking living objects are lapses called *dāyaka*.

पुरकम्मेण हत्थेण दव्वीए भायणेण वा ।
देंतियं पडियाइक्खे न मे कप्पइ तारिसं ॥३२॥

पुरः कर्मणा हस्तेन दर्व्या भाजनेन वा ।
ददतीं प्रत्याचक्षीत न मे कल्पते तादृशम् ॥३२॥

If before giving out food
Hands are washed or the laddle
Or vessel made of bell-metal
When the *muni* prohibits the donor-lady—
"Such food is not acceptable to me." 32

Note : The word *bhāyaṇa* (*bhājana*) in the *sūtra* stands for bell-metal. It is interesting that even at such early period, the use of bell-metal was quite common. Since the act of washing involves the use of water which is considered to be a live object, the outcome is *hiṁsā* and hence the prohibition. This act of washing prior to giving out food is called *purā-kamma* or prior acts.

एवं उदूओल्ले ससिणिद्धे ससरक्खे मट्टिया ऊसे ।
हरियाले हिंगुलए मणोसिला अंजणे लोणे ॥३३॥

एवं उदकार्द्रः सस्निग्धः ससरक्षो मृत्तिका ऊषः ।
हरितालं हिङ्गुलकं मनःशिला अञ्जनं लवणम् ॥३३॥

गेरुय वण्णिय सेडिय सोरट्ठिय पिट्ठ कुक्कुस कए य ।
उक्कट्ठमसंसट्ठे संसट्ठे चेव बोधव्वे ॥३४॥

गैरिकं वर्णिका-सेटिका सौराष्ट्रिका-पिष्टं कुक्कुसकृतश्च ।
उत्कृष्टमसंसृष्टः संसृष्टश्चैव बोद्धव्यः ॥३४॥

Likewise (if hand, laddle or vessel)
Is wet or oozing water
Or has particles of living sand or clay
Or alkaline soil
Or *haritāla, hiṁgula, manaḥśilā, añjana*
Or salt or laterite soil
Or soil that is yellow or white
Or even the soil of Saurashtra
Or flour just crushed from wheat
Or raw rice meant for sweet cakes
Or be infested with husk or skin of corn
Or particles of fruits
Or juice of leaves green
Then the *muni* **prohibits the donor-lady—**
"Such food is not acceptable to me."
And he should know to distinguish
Besmeared from the non-besmeared. 33-34

Note : *Soraṭṭhiya* (*Saurāṣṭrika*) or the soil of Saurashtra is popularly called *gopi-candana* which is used by the goldsmiths to impart glaze to ornaments. *Piṭṭha (piṣṭa)* is the cake prepared from raw rice flour. Such cakes are even now ceremonially used in northern India but are a staple food in the south. The word *kukkusa* stands for paddy husk. The word *ukkaṭṭha* (alternately *ukkiṭṭha* or *ukkuṭṭha)*, has been used at several places. This implies small particles of fruits or paste of green leaves, gourd or water-melon. *Saṁsaṭṭha (Saṁsṛṣṭa)* and *a-saṁsaṭṭha (a-saṁsṛṣṭa)* have been translated as besmeared and non-besmeared. With the contact of living earth, water or vegetable, a hand, a laddle or a pot becomes besmeared. Just the reverse when these have no such contacts. In other *sūtras* and *cūrṇis*, innumerable varieties of besmearing have been indicated.

असंसट्ठेण हत्थेण दव्वीए भायणेण वा ।
दिज्जमाणं न इच्छेज्जा पच्छाकम्मं जहिं भवे ॥३५॥

असंसृष्टेन हस्तेन दर्व्या भाजनेन वा ।
दीयमानं नेच्छेत् पश्चात्कर्म यत्र भवेत् ॥३५॥

When there is scope for a posterior act
The *muni* accepts not the gift of food
Offered by hand, laddle or vessel
That is not already so besmeared. 35

Note: The contrast with *sūtra* 32 above is worthy of note. In that *sūtra* the prohibition relates to *purā-karma* but in the present *sūtra* it relates to the *pacchā-kamma* (*paścāt-karma*) or posterior acts which may be an occasion of violence. For instance, if a lady offers food to a *muni* which sticks to her hand because of which the hand needs a wash with live water after the offer is made, such food is unacceptable. But if the hand, laddle or vessel is already besmeared, and not besmeared for making the offer to the *muni*, then the food offered by the besmeared hand, laddle or vessel is acceptable. The idea is that the hand, laddle or vessel being already besmeared will later have to be washed but such wash is not occasioned by the offer of food to the *muni* and so the *muni* is absolved. The rule does not apply in case of dry food like bread.

संसट्ठेण हत्थेण दव्वीए भायणेण वा ।
दिज्जमाणं पडिच्छेज्जा जं तत्थेसणियं भवे ॥३६॥

संसृष्टेन हस्तेन दर्व्या भाजनेन वा ।
दीयमानं प्रतीच्छेत् यत्तत्रैषणीयं भवेत् ॥३६॥

When the food is offered
With a hand, laddle or vessel

Provided it be pure
It is acceptable to the *muni*. 36

दोण्हं तु भुंजमाणाणं एगो तत्थ निमंतए ।
दिज्जमाणं न इच्छेज्जा छंदं से पडिलेहए ॥३७॥

द्वयोस्तु भुञ्जानयोः एकस्तत्र निमन्त्रयेत् ।
दीयमानं न इच्छेत् छन्दं तस्य प्रतिलेखयेत् ॥३७॥

When there are two masters
And the offer is extended by one
The *muni* accepts not the food
But watches the will of the other
And accepts not, if the gift
Is not dear to him
But accepts if it be dear. 37

दोण्हं तु भुंजमाणाणं दोवि तत्थ निमंतए ।
दिज्जमाणं पडिच्छेज्जा जं तत्थेसणियं भवे ॥३८॥

द्वयोस्तु भुञ्जानयोः द्वावपि तत्र निमन्त्रयेयाताम् ।
दीयमानं प्रतीच्छेत् यत्तत्रैषणीयं भवेत् ॥३८॥

When there are two masters
And invitation is extended by both
Then the *muni* accepts the offer
Provided the food is pure. 38

गुव्विणीए उवन्नत्थं विविहं पाणभोयणं ।
भुज्जमाणं विवज्जेज्जा भुत्तसेसं पडिच्छए ॥३९॥

गुर्विण्या उपन्यस्तं विविधं पानभोजनम् ।
भुज्यमानं विवर्जयेत् भुक्तशेषं प्रतीच्छेत् ॥३९॥

If a pregnant spouse
Prepares dainties for her use
And be immersed in eating
Then the *muni* accepts not that
But takes what remains after her use. 39

सिया य समणट्ठाए गुव्विणी कालमासिणी ।
उट्ठिया वा निसीएज्जा निसन्ना वा पुणुट्ठए ॥४०॥

स्याच्च श्रमणार्थं गुर्विणी कालमासिनी ।
उत्थिता वा निषीदेत निषण्णा वा पुनरुत्तिष्ठेत् ॥४०॥

तं भवे भत्तपाणं तु संजयाण अकप्पियं ।
देंतियं पडियाइक्खे न मे कप्पइ तारिसं ॥४१॥

तद्भवेद् भक्तपानं तु संयतानामकल्पिकम् ।
ददतीं प्रत्याचक्षीत न मे कल्पते तादृशम् ॥४१॥

If a pregnant spouse
For whom the time to deliver is near
If from standing posture she sits
Or stands if already seated
Then the food and drink offered by her
Are unacceptable for the restrained
So the *muni* prohibits the donor-lady—
"This food is not acceptable to me." 40-41

Note: According to some commentators, food offered by any pregnant woman is unacceptable irrespective of the proximity or otherwise of the time of her delivery. The acceptance of food from a woman whose delivery time is near is a lapse also called *dāyaka*. (See note on *sūtra* 30-31)

थणगं पिज्जेमाणी दारगं वा कुमारियं ।
त निक्खिवित्तु रोयंतं आहरे पाणभोयणं ॥४२॥

स्तनकं पाययन्ती दारकं वा कुमारिकाम् ।
तं निक्षिप्य रुदन्तम् आहरेत् पान-भोजनम् ॥४२॥

तं भवे भत्तपाणं तु संजयाण अकप्पियं ।
देंतियं पडियाइक्खे न मे कप्पइ तारिसं ॥४३॥

तद्भवेद् भुक्तपानं तु संयतानामकल्पिकम् ।
ददतीं प्रत्याचक्षीत न मे कल्पते तादृशम् ॥४३॥

If a spouse is in the midst of breast-feeding
And discards she a weeping child
To offer food and drink to a *muni*
Then that is unacceptable to the restrained
So the *muni* debars the donor-lady—
"This food is not acceptable to me." 42-43

Note : The lapse involved here has been called *paritāpa*. It is incurred in the process of placing the child on the hard ground and in picking it up again.

जं भवे भत्तपाणं तु कप्पाकप्पम्मि संकियं ।
देंतियं पडियाइक्खे न मे कप्पइ तारिसं ॥४४॥

यद्भवेद् भक्त-पानं तु कल्प्याकल्प्ये शङ्कितम् ।
ददतीं प्रत्याचक्षीत न मे कल्पते तादृशम् ॥४४॥

When there is room for doubt
Whether the food and drink is good
The *muni* then debars the donor-lady—
"This food is not acceptable to me." 44

Note : The lapse involved here is called *śaṅkita*. The food may be pure but because of the association of doubt, it becomes impure. Hence the acceptance of such food leads to bondage. If food is taken after proper care and then it is discovered that it is not pure, such acceptance causes no bondage.

दगवारएण पिहियं नीसाए पीढएण वा ।
लोढेण वा वि लेवेण सिलेसेण व केणइ ॥४५॥

'दगवारएण' पिहितं 'नीसाए' पीठकेन वा ।
'लोढेण' वाऽपि लेपेन श्लेषेण वा केनचित् ॥४५॥

तं च उब्भिंदिया देज्जा समणट्ठाए व दावए ।
देंतियं पडियाइक्खे न मे कप्पइ तारिसं ॥४६॥

तच्चोद्भिद्य दद्यात् श्रमणार्थं वा दायकः ।
ददतीं प्रत्याचक्षीत न मे कल्पते तादृशम् ॥४६॥

If a jar is covered with a slab, wood or stone
Or sealed with a paste of mud or shellac

And if to make the offer
The donor-lady removes the cover or the seal
Then the *muni* debars her—
"This food (drink) is not acceptable to me." 45-46

Note : The lapse involved here has been called *udbhinna.* One type of *udbhinna* called *kapāṭa-udbhinna* is involved in the opening and shutting of doors for making the offer of food to a *muni.* This has been noted above in *sūtra* 18. Here is mentioned a second type, *pihita-udbhinna,* in which is involved the opening of a seal or removal of a cover of wood or stone or slab to take out the food. In both the *udbhinnas*, the possibility of *hiṁsā* is apprehended.

असणं पाणगं वा वि खाइमं साइमं तहा ।
जं जाणेज्ज सुणेज्जा वा दाणट्ठा पगडं इमं ॥४७॥

अशनं पानकं वाऽपि खाद्यं स्वाद्यं तथा ।
यज्जानीयात् शृणुयाद्वा दानार्थं प्रकृतमिदम् ॥४७॥

तं भवे भत्तपाणं तु संजयाण अकप्पियं ।
देंतियं पडियाइक्खे न मे कप्पइ तारिसं ॥४८॥

तद्भवेद् भक्त-पानं तु संयतानामकल्पिकम् ।
ददतीं प्रत्याचक्षीत न मे कल्पते तादृशम् ॥४८॥

'This food, brew, cake and dainty
Are prepared to make the offer'—
If the *muni* learns or hears
Then that food or drink is unacceptable
And the *muni* debars the donor-lady—
"This is not acceptable to me." 47-48

Note : Upto this time, the word *pāṇabhoyanam* or *bhattapānam* has been more commonly used. Now we come across a new word *pānagam* (*pānakam)* which has been translated above as 'brew'; for, this is no ordinary drink of water. *Ācārāṅga Sūtra* mentions several types of *pānagas*. Among the commonest are boiled water, husk water, barley water, ash water, etc. *Pravacanasāroddhāra* has three words : *pāna* to indicate alcohol, *pānīya* to indicate water and *pānaka* which is special drink prepared from dry vine or date. *Pānaka* was widely used by the householders and the method of brewing it is indicated in some of the texts on *Āyurveda*. It was used by the ailing and also by those in full health in prescribed doses. From this *sūtra* it appears that a wide range of liquor covered by the word *pānaga* was acceptable to a *muni*. Another notable word to support the above interpretation is *dānaṭṭha (dānārtha)* which means 'for offer'.

असणं पाणगं वा पि खाइमं साइमं तहा ।
जं जाणेज्ज सुणेज्जा वा पुण्णट्ठा पगडं इमं ॥४९॥

अशनं पानकं वाऽपि खाद्यं स्वाद्यं तथा ।
यज्जानीयात् शृणुयाद्वा पुण्यार्थं प्रकृतमिदम् ॥४९॥

तं भवे भत्तपाणं तु संजयाण अकप्पियं ।
देंतियं पडियाइक्खे न मे कप्पइ तारिसं ॥५०॥

तद्भवेद् भक्त-पानं तु संयतानामकल्पिकम् ।
ददतीं प्रत्याचक्षीत न मे कल्पते तादृशम् ॥५०॥

'This food, brew, cake and dainty
Are prepared to celebrate a holy occasion'
If the *muni* comes to know this or even hears
He debars the donor-lady—
"This is not acceptable to me." 49-50

Note : The prohibition applies to food and brew prepared to celebrate some special occasion which is not a preparation for the daily use. If, however, in the more affluent houses extra or special food is prepared for offer to departed forefathers, then the prohibition does not apply, since this one is as good as daily preparation.

असणं पाणगं वा वि खाइमं साइमं तहा।
जं जाणेज्ज सुणेज्जा वा वणिमट्ठा पगडं इमं ॥५१॥

अशनं पानकं वाऽपि खाद्यं स्वाद्यं तथा।
यज्जानीयात् शृणुयाद्वा वनीपकार्थं प्रकृतमिदम् ॥५१॥

तं भवे भत्तपाणं तु संजयाण अकप्पियं।
देंतियं पडियाइक्खे न मे कप्पइ तारिसं ॥५२॥

तद्भवेद् भुक्तपानं तु संयतानामकल्पिकम्।
ददतीं प्रत्याचक्षीत न मे कल्पते तादृशम् ॥५२॥

'This food, brew, cake and dainty
Are prepared for beggars'
If the *muni* comes to know this
Or even hears, then these items
Become non-acceptable to the *muni*
And he debars the donor-lady—
"This is not acceptable to me." 51-52

Note: The word 'beggar' here means any other who is not a *muni* and who still begs to support himself. The *sūtra* uses the word *vaṇimaṭhā* (*vanīpakā*) which means one who obtains a gift by appealing to compassion on the ground of poverty or wretchedness. A *muni* surely begs food but he appeals not to anybody's compassion. His renunciation is voluntary and his begging is a part of spiritual austerity.

असणं पाणगं वा वि खाइमं साइमं तहा।
जं जाणेज्ज सुणेज्जा वा समणट्ठापगडं इमं ॥५३॥

अशनं पानकं वाऽपि खाद्यं स्वाद्यं तथा।
यज्जानीयात् शृणुयाद्वा श्रमणार्थं प्रकृतमिदम् ॥५३॥

तं भवे भत्तपाणं तु संजयाण अकप्पियं।
देंतियं पडियाइक्खे न मे कप्पइ तारिसं ॥५४॥

तद्भवेद् भक्त-पानं तु संयतानामकल्पिकम् ।
ददतीं प्रत्याचक्षीत न मे कल्पते तादृशम् ।।५४।।

'This food and brew, cake and dainty,
Are specially prepared for a *śramaṇa*'
If the *muni* comes to know this
Or even hears, then these items
Become non-acceptable to the *muni*.
And he debars the donor-lady—
"This is not acceptable to me." 53-54

उद्देसियं कीयगडं पूईकम्मं च आहडं ।
अज्झोयर पामिच्चं मीसजायं च वज्जए ।।५५।।

औद्देशिकं क्रीतकृतं पूतिकर्म चाहृतम् ।
अध्यवतर प्रामित्यं मिश्रजातं च वर्जयेत् ।।५५।।

If prepared for the *śramaṇa*
Or bought for him
Or when in food and brew are mixed
Items prepared for the monk
Or these are brought to his presence
Or are prepared in excess of need
Keeping in view the offer to be made
Or food and brew borrowed to make a gift
Or those for monk and laity cooked together
None of these is acceptable to a *muni*. 55

Note : The above *sūtra* is full of technical words. *Uddesiya* (*auddeśika*) points to some object, here the object being the preparation of food for a *śramaṇa*. *Kīyagaḍa* (*Krītakṛta*) is the bringing of food for the *śramaṇa*. *Pūyīkamma* (*Pūtikarma*) is the third lapse in the category of *udgama*. When food and drink are prepared for the *śramaṇa*, this is *ādhākarma* and when this food and drink get mixed with other food and drink, even these become impure and the house remains impure for three days so that from such a house the *muni* cannot accept food and drink before the fourth day. *Ajjhoyara* (*adhyavatara*) is the sixteenth lapse in the category of *udgama*. In this lapse, the householder who in the beginning is making food for his own use increases its quantity when he remembers of the *muni*. This sort of lapse is to be distinguished from another, *miśra-jāta*, where food is prepared for self and *muni*. In other words, in *miśra-jāta* the quantity of food to be cooked is enhanced at the beginning; in *ajjhoyara*, the mixture takes place in the middle of the process. *Miśra-jāta* is the fourth lapse in *udgama*. *Pāmicca (prāmitya)* is the ninth lapse in which food is borrowed in order to make an offer to the *muni*.

उग्गमं से पुच्छेज्जा कस्सट्ठा केरण वा कडं ।
सोच्चा निस्संकियं सुद्धं पडिगाहेज्ज संजए ॥५६॥

उद्गमं तस्य पृच्छेत् कस्यार्थं केन वा कृतम् ।
श्रुत्वा निःशङ्कितं शुद्धं प्रतिगृह्णीयात् संयतः ॥५६॥

The restrained one asks the source of food
Why has it been made and by whom.
Hearing that it is pure,
Carefree, accepts he the offer. 56

असणं पाणगं वा वि खाइमं साइमं तहा ।
पुप्फेसु होज्ज उम्मीसं बीएसु हरिएसु वा ॥५७॥

अशनं पानकं वाऽपि खाद्यं स्वाद्यं तथा ।
पुष्पैर्भवेदुन्मिश्रं बीजैर्हरितैर्वा ॥५७॥

तं भवे भत्तपाणं तु संजयाण अकप्पियं ।
देंतियं पडियाइक्खे न मे कप्पइ तारिसं ॥५८॥

तद्भवेद् भक्त-पानं तु संयतानामकल्पिकम् ।
ददतीं प्रत्याचक्षीत न मे कल्पते तादृशम् ॥५८॥

If food and brew, cake and dainty
Get mixed with flower, seed or greenery
Then these are unacceptable for the restrained
And so debars the *muni* a donor-lady
'Such food is not acceptable to me.' 57-58

Note : This sort of mixture is called *unmiśra* which is the seventh lapse.

असणं पाणगं वा वि खाइमं साइमं तहा ।
उदगम्मि होज्ज निक्खित्तं उत्तिगपणगेसु वा ॥५९॥

अशनं पानकं वाऽपि खाद्यं स्वाद्यं तथा ।
उदके भवेन्निक्षिप्तं 'उत्तिङ्ग'-'पनकेषु' वा ॥५९॥

तं भवे भत्तपाणं तु संजयाण अकप्पियं ।
देंतियं पडियाइक्खे न मे कप्पइ तारिसं ॥६०॥

तद्भवेद् भक्त-पानं तु संयतानामकल्पिकम् ।
ददतीं प्रत्याचक्षीत न मे कल्पते तादृशम् ॥६०॥

If food or brew, cake or dainty
Be placed on water, ant-concentration or moss
Then these are unacceptable to the restrained
And so debars the *muni* a donor-lady
'Such food is not acceptable to me.' 59-60

Note : The Jainas make a distinction between two types of contacts. When, for instance, butter is placed inside water, the contact is visible and direct and this has been called *anantara nikṣipta*. But when we place a pot containing sweets inside water in order to save it from invasion by insects or ants, it is called *paramparā nikṣipta*, the contact being indirect. The lapse involved here has been named *grahaiṣana doṣa*.

असणं पाणगं वा वि खाइमं साइमं तहा ।
तेउम्मि होज्ज निक्खित्तं तं च संघट्टिया दए ॥६१॥

अशनं पानकं वाऽपि खाद्यं स्वाद्यं तथा ।
तेजसि भवेन्निक्षिप्तं तच्च सङ्घट्य दद्यात् ॥६१॥

तं भवे भत्तपाणं तु संजयाण अकप्पियं ।
देंतियं पडियाइक्खे न मे कप्पइ तारिसं ॥६२॥

तद्भवेद् भक्त-पानं तु संयतानामकल्पिकम् ।
ददतीं प्रत्याचक्षीत न मे कल्पते तादृशम् ॥६२॥

If food, brew, cake or dainty
Be placed on fire, and from such contact
If there be concern of their being burnt
Then these are unacceptable to the restrained
And says *muni* to the donor-lady
'This is not acceptable to me.' 61-62

Note: If bread be placed on the oven or if milk be placed on the oven, and if the donor-lady is coming forward to offer food to the *muni* and if she is still anxious about the fate of the bread or milk on the oven, then the food is unacceptable because of a lapse called *samghaṭṭya*.

एवं उस्सक्किया ओसक्किया उज्जालिया पज्जालिया निव्वाविया ।
उस्सिंचिया निस्संचिया ओवत्तिया ओयारिया दए ॥६३॥

एवमुत्ष्वक्य अवष्वक्य उज्ज्वाल्य प्रज्वाल्य निर्वाप्य ।
उत्सिच्य निषिच्य अपवर्त्य अवतार्य दद्यात् ॥६३॥

तं भवे भत्तपाणं तु संजयाण अकप्पियं ।
देंतियं पडियाइक्खे न मे कप्पइ तारिसं ॥६४॥

तद्भवेद् भक्त-पानं तु संयतानामकल्पिकम् ।
ददतीं प्रत्याचक्षीत न मे कल्पते तादृशम् ॥६४॥

Likewise, if a log be added in the oven
Or taken out, or if flame is lighted or brightened,
Or put out, or if food is taken from a pot on the fire,

If water is poured or vessel turned
Or taken off from the fire
In all such cases the food is unacceptable
And so debars the *muni* a donor-lady
'This food is not acceptable to me.' 63-64

Note : This *sūtra* records a number of concerns on the part of the house-wife because of which the food becomes unacceptable. What are these concerns ? One is that the fire may go out because of which a log is added before the lady proceeds to make the offer. Another such concern is expressed when a log is taken out lest the food on the oven should be burnt. When the flame is lightened it is a fresh act; it is brightened when it is already in the process of burning.

होज्ज कट्ठं सिलं वा वि इट्टालं वा वि एगया ।
ठवियं संकमट्ठाए तं च होज्ज चलाचलं ।।६५।।

भवेत् काष्ठं शिला वाऽपि 'इट्टालं' वाऽपि एकदा ।
स्थापितं संक्रमार्थं तच्च भवेच्चलाचलम् ।।६५।।

न तेण भिक्खू गच्छेज्जा दिट्ठो तत्थ असंजमो ।
गंभीरं झुसिरं चेव सव्विंदियसमाहिए ।।६६।।

न तेन भिक्षुर्गच्छेद् दृष्टस्तत्रासंयमः ।
गंभीरं शुषिरं चैव सर्वेन्द्रिय-समाहितः ।।६६।।

If a log, slab or brick
Be placed to provide a link
And if it be in a swinging state
Then a *bhikṣu* whose senses are calmed
Never goes across any one of these.
Likewise, he goes not to a place
Which is dark or which is soft,
For the Lord has seen in these a lack of restraint.
65-66

निस्सेणिं फलगं पीढं उस्सवित्ताणमारुहे ।
मंचं कीलं च पासायं समणट्ठाए व दावए ॥६७॥

निश्रेणिं फलकं पीठं उत्सृत्य आरोहेत् ।
मञ्चं कीलं च प्रासादं श्रमणार्थं वा दायकः ॥६७॥

दुरूहमाणी पवडेज्जा हत्थं पायं व लूसए ।
पुढविजीवे वि हिंसेज्जा जे य तन्निस्सिया जगा ॥६८॥

आरोहन्ती प्रपतेत् हस्तं पादं वा लूषयेत् ।
पृथिवी-जीवान् विहिंस्यात् याश्च तन्निश्रितान् 'जगा' ॥६८॥

एयारिसे महादोसे जाणिऊण महेसिणो ।
तम्हा मालोहडं भिक्खं न पडिगेण्हंति संजया ॥६९॥

एतादृशान्महादोषान् ज्ञात्वा महर्षयः ।
तस्मान्मालापहृतां भिक्षां न प्रतिगृह्णन्ति संयताः ॥६९॥

The donor, if for *śramaṇa's* sake
Uses a staircase, a flat plank or a wooden bed
Or climbs on a scaffold, pillar or palace
Or a lady climbing with the help of a staircase
May fall or fracture her hand or leg
Or may crush under her body's weight
Living beings sheltered on earth—
Knowing these mighty lapses
A *maharṣi*, a restrained,
Accepts not a gift drawn from a height. 67-69

कंदं मूलं पलंबं वा आमं छिन्नं व सन्निरं ।
तुंबागं सिंगबेरं च आमगं परिवज्जए ॥७०॥

कन्दं मूलं प्रलम्बं वा आमं छिन्नं वा 'सन्निरम्' ।
तुम्बकं शृङ्गबेरञ्च आमकं परिवर्जयेत् ॥७०॥

Discards a *muni* an unripe trunk
Root or fruit or leafy vegetable with peeled skin
Or even pumpkin or ginger. 70

तहेव सत्तुचुण्णाइं कोल चुण्णाइं आवणे ।
सक्कुलिं फाणियं पूयं अन्नं वा वि तहाविहं ॥७१॥

तथैव सक्तु-चूर्णानि कोल-चूर्णानि आपणे ।
शष्कुलीं फाणितं पूपं अन्यद्वाऽपि तथाविधम् ॥७१॥

विक्कायमाणं पसढं रएण परिफासियं ।
देंतियं पडियाइक्खे न मे कप्पइ तारिसं ॥७२॥

विक्रीयमाणं प्रसृतं रजसा परिस्पृष्टम् ।
ददतीं प्रत्याचक्षीत न मे कल्पते तादृशम् ॥७२॥

Likewise barley powder or powder of berry
Sweets made with sesamum or liquid jaggery
Or *pua* or other things displayed in a shop
For sale, and yet unsold,
Contacted with particles of dust
Such things a *muni* debars a lady from offering
'This is not acceptable to me.' 71-72

बहु-अट्ठियं पुग्गलं अणिमिसं वा बहु-कंटयं ।
अत्थियं तिंदुयं बिल्लं उच्छुखंडं व सिंबलिं ॥७३॥

बह्वस्थिकं पुद्गलं अनिमिषं वा बहुकण्टकम् ।
अस्थिकं तिन्दुकं बिल्वं इक्षुखण्डं वा शिम्बिम् ॥७३॥

अप्पे सिया भोयणजाए बहु-उज्झिय-धम्मिए ।
देंतियं पडियाइक्खे न मे कप्पइ तारिसं ॥७४॥

अल्पं स्याद् भोजन-जातं बहु-उज्झित-धर्मकम् ।
ददतीं प्रत्याचक्षीत न मे कल्पते तादृशम् ॥७४॥

A *pudgala* with many bones
Pine-apple with many thorns
Aṭṭhiya (asthika) **fruit,** *tendu* **or** *bael*
Pieces of sugarcane and beans
Of which edible portion is small
And discardable substance more
Such things a *muni* debars a lady from offering
'This is not acceptable to me.' 73-74

Note : Two words in the *sūtra* that are likely to raise a controversy are *bahu-aṭṭhiya puggala (bahvasthika-pudgala)*, i. e., object with many bones and *bahu-kaṇṭaya aṇimisa (bahu-kaṇṭaka animiṣa)*, i. e., pine-apple with many thorns. According to some, these are living organs from the animal world while others have interpreted these as being some portions of fruits. Maybe because of divergent food habits in different parts of the country, non-vegetarian food was taken in certain regions.

तहेवुच्चावयं पाणं अदुवा वारधोयणं ।
संसेइमं चाउलोदगं अहुणाधोयं विवज्जए ॥७५॥

तथैवोच्चावचं पानं अथवा वार-धावनम् ।
संस्वेदजं तण्डुलोदकं अधुना-धौतं विवर्जयेत् ॥७५॥

जं जाणेज्ज चिराधोयं मईए दंसणेण वा ।
पडिपुच्छिऊण सोच्चा वा जं च निस्संकियं भवे ॥७६॥

यज्जानीयाच्चिराद्धौतं मत्या दर्शनेन वा ।
प्रतिपृच्छ्य श्रुत्वा वा यच्च निःशङ्कितं भवेत् ॥७६॥

अजीवं परिणयं नच्चा पडिगाहेज्ज संजए ।
अह संकियं भवेज्जा आसाइत्ताण रोयए ॥७७॥

अजीवं परिणतं ज्ञात्वा प्रतिगृह्णीयात् संयतः ।
अथ शंकितं भवेत् आस्वाद्य रोचयेत् ॥७७॥

Likewise, water pure or impure
Or wash-off from a jaggery jar
Or of flour or of rice just washed
A *muni* accepts not;

Guided is he in this by knowledge or faith
Or by asking or hearing.
But when the wash-off water is old
And the *muni* doubts not its purity
Then knowing it to be bacteria-free
And duly changed in taste and colour
Accepts he; but if there be occasion for doubt
Then before accepting he decides to taste. 75-77

Note : Water which has not changed its taste, colour, smell, touch etc., has been called *ahuṇādhoya* (*adhunā dhauta*), but water which has duly changed in these respects is *cira dhauta*.

थोवमासायणट्ठाए हत्थगम्मि दलाहि मे ।
मा मे अच्चंबिलं पूइं नालं तण्हं विणित्तए ॥७८॥

स्तोकमास्वादनार्थं हस्तके देहि मे ।
मा मे अत्यम्लं पूति नालं तृष्णां विनेतुम् ॥७८॥

To donor says he,
'Pour some water on my palm
So that I may have a taste.
Of no use to me is water
Which is too sour or emits foul smell
Or is unfit to quench my thirst. 78

तं च अच्चंबिलं पूइं नालं तण्हं विणेत्तए ।
देंतियं पडियाइक्खे न मे कप्पइ तारिसं ॥७९॥

तच्चात्यम्लं पूति नालं तृष्णां विनेतुम् ।
ददतीं प्रत्याचक्षीत न मे कल्पते तादृशम् ॥७९॥

If water is too sour to taste
Or emits foul smell
Or is unable to quench thirst
Then the *muni* debars the donor-lady
'This is not acceptable to me.' 79

तं च होज्ज अकामेणं विमणेण पडिच्छियं ।
तं अप्पणा न पिबे नो वि अन्नस्स दावए ॥८०॥

तच्च भवेदकामेन विमनसा प्रतीप्सितम् ।
तद् आत्मना न पिबेत् नो अपि अन्यस्मै दापयेत् ॥८०॥

एगंतमवक्कमित्ता अचित्तं पडिलेहिया ।
जयं परिट्ठवेज्जा परिट्ठप्प पडिक्कमे ॥८१॥

एकान्तमवक्रम्य अचित्तं प्रतिलेख्य ।
यतं परिस्थापयेत् परिस्थाप्य प्रतिक्रामेत् ॥८१॥

If such water is acquired
Against the will or due to carelessness
Then the *muni* drinks it not himself
Nor offers it to other *munis*
But deposits it on land
Lonely and free from living objects
And this he does with due care,
Returns to his place and offers *paḍikkama*. 80-81

Note : The *paḍikkama* (*pratikramana*) is prescribed as a penance so that in future he exercises a little more restraint.

(*On the method of eating food*)

सिया य गोयरग्गगओ इच्छेज्जा परिभोत्तुयं ।
कोट्ठगं भित्तिमूलं वा पडिलेहित्ताण फासुयं ॥८२॥

स्याच्च गोचराग्रगतः इच्छेत् परिभोक्तुम् ।
कोष्ठकं भित्तिमूलं वा प्रतिलेख्य प्रासुकम् ॥८२॥

अणुन्नवेत्तु मेहावी पडिच्छन्नम्मि संवुडे ।
हत्थगं संपमज्जित्ता तत्थ भुंजेज्ज संजए ॥८३॥

अनुज्ञाप्य मेधावी प्रतिच्छन्ने संवृते ।
हस्तकं संप्रमृज्य तत्र भुञ्जीत संयतः ॥८३॥

If a *muni* when in search of food
Feels hungry and desires to eat
Then finding a chamber free from live objects
Or a foundation between two houses
And obtaining permission of the master
He sits in a place enclosed and covered
Loosens his mouth-cover
And then the restrained takes food. 82-83

Note : A *muni* in search of food is not usually expected to take it on the way. He must return to his place and then only he is to take food. But exception is made for a child *muni*, an old one or for one who has gone to another village at a distance in search of food and is tired and feels hungry. Even in this case it is desired that he goes to a place where there are other *munis* of the order. But when that too is not possible, then the above prescription applies. The word *bhittimula* has been variously interpreted. We have taken it to mean a foundation or elevation between two houses. Perhaps a more plausible interpretation would be an elevated portion in front of a house which is very much commonplace. *Hatthaga* (*hastaka*) means a piece of cloth covering the mouth of the *muni*. The idea should be to wipe the mouth before taking food or just to loosen it. The idea of wiping or rubbing the whole body with this piece of cloth as suggested by some commentators does not appeal nor does it seem necessary. Some commentators have taken it to be synonymous with *pramārjani* or the soft broom carried by a *muni*. This too does not appear as a good enough explanation, since this is never used by a *muni* to rub the body. Maybe the suggestion is that the *muni* cleans the place before he takes his seat but this too does not stand, since the *muni* is already seated. Considering all these it appears that the *muni* loosens the cloth before he starts taking some food.

तत्थ से भुंजमाणस्स अट्ठियं कंटओ सिया ।
तण-कट्ठ-सक्करं वा वि अन्नं वा वि तहाविहं ॥८४॥

तत्र तस्य भुञ्जानस्य अस्थिकं कण्टकः स्यात् ।
तृण-काष्ठ-शर्करा वाऽपि अन्यद्वाऽपि तथाविधम् ॥८४॥

तं उक्खिवित्तु न निक्खिवे श्रासएण न छड्डुए ।
हत्थेण तं गहेऊणं एगंतमवक्कमे ॥८५॥

तद्उत्क्षिप्य न निक्षिपेत् श्रास्यकेन न छर्दयेत् ।
हस्तेन तद् गृहीत्वा एकान्तमवक्रामेत् ॥८५॥

एगंतमवक्कमित्ता श्रचित्तं पडिलेहिया ।
जयं परिट्ठवेज्जा परिट्ठप्प पडिक्कमे ॥८६॥

एकान्तमवक्रम्य श्रचित्तं प्रतिलेख्य ।
यतं परिस्थापयेत् परिस्थाप्य प्रतिक्रामेत् ॥८६॥

While thus taking his food
If a seed, thorn or straw
A piece of wood, stone-cheap or any other strikes
Then he throws it not aside
Nor drops it from his mouth
But places it on his palm
And repairs to a lonely place
Looks for a suitable spot
Whereon he deposits it with due care
And then returns, to his own station
To say *paḍikkama*. 84-86

Note : According to some commentators *aṭṭhiyam* (st 84) is not seed but bone in meat and *kanṭao* (st 84) is no thorn but scale of fish. We have noted above that due to local food habits in certain parts of the country, non-vegetarian food was perhaps not totally prohibited but was taken by a *muni*.

सिया य भिक्खू इच्छेज्जा सेज्जमागम्म भोत्तुयं ।
सपिंडपायमागम्म उंडुयं पडिलेहिया ॥८७॥

स्याच्च भिक्षुरिच्छेत् शय्यामागम्य भोक्तुम् ।
सपिण्डपातमागम्य 'उंडुयं' प्रतिलेख्य ॥८७॥

विणएण पविसित्ता सगासे गुरुणो मुणी ।
इरियावहियमायाय श्रागश्रो य पडिक्कमे ॥८८॥

विनयेन प्रविश्य सकाशे गुरोर्मुनिः ।
ऐर्यापथिकीमादाय आगतश्च प्रतिक्रामेत् ॥८८॥

And sometimes the *bhikṣu* desires
To take food on return to his abode
Then comes he back with his food
And after due observation enters the abode
Presents himself before his *guru*
Reads the *sūtra Iryā-pathikī*
And then says *paḍikkama*. 87-88

Note : *Upāśraya* is the name given to a *muni's* abode, temporary or permanent, and the two *sūtras* above prescribe the mode of carrying food to and inside the shelter. In this mode the first place is of course given to the purification of food that has been obtained; but before this can be done it is necessary to exercise proper selection of the place where the process may be carried out. Three places are usually prescribed, viz., an empty chamber, the niche at the porch and the entrance-gate of the *upāśraya*. At any one of these places the food may be purified before it is taken in. The process of entrance too is prescribed. First, the *muni* is to wipe his feet with his duster and then utter thrice '*nisihiyā*' (I desist from necessary act). After this he presents himself before his *guru* and says with folded palms, *namokṣamāsamaṇāṇang*. This entire process is humility or *vinaya*. Then he goes inside, observes the spot closely before placing the bowl on the spot, returns to the *guru*, recites the *iryā-pathikī sūtra*, and then stands in prescribed posture and recites *tassottari karaṇenang sūtra* and once again stands motionless. Now he recollects any overdoings and thinks of the *logassa ujjoyagareya sūtra*. Then it is the duty of the *muni* to acquaint his *guru* with all that had happened since his going out in search of food till return, if possible, in details, otherwise in brief. If the *guru* be busy, this confession of experience may be presented to another senior *muni*. In this way a very elaborate process is prescribed which may be read in the following :

आभोएत्ताण नीसेसं अइयारं जहक्कमं ।
गमणागमणे चेव भत्तपाणे व संजए ॥८९॥

आभोग्य निश्शेषम् अतिचारं यथाक्रमम् ।
गमनागमने चैव भक्तपाने च संयतः ॥८९॥

उज्जुप्पन्नो अणुव्विग्गो अव्वक्खित्तेण चेयसा ।
आलोए गुरुसगासे जं जहा गहियं भवे ॥९०॥

ऋजुप्रज्ञः अनुद्विग्नः अव्याक्षिप्तेन चेतसा ।
आलोचयेत् गुरुसकाशे यद् यथा गृहीतं भवेत् ॥९०॥

In going and coming
And in accepting food articles
All overdoings are remembered in order
By the restrained, calm, *ujjuppanno (ṛju-prajña) muni*
And these he presents to the *guru*
To whom he delineates the method
That was used in accepting the offer. 89-90

न सम्ममालोइयं होज्जा पुव्विं पच्छा व जं कडं ।
पुणो पडिक्कमे तस्स वोसट्ठो चिंतए इमं ॥९१॥

न सम्यगालोचितं भवेत् पूर्वं पश्चाद्वा यत्कृतम् ।
पुनः प्रतिक्रामेत्तस्य व्युत्सृष्टश्चिन्तयेदिदम् ॥९१॥

अहो जिणेहिं असावज्जा वित्ती साहूण देसिया ।
मोक्खसाहणहेउस्स साहुदेहस्स धारणा ॥९२॥

अहो ! जिनैः असावद्या वृत्तिः साधुभ्यो देशिता ।
मोक्षसाधनहेतोः साधुदेहस्य धारणाय ॥९२॥

Apprehending lapse in delineation
Or transgression in the order of events
A *muni* **offers** *paḍikkama* **again**
And with his body motionless he thinks—
'What a good fortune !
The victor *jina* **has given prescription**
Of practices flawless
For maintaining the body restrained
Which is shelter for practising penance
That leads to liberation.' 91-92

नमोक्कारेण पारेत्ता करेत्ता जिणसंथवं ।
सज्झायं पट्ठवेत्ताणं वीसमेज्ज खणं मुणी ॥९३॥

नमस्कारेण पारयित्वा कृत्वा जिनसंस्तवम् ।
स्वाध्यायं प्रस्थाप्य विश्राम्येत् क्षणं मुनिः ॥९३॥

Then completing this thoughtful dedication
By the chanting of the *namokkāra mantra*
He sings in praise of the *tīrthaṅkaras* *(jinas)*
And practises pious reading. 93.

वीसमंतो इमं चिंते हियमट्ठं लाभमट्ठिओ ।
जइ मे अणुग्गहं कुज्जा साहू होज्जामि तारिओ ॥९४॥

विश्राम्यन् इमं चिन्तयेत् हितमर्थं लाभार्थिकः ।
यदि मेऽनुग्रहं कुर्युः साधवो भवामि तारितः ॥९४॥

While resting, a *muni* **desirous of liberation,**
Thinks on this helpful line—
'Obliged shall be my self
If *ācārya* **and** *sādhus* **are favourable to me**
Methink they have helped me to cross
The ocean of earthly existence'. 94

Note : The prescription of rest has two aspects. When the *muni* is to dine alone, he is to rest a while before meal. But when there are others in the group who have not yet come back, then the *muni* who has returned earlier needs wait a while.

साहवो तो चियत्तेणं निमंतेज्ज जहक्कमं ।
जेइ तत्थ केइ इच्छेज्जा तेहिं सद्धिं तु भुंजए ॥९५॥

साधूंस्ततः 'चियत्तेण' निमन्त्रयेद् यथाक्रमम् ।
यदि तत्र केचित् इच्छेयुः तैः सार्धं तु भुञ्जीत ॥९५॥

Then he invites in order
And with due politeness
All *sādhus* to partake of food
And if any *sādhu* so invited
Desires to do so
He shares his meal with him. 95

अह कोइ न इच्छेज्जा तओ भुंजेज्ज एक्कओ ।
आलोए भायणे साहू जयं अपरिसाडयं ॥९६॥

अथ कोऽपि नेच्छेत् ततः भुञ्जीत एककः ।
आलोके भाजने साधुः यतमपरिशाटयन् ॥९६॥

If no *sādhu* desires to partake
Then he takes his food alone
From pot uncovered with care,
And not dropping it on the ground. 96.

तित्तगं व कडुपं व कसायं अंबिलं व महुरं लवणं वा ।
एय लद्धमन्नट्ठ-पउत्तं महु-घयं व भुंजेज्ज संजए ॥९७॥

तिक्तकं वा कटुकं वा कषायं अम्लं वा मधुरं लवणं वा ।
एतल्लब्धमन्यार्थप्रयुक्तं मधुघृतमिव भुञ्जीत संयतः ॥९७॥

A food prepared for householder
May be sour in taste, bitter, pungent or hot
It may be sweet or salted—
Whatever has been obtained
The restrained *sādhu* takes it
As if it is butter and honey. 97

अरसं विरसं वा वि सूइयं वा असुइयं ।
उल्लं वा जइ वा सुक्कं मन्थु-कुम्मास-भोयणं ॥९८॥

अरसं विरसं वाऽपि सूपितं वा असूपितम् ।
आर्द्रं वा यदि वा शुष्कं मन्थु-कुल्माष-भोजनम् ॥९८॥

उप्पण्णं नाइहीलेज्जा अप्पं पि बहु फासुयं ।
मुहालद्धं मुहाजीवी भुंजेज्जा दोसवज्जियं ॥९९॥

उत्पन्नं नातिहीलयेत् अल्पं वा बहु प्रासुकम् ।
मुधालब्धं मुधाजीवी भुञ्जीत दोषवर्जितम् ॥९९॥

A *muni* who lives with non-attachment
Speaks not ill of food
Obtained as per prescription
No matter whether it is juicy or devoid of it
With curry or without, dry or wet,
Manthu or *kummāsa (kulmāṣa)*
For, food which is pure
Even though scanty and without juice
Is really much and tasty
So he takes with equanimity
The food which is free from fault
And which is acquired without attachment. 98-99

दुल्लहा उ मुहादाई मुहाजीवी वि दुल्लहा ।
मुहादाई मुहाजीवी दो वि गच्छंति सोग्गइं ॥१००॥
ति बेमि ॥

दुर्लभास्तु मुधादायिनः मुधाजीविनोऽपि दुर्लभाः ।
मुधादायिनो मुधाजीविनः द्वावपि गच्छतः सुगतिम् ॥१००॥
इति ब्रवीमि ॥

A donor with non-attachment is rare
So is one living on non-attachment
A non-attached donor and a non-attached being
Both attain a high level. 10
so say I

Note : Most noteworthy in the three *sūtras* is the word *muhā* which is used in three contexts, viz., *muhājīvī*, *muhāladdha* and *muhādāī*. This is an expression of non-attachment. With non-attachment a donor as well as a receiver attains higher spiritual status.

पंचमं अज्झयणं (पञ्चममध्ययनम्)

PRESCRIPTION FIVE

पिण्डेसरणा (पिण्डैषणा)

Selection of Right Food (Continued)

Second Part *(uddesa or uddeśaka)*

पडिग्गहं संलिहित्ताणं लेव-मायाए संजए ।
दुगंधं वा सुगंधं वा सव्वं भुंजे न छड्डुए ॥१॥

प्रतिग्रहं संलिह्य लेपमात्रया संयतः ।
दुर्गन्धं वा सुगन्धं वा सर्वं भुञ्जीत न छर्दयेत् ॥१॥

The *muni* who is restrained
Eats clean till the last particle
And leaves nothing (in the pot)
No matter whether it tastes ill or well. 1

Note : *Dugandham* and *sugandham*—these two words do not appear to have much to do with smell, since the *muni* has already applied necessary precaution in this respect. The prescription is, therefore, about taste, whether the food is coarse or fine. Even if it tastes coarse, the *muni* must take it without any feeling, with perfect non-attachment.

सेज्जा निसीहियाए समावन्नो व गोयरे ।
अयावयट्ठा भोच्चाणं जइ तेणं न संथरे ॥२॥

शय्यायां नैषेधिक्यां समापन्नो वा गोचरे ।
अयावदर्थं भुक्त्वा 'णं' यदि तेन न संस्तरेत् ॥२॥

तओ कारणमुप्पन्ने भत्तपाणं गवेसए ।
विहिणा पुव्व-उत्तेण इमेणं उत्तरेण य ॥३॥

ततः कारणे उत्पन्ने भक्त-पानं गवेषयेत् ।
विधिना पूर्वोक्तेन अनेन उत्तरेण च ॥३॥

If a *muni*
In *upāśraya* or place of *svādhyāya*
Or when out for begging food
Is unable to live

With food inadequate
Then, under special circumstances,
In manner aforesaid, and that follows,
He again looks for food and drink. 2-3

Note : *Sejjā* in the *sūtra* should mean *upāśraya* or the abode of a monk. The place of *svādhyāya* is a place of study or meditation and is not frequented by others. It is a lonely place and may be even the root of a tree. It is evident that a *muni* is not debarred from using the root of a tree for practising *svādhyāya*. The prescription here is about a second search for food in the course of a day. According to commentators, this relaxation is applicable to a *muni* in penance and not to one who takes a full meal every day and is in good health.

कालेण निक्खमे भिक्खु कालेण य पडिक्कमे ।
अकालं च विवज्जेत्ता काले कालं समायरे ॥४॥

कालेन निष्क्रामेद् भिक्षुः कालेन च प्रतिक्रामेत् ।
अकालं च विवर्ज्य काले कालं समाचरेत् ॥४॥

In search of food
A *bhikṣu* goes in time
And comes back in time.
By avoiding unpunctuality
He does his work at right time. 4

अकाले चरसि भिक्खू कालं न पडिलेहसि ।
अप्पाणं च किलामेसि सन्निवेसं च गरिहसि ॥५॥

अकाले चरसि भिक्षो ! कालं न प्रतिलिखसि ।
आत्मानं न क्लामयसि सन्निवेशं च गर्हसे ॥५॥

"Oh *bhikṣu*, goeth ye at improper hour
Observeth not the time
And so maketh thyself weary
And speaketh ill of the village." 5

Note : It is a quotation of what a punctual *muni* said to another who did not observe punctuality. The latter had gone out for begging but got nothing. When the two had a chance meeting, the punctual *muni* enquired if he could get some food. The unpunctual *muni* said, "Sorry, no. This is a village of beggars. Who is then to make an offer ?" Thus by being unpunctual, he tired himself, spoke ill of the villagers and yet could get no food.

सइ काले चरे भिक्खू कुज्जा पुरिसकारियं ।
अलाभो त्ति न सोएज्जा तवो त्ति अहियासए ॥६॥

सति काले चरेद् भिक्षुः कुर्यात् पुरुषकारकम् ।
'अलाभ' इति न शोचेत् तप इति अधिसहेत ॥६॥

A *Bhikṣu* goes out for food at right hour
Strives for it but grieves not
Even if he gets none, thinking—
"I endure this natural penance'—
And bears he the pain of foodlessness. 6

Note : The word *sai kāle* of which the sanskrit equivalent is sati kāle, alternatively *smṛti kāle,* is the hour when the donor expects the appearance of a *muni* in search of food.

तहेवुच्चावया पाणा भत्तट्ठाए समागया ।
तउज्जुयं न गच्छेज्जा जयमेव परक्कमे ॥७॥

तथैवोच्चावचाः प्राणाः भक्तार्थं समागताः ।
तदृजुकं न गच्छेत् यतमेव पराक्रामेत् ॥७॥

Where animals are assembled
For the sake of feeding them,
A *muni* goes not in their presence
But passes carefully causing 'em no terror. 7

गोयरग्ग-पविट्ठो उ न निसीएज्ज कत्थई ।
कहं च न पबंधेज्जा चिट्ठित्ताण व संजए ॥८॥

गोचराग्र-प्रविष्टस्तु न निषीदेत् कुत्रचित् ।
कथां च न प्रबध्नीयात् स्थित्वा वा संयतः ॥८॥

The restrained, out for begging food
Takes not a seat anywhere
Nor does he, while standing
Indulge in any gossip. 8

अग्गलं फलिहं दारं कवाडं वा वि संजए ।
अवलंबिया न चिट्ठेज्जा गोयरग्गगओ मुणी ॥९॥

अर्गलां परिघं द्वारं कपाटं वाऽपि संयतः ।
अवलम्ब्य न तिष्ठेत् गोचराग्र-गतो मुनिः ॥९॥

The restrained, out for begging food,
Stands not reclining against a latch,
Door-support of city portal, door-frame or a door. 9

समणं माहणं वा वि किविणं वा वणीमगं ।
उवसंकमंतं भत्तट्ठा पाणट्ठाए व संजए ॥१०॥

श्रमणं ब्राह्मणं वाऽपि कृपणं वा वनीपकम् ।
उपसंक्रामन्तं भक्तार्थं पानार्थं वा संयतः ॥१०॥

तं अइक्कमित्तु न पविसे न चिट्ठे चक्खु-गोयरे ।
एगंतमवक्कमित्ता तत्थ चिट्ठेज्ज संजए ॥११॥

तमतिक्रम्य न प्रविशेत् न तिष्ठेत् चक्षुर्गोचरे ।
एकान्तमवक्रम्य तत्र तिष्ठेत् संयत. ॥११॥

The restrained, while out for food and drink
Bypasses not a *śramaṇa* or a *brāhmaṇa*,
Or a miser (who lives on others support),
To enter the quarter of a householder,
Nor does he stand under the eyes
Of a master, a *śramaṇa* or any other
But stands humbly apart. 10-11

वणीमगस्स वा तस्स दायगस्सुभयस्स वा ।
अप्पत्तियं सिया होज्जा लहुत्तं पवयणस्स वा ॥१२॥

वनीपकस्य वा तस्य दायकस्योभयोर्वा ।
अप्रीतिकं स्याद् भवेत् लघुत्वं प्रवचनस्य वा ॥१२॥

In entering a house by by-passing other seekers
He may incur displeasure of the master.
Such act may even undermine
The prestige of the Jaina order. 12.

पडिसेहिए व दिन्ने वा तओ तम्मि नियत्तिए ।
उवसंकमेज्ज भत्तट्ठा पाणट्ठाए व संजए ॥१३॥

प्रतिषिद्धे वा दत्ते वा ततस्तस्मिन् निवृत्ते ।
उपसंक्रामेद् भक्तार्थं पानार्थं वा संयतः ॥१३॥

When the aforesaid depart
After being entertained or refused
The restrained *muni* enters the household
To seek food and drink. 13

उप्पलं पउमं वा वि कुमुयं वा मगदंतियं ।
अन्नं वा पुप्फ सच्चित्तं तं च संलुंचिया दए ॥१४॥

उत्पलं पद्मं वाऽपि कुमुदं वा 'मगदन्तिकाम्' ।
अन्यद्वा पुष्प सचित्तं तच्च संलुञ्च्य दद्यात् ॥१४॥

तं भवे भत्तपाणं तु संजयाण अकप्पियं ।
देंतियं पडियाइक्खे न मे कप्पइ तारिसं ॥१५॥

तद्भवेद् भक्त-पानं तु संयतानामकल्पिकम् ।
ददतीं प्रत्याचक्षीत न मे कल्पते तादृशम् ॥१५॥

If blue, red or lotus white
Or *mālati* or any other fresh flower
Be plucked in the process of offering
Then that food and drink are not acceptable
And the *muni* debars the donor-lady—
"These are not acceptable to me." 14-15

उप्पलं पउमं वा वि कुमुयं वा मगदंतियं ।
अन्नं वा पुप्फ सच्चित्तं तं च सम्मद्दिया दए ॥१६॥

उत्पलं पद्मं वाऽपि कुमुदं वा 'मगदन्तिकाम्' ।
अन्यद्वा पुष्प-सचित्तं तच्च संमृद्य दद्यात् ॥१६॥

तं भवे भत्तपाणं तु संजयाण अकप्पियं ।
देंतियं पडियाइक्खे न मे कप्पइ तारिसं ॥१७॥

तद्भवेद् भक्त-पानं तु संयतानामकल्पिकम् ।
ददतीं प्रत्याचक्षीत न मे कल्पते तादृशम् ॥१७॥

If blue, red or lotus white
Or *mālati* or any other flower fresh
Be molested in the process of offering
Then that food and drink are not acceptable
And the *muni* debars the donor-lady—
"These are not acceptable to me."   16-17

सालुयं वा विरालियं कुमुदुप्पलनालियं ।
मुणालियं सासवनालियं उच्छुखंडं अनिव्वुडं ॥१८॥

शालूकं वा विरालिकां कुमुदोत्पलनालिकाम् ।
मृणालिकां सर्षपनालिकां इक्षु-खण्डमनिर्वृतम् ॥१८॥

तरुणगं वा पवालं रुक्खस्स तणगस्स वा ।
अन्नस्स वा वि हरियस्स आमगं परिवज्जए ॥१९॥

तरुणकं वा प्रवालं वृक्षस्य तृणकस्य वा ।
अन्यस्य वाऽपि हरितस्य आमकं परिवर्जयेत् ॥१९॥

A *muni* accepts not
The roots of *kamala* and *palāśa*
The stalks of *kumuda*, *utpala* or lotus
Or of mustard, or pieces of unripe sugarcane
Or fresh twigs of trees, grass or other flora.
18-19

तरुणियं व छिवाडिं आमियं भज्जियं सइं ।
देंतियं पडियाइक्खे न मे कप्पइ तारिसं ॥२०॥

तरुणां वा 'छिवाड़िं' आमिकां भर्जितां सकृत् ।
ददतीं प्रत्याचक्षीत न मे कल्पते तादृशम् ॥२०॥

A *muni* debars a lady from giving
Beans that are green or half-fried.
Says he, "Such is not acceptable to me." 20

तहा कोलमणुस्सिन्नं वेलुयं कासवनालियं ।
तिलपप्पडगं नीमं आमगं परिवज्जए ॥२१॥

तथा कोलमनुत्स्विन्नं वेणुकं काश्यपनालिकाम् ।
तिलपर्पटकं नीपं आमकं परिवर्जयेत् ॥२१॥

A *muni* accepts not
If not duly boiled, jujube or *bel*,
***Kāsabanāliyā (kāśyapanālikā)*, sesamum-sweet unripe**
Of unripe fruit of *kadamba*. 21

तहेव चाउलं पिट्ठं वियडं वा तत्तनिव्वुडं ।
तिलपिट्ठं पूइपिण्णागं आमगं परिवज्जए ॥२२॥

तथैव 'चाउलं' पिष्टं विकटं वा तप्त-निर्वृतम् ।
तिलपिष्टं पूतिपिण्याकं आमकं परिवर्जयेत् ॥२२॥

Likewise he accepts not, if not duly boiled
Rice-cake, hot water, sesamum-cake,
Basil or mustard-cake. 22

कविट्ठं माउलिंगं च मूलगं मूलगत्तियं ।
आमं असत्थपरिणयं मणसा वि न पत्थए ॥२३॥

कपित्थं मातुलिङ्गं च मूलकं मूलकर्त्तिकाम् ।
आमामशस्त्र-परिणतां मनसाऽपि न प्रार्थयेत् ॥२३॥

Nor does he desire in mind to receive
***Kaviṭṭha (kapittha)*, shaddock, raddish or its round pieces**
That are unripe or not deprived of freshness. 23

तहेव फलमंथूणि बोयमंथूणि जाणिया ।
बिहेलगं पियालं च आमगं परिवज्जए ॥२४॥

तथैव फलमन्थून् बीजमन्थून् ज्ञात्वा ।
बिभीतकं प्रियालं च आमकं परिवर्जयेत् ॥२४॥

A *muni* accepts not
The powder of unripe fruit
Powder of seed, *bihelaga (bibhītaka)* or *piyāla (priyāla)* **fruit. 24**

समुयाणं चरे भिक्खू कुलं उच्चावयं सया ।
नीयं कुलमइकम्म ऊसढं नाभिधारए ॥२५॥

समुदानं चरेद् भिक्षुः कुलमुच्चावचं सदा ।
नीचं कुलमतिक्रम्य उत्सृतं नाभिधारयेत् ॥२५॥

In seeking food a *bhikṣu* discriminates not
But goes he to high and low
He goes not to the high alone
By discarding the low. 25

अदीणो वित्तिमेसेज्जा न विसीएज्ज पंडिए ।
अमुच्छिओ भोयणम्मि मायन्ने एसणारए ॥२६॥

अदीनो वृत्तिमेषयेत न विषीदेत पण्डितः ।
अमूर्च्छितो भोजने मात्राज्ञ एषणारतः ॥२६॥

With full alertness about food
And fully aware of the prescriptions
A learned *muni* who is out for food
Looks for it without feeling wretched
And feels not sad if he gets none. 26

बहुं परघरे अत्थि विविहं खाइमसाइमं ।
न तत्थ पंडिओ कुप्पे इच्छा देज्ज परो न वा ॥२७॥

बहु परगृहेऽस्ति विविधं खाद्यं स्वाद्यम् ।
न तत्र पण्डितः कुप्येत इच्छा दद्यात् परो न वा ॥२७॥

Food and dainty of various sorts
Are prepared by householders in large quantity
But a *muni* loses not temper (if not offered)
(Thinks) it is householder's discretion
Whether he offers or does not. 27

सयणासणवत्थं वा भत्तपाणं व संजए ।
अदेंतस्स न कुप्पेज्जा पच्चक्खे वि य दीसओ ॥२८॥

शयनासन-वस्त्रं वा भक्त-पानं वा संयतः ।
अददते न कुप्येत् प्रत्यक्षेऽपि च दृश्यमाने ॥२८॥

A restrained *muni* loses not temper
Against one who has not offered
A bed, a seat, cloth, food or drink. 28

इत्थियं पुरिसं वा वि डहरं वा महल्लगं ।
वंदमाणो न जाएज्जा नो य णं फरुसं वए ॥२९॥

स्त्रियं पुरुषं वाऽपि डहरं वा महान्तम् ।
वन्दमानो न याचेत नो चैनं परुषं वदेत् ॥२९॥

A *muni* flatters not, while seeking food,
Man or woman, young or aged
Not does he express harsh words
(If not offered or even refused.) 29

जे न वंदे न से कुप्पे वंदिओ न समुक्कसे ।
एवमन्नेसमाणस्स सामण्णमणुचिट्ठई ॥३०॥

यो न वन्दते न तस्मै कुप्येत् वन्दितो न समुत्कर्षेत् ।
एवमन्वेषमाणस्य श्रामण्यमनुतिष्ठति ॥३०॥

Get not angry if not offered obeisance
Is not overwhelmed when so offered
Feels no pride, nor discriminates,
And preserves his monkhood without lapse. 3

सिया एगइओ लद्धुं लोभेण विणिगूहई ।
मा मेयं दाइयं संतं दट्ठूणं सयमायए ॥३१॥

स्यादेकको लब्ध्वा लोभेन विनिगूहते ।
मा ममेदं दर्शितं सत् दृष्ट्वा स्वयमाददद्यात् ॥३१॥

अत्तट्ठगुरुओ लुद्धो बहुं पावं पकुव्वई ।
दुत्तोसओ य से होइ निव्वाणं च न गच्छई ॥३२॥

आत्मार्थगुरुको लुब्धः बहुपापं प्रकरोति ।
दुस्तोषकश्च स भवति निर्वाणं च न गच्छति ॥३२॥

Sometimes he gets a delicious food
And greedily hides, lest it should be shared
If shown to *ācārya* or other monks—
Such one who rates high his own gratification
And who is greedy of delicacies
Incurs much sin.
Pleased not is he of plain things
And attains he not the liberation. 31-32

सिया एगइओ लद्धुं विविहं पाणभोयणं ।
भद्दगं भद्दगं भोच्चा विवण्णं विरसमाहरे ॥३३॥

स्यादेकको लब्ध्वा विविधं पान-भोजनम् ।
भद्रकं भद्रकं भुक्त्वा विवर्णं विरसमाहरेत् ॥३३॥

Sometimes a *muni* who has received
Food and drink of various sorts
Eats himself the dainties in private
And carries only what is tasteless and colourless. 33

जाणंतु ता इमे समणा आययट्ठी अयं मुणी ।
संतुट्ठो सेवई पंतं लूहवित्ती सुतोसओ ॥३४॥

जानन्तु तावदिमे श्रमणा आयतार्थी अयं मुनिः ।
सन्तुष्टः सेवते प्रान्तं रूक्षवृत्तिः सुतोषकः ॥३४॥

पूयणट्ठी जसोकामी माणसम्माणकामए ।
बहुं पसवई पावं मायासल्लं च कुव्वई ॥३५॥

पूजनार्थी यशस्कामी मान-सम्मान-कामकः ।
बहु प्रसूते पापं मायाशल्यञ्च करोति ॥३५॥

"Let other *śramaṇas* know me
To be desirous of liberation, always contented,
As taker of coarse food,
Highly restrained, pleased with anything"—
A *muni* thus covetous of honour,
Fame, status, respect, acquires much sin
And yet strives he to hide all his sinful acts.34-35

Note : The word *māyāsalla* (*māyāśalya*) deserves a note. *Salla* (*Śalya*) stands for surgery. Just as a foreign object penetrated into the body causes pain, so sinful deeds always cause hurt to the doer's mind. The idea is that a *muni* greedy of status, fame and respect indulges in sinful acts, and still in order to preserve these untarnished, he seeks to hide them.

सुरं वा मेरगं वा वि अन्नं वा मज्जगं रसं ।
ससक्खं न पिबे भिक्खू जसं सारक्खमप्पणो ॥३६॥

सुरां वा मेरकं वाऽपि अन्यद्वा माद्यकं रसम् ।
ससाक्ष्यं न पिबेद्भिक्षुः यशः संरक्षन्नात्मनः ॥३६॥

While preserving his own restraint
A *bhikṣu* drinks not *surā*, *meraga* or liquor
Even in the presence of his own self. 36

Note : The word *sasakkhang (sasākṣyam)* has been rendered "in the presence of his own self." Literally it should mean "by keeping his own self as witness." In other words, it means, in privacy when others are absent.

पिया एगइग्रो तेणो न मे कोइ वियाणई ।
तस्स पस्सह दोसाइं नियडिं च सुणेह मे ॥३७॥

पिबति एककः स्तेनः न मां कोऽपि विजानाति ।
तस्य पश्यत दोषान् निकृतिं च शृणुत मे ॥३७॥

Now behold, and listen from me
The misdeeds of a *muni*
Who, considering himself to be in privacy,
Drinks liquor out of attachment. 37

वड्ढई सोंडिया तस्स मायामोसं च भिक्खुणो ।
ग्रयसो य ग्रनिव्वाणं सययं च ग्रसाहुया ॥३८॥

वर्धते शौण्डिता तस्य माया-मृषा च भिक्षोः ।
ग्रयशश्चानिर्वाणं सततं च ग्रसाधुता ॥३८॥

His intoxication and deceitful untruth
His evil name and lack of contentment
His perpetual state of dishonesty—
These lapses are on the wax. 38

निच्चुव्विग्गो जहा तेणो ग्रत्तकम्मेहि दुम्मई ।
तारिसो मरणंते वि नाराहेइ संवरं ॥३९॥

नित्योद्विग्नो यथा स्तेनः ग्रात्मकर्मभिर्दुर्मतिः ।
तादृशो मरणान्तेऽपि नाराधयति सम्वरम् ॥३९॥

Wrong-witted because of his misdeeds
A *muni* is ever restless like a thief,
An addict *muni*, even when approaching death
Is unable to prevent influx. 39

आयरिए नाराहेइ समणे यावि तारिसो ।
गिहत्था वि णं गरहंति जेण जाणंति तारिसं ॥४०॥

आचार्यान्नाराधयति श्रमणानपि तादृशः ।
गृहस्था अप्येनं गर्हन्ते येन जानन्ति तादृशम् ॥४०॥

Such one worships not the *ācārya*
Nor does he worship the *śramaṇas*
Even householders knowing him an addict
They speak ill of him. 40

एवं तु अगुणप्पेही गुणाणं च विवज्जओ ।
तारिसो मरणंते वि नाराहेइ संवरं ॥४१॥

एवन्तु अगुणप्रेक्षी गुणानां च विवर्जकः ।
तादृशो मरणान्तेऽपि नाराधयति संवरम् ॥४१॥

Thus a *muni* who practises misdeeds
And has discarded his pious conduct
Even when he approaches death
Is unable to prevent influx. 41

तवं कुव्वइ मेहावी पणीयं वज्जए रसं ।
मज्जप्पमायविरओ तवस्सी अइउक्कसो ॥४२॥

तपः करोति मेधावी प्रणीतं वर्जयेद् रसम् ।
मद्यप्रमादविरतः तपस्वी अत्युत्कर्षः ॥४२॥

तस्स पस्सह कल्लाणं अणेगसाहुपूइयं ।
विउलं अत्थसंजुत्तं कित्तइस्सं सुणेह मे ॥४३॥

तस्य पश्यत कल्याणं अनेक-साधु-पूजितम् ।
विपुलमर्थ-संयुक्तं कीर्तयिष्ये शृणुत मे ॥४३॥

And contrariwise, listen and behold
A *muni* who is adored by other *munis*,
Who possesses vast and meaningful welfare
(Which is Liberation)
Of him I speak now :

He is one who is full of wit,
Who practises penance,
Accepts not fatty substance
Desists from alcohol
And indulges not in eulogy of self. 42-43

एवं तु गुणप्पेही अगुणाणं च विवज्जओ ।
तारिसो मरणंते वि आराहेइ संवरं ॥४४॥

एवं तु गुण-प्रेक्षी अगुणानां च विवर्जकः ।
तादृशो मरणान्तेऽपि आराधयति संवरम् ॥४४॥

Such a *muni* who practises pious deeds
And scrupulously avoids all misdeeds
Accepts pure food
Prevents influx even at the time of death. 44

आयरिए आराहेइ समणे यावि तारिसो ।
गिहत्था वि णं पूयंति जेण जाणंति तारिसं ॥४५॥

आचार्यानाराधयति श्रमणांश्चापि तादृशः ।
गृहस्था अप्येनं पूजयन्ति येन जानन्ति तादृशम् ॥४५॥

Worships he the *ācārya*
Adores he the *śramaṇas*
And such one is respected by householders
Who know him to be the taker of pure food. 45

तवतेणे वयतेणे रूवतेणे य जे नरे ।
आयारभावतेणे य कुव्वइ देवकिब्बिसं ॥४६॥

तपः स्तेनः वचः स्तेनः रूपस्तेनस्तु यो नरः ।
आचार-भावस्तेनश्च करोति देव-किल्बिषम् ॥४६॥

A *muni* committing theft of penance,
Of word, shape, behaviour and subjective sense,
Performs acts befitting a *deva*
Who is only of the lowest order. 46

Note : The word *deba-kibbisa* means *kibbisa* (low caste) among the gods.

लद्धूण वि देवत्तं उववन्नो देवकिब्बिसे ।
तत्था वि से न याणाइ किं मे किच्चा इमं फलं ।।४७।।

लब्ध्वाऽपि देवत्वं उपपन्नो-दैव-किल्बिषे ।
तत्राऽपि स न जानाति किं मे कृत्वा इदं फलम् ।।४७।।

A *jiva* **born as** *deva-kibbisa*
Even though he attains a celestial life
Yet he knows not
For what is he so stationed. 47

तत्तो वि से चइत्ताणं लब्भिही-एलमूयगं ।
नरयं तिरिक्खजोणिं वा बाही जत्थ सुदुल्लहा ।।४८।।

ततोऽपि सः च्युत्वा लप्स्यते एडमूकताम् ।
नरकं तिर्यग्योनिं वा बोधिर्यत्र सुदुर्लभा ।।४८।।

Falling from there he may come to earth
The abode of men, and be born dumb,
Or (going further down) he reaches hells
Or acquires the body of bird or beast
Where understanding is very rare. 48

एयं च दोसं दट्ठूणं नायपुत्तेण भासियं ।
अणुमायं पि मेहावो मायामोसं विवज्जए ।।४९।।

एनं च दोषं दृष्ट्वा ज्ञातपुत्रेण भाषितम् ।
अणुमात्रमपि मेधावी माया-मृषा विवर्जयेत् ।।४९।।

Seeing the fault, says Nayaputta Mahavira,
A gifted *muni* **indulges not**
Even a little in deceitful untruth. 49

सिक्खिऊण भिक्खेसणसोहिं संजयाण बुद्धाण सगासे ।
तत्थ भिक्खू सुप्पणिहिंदिए तिव्वलज्ज गुणवं विहरेज्जासि
॥५०॥
॥त्तिबेमि॥

शिक्षित्वा भिक्षैषणाशुद्धिं संयतानां बुद्धानां सकाशे ।
तत्र भिक्षुः सुप्रणिहितेन्द्रियः तीव्रलज्जो गुणवान् विहरेत ॥५०॥
इति ब्रवीमि ।

Learning the pure way of begging
From the restrained and enlightened *śramaṇas*
A *bhikṣu* **with senses under control**
Acquiring restraint of the highest order
And also virtue, continues to move 50
So say I

छट्ठमज्झयणं (षष्ठमध्ययनम्)

PRESCRIPTION SIX

महायारकहा (महाचारकथा)

On Great Conduct

(Determining great conduct)

नाणदंसणसंपन्नं संजमे य तवे रयं ।
गणिमागमसंपन्नं उज्जाणम्मि समोसढं ॥१॥

ज्ञानदर्शनसंपन्नं संयमे च तपसि रतम् ।
गणिमागमसंपन्नम् उद्याने समवसृतम् ॥१॥

रायाणो रायमच्चा य माहणा अदुव खत्तिया ।
पुच्छंति निहुअप्पाणो कहं भे आयारगोयरो ॥२॥

राजानो राजामात्याश्च ब्राह्मणा अथवा क्षत्रियाः ।
पृच्छन्ति निभृतात्मानः कथं भवतामाचारगोचरः ॥२॥

Seeing the wise stationed in the garden—
The wise endowed with knowledge and faith
Immersed in restraint and penance
And enriched with learning of the *Āgamas*—
The king, his ministers, the *brāhmins* **and the** *kṣatriyas*
Ask him with humility—"What may be the base of conduct ? 1-2

तेसिं सो निहुओ दंतो सव्वभूयसुहावहो ।
सिक्खाए सुसमाउत्तो आइक्खइ वियक्खणो ॥३॥

तेभ्यः स निभृतो दान्तः सर्वभूतसुखावहः ।
शिक्षया सुसमायुक्तः आख्याति विचक्षणः ॥३॥

Being so asked, the wise,
Who is balanced in soul
Whose senses are conquered
Who is a pleasure to living beings
And who is dedicated to learning
Scholarly, quoth he 3

हंदि धम्मत्थकामाणं निग्गंथाणं सुणेह मे ।
आयारगोयरं भीमं सयलं दुरहिट्ठियं ॥४॥

हंदि धर्मार्थकामानां निर्ग्रन्थानां शृणुत मे ।
आचारगोचरं भीमं सकलं दुरधिष्ठितम् ॥४॥

Listen to me about the conduct
Difficult, mighty and full
Of a *nirgrantha* monk
Who is desirous of attaining *mokṣa*. 4

नन्नत्थ एरिसं वुत्तं जं लोए परमदुच्चरं ।
विउलट्ठाणभाइस्स न भूयं न भविस्सई ॥५॥

नान्यत्र ईदृशमुक्तं यल्लोके परमदुश्चरम् ।
विपुलस्थानभागिनः न भूतं न भविष्यति ॥५॥

"This sort of highly difficult conduct
For the world of human beings
Is delineated nowhere save in *nirgrantha* philosophy.
For those covetous of *mokṣa*
Such conduct has nowhere been prescribed in the past
Nor will it ever be prescribed in future. 5

सखुड्डगवियत्ताणं वाहियाणं च जे गुणा ।
अखंडफुडिया कायव्वा तं सुणेह जहा तहा ॥६॥

सक्षुल्लक-व्यक्तानां व्याधितानां च ये गुणाः ।
अखण्डास्फुटिताः कर्तव्याः तान् शृणुत यथा तथा ॥६॥

**"Listen in proper order
Those virtues which are to be practised
Undivided and as a whole
By young and old, healthy and ailing,
By all that are covetous of heaven. 6**

दस अट्ठ य ठाणाइं जाइं बालोऽवरज्झई ।
तत्थ अन्नयरे ठाणे निग्गंथत्ताओ भस्सई ॥७॥

दशाष्टौ च स्थानानि यानि बालोऽपराध्यति ।
तत्रान्यतरस्मिन् स्थाने निर्ग्रन्थत्वाद् भ्रश्यति ॥७॥

[वयछक्कक्कं कायछक्कं अकप्पो गिहिभायणं ।
पलियकं निसेज्जा य सिणाणं सोहवज्जणं ॥]

[व्रतषट्कं कायषट्कं अकल्पो गृहिभाजनम् ।
पर्यङ्को निषद्या च स्नानं शोभावर्जनम् ॥]

**"Conduct has eighteen items.
The ignoramous who transgresses even one
Falls he from the state of** *nirgrantha*.
**(These eighteen are as follows :
Six are** *bratas*, **six** *kāyas*—
**That are to be protected from injury
And the remaining six are
Avoidance of things unacceptable,
Of householders' utensils, his cushion
Of sitting in his residence, of bath and of decoration.) 7**

तत्थिमं पढमं ठाणं महावीरेण देसियं ।
अहिंसा निउणं दिट्ठा सव्वभूएसु संजमो ॥८॥

तत्रेदं प्रथमं स्थानं महावीरेण देशितम् ।
अहिंसा निपुणं दृष्टा सर्वभूतेषु संयमः ॥८॥

**"Of the eighteen items
Mahavira placed** *ahiṁsā* **first**

He has viewed it in minutest form
Restraint towards all animals is *ahiṁsā*. 8

जावंति लोए पाणा तसा अदुव थावरा ।
ते जाणमजाणं वा न हणे णो वि घायए ॥९॥

यावन्तो लोके प्राणाः त्रसाः अथवा स्थावराः ।
तान् जानन्नजानन् वा न हन्यात् नो अपि घातयेत् ॥९॥

"Knowing or without knowledge
A *nirgrantha* kills not nor orders the slaughter
Of any animal moving or without movement
That may exist in all the *logas*. 9

सव्वे जीवा वि इच्छन्ति जीविउं न मरिज्जिउं ।
तम्हा पाणवहं घोरं निग्गंथा वज्जयंति णं ॥१०॥

सर्वे जीवा अपीच्छन्ति जीवितुं न मर्तुम् ।
तस्मात् प्राणवधं घोरं निर्ग्रन्था वर्जयन्ति 'णं' ॥१०॥

"All living beings want to live
And none is desirous of dying
For this, knowing slaughter to be terrific,
A *nirgrantha* avoids it. 10

अप्पणट्ठा परट्ठा वा कोहा वा जइ व भया ।
हिंसगं न मुसं बूया नो वि अन्नं वयावए ॥११॥

आत्मार्थं परार्थं वा क्रोधाद्वा यदि वा भयात् ।
हिंसकं न मृषा ब्रूयात् नो अप्यन्यं वादयेत् ॥११॥

"A *nirgrantha* says not
Nor asks others to say
For his own self or for others
Out of passion or fear
Truth that is painful, or untruth. 11

मुसावाओ य लोगम्मि सव्वसाहूहिं गरहिओ ।
अविस्सासो य भूयाणं तम्हा मोसं विवज्जए ॥१२॥

मृषावादश्च लोके सर्वसाधुभिर्गर्हितः ।
अविश्वास्यश्च भूतानां तस्मान्मृषा विवर्जयेत् ॥१२॥

"In this entire *loga*
Falsehood is decried by all *monks*
And that is unworthy to the living being
So a *nirgrantha* utters not falsehood. 12

चित्तमंतमचित्तं वा अप्पं वा जइ वा बहुं ।
दंतसोहणमेत्तं पि ओग्गहंसि अजाइया ॥१३॥

चित्तवदचित्तं वा अल्पं वा यदि वा बहु ।
दन्तशोधनमात्रमपि अवग्रहे अयाचित्वा ॥१३॥

तं अप्पणा न गेण्हंति नो वि गेण्हावए परं ।
अन्नं वा गेण्हमाणं पि नाणु जाणंति संजया ॥१४॥

तदात्मना न गृह्णन्ति नाऽपि ग्राहयन्ति परम् ।
अन्यं वा गृह्णन्तमपि नानुजानन्ति संयताः ॥१४॥

"A *muni* who is restrained
Takes not, nor orders acceptance
By others, not approves of it,
Of things living or without life
More or less
Not even as insignificant
As may serve as tooth paste,
Without the permission of the owner. 13-14

अबंभचरियं घोरं पमायं दुरहिट्ठियं ।
नायरंति मुणी लोए भेयाययणवज्जिणो ॥१५॥

अब्रह्मचर्यं घोरं प्रमादं दुरधिष्ठितम् ।
नाचरन्ति मुनयो लोके भेदायतनवर्जिनः ॥१५॥

"Indulging in sex is dangerous
It causes illusion and generates hatred

A *muni* anxious to safeguard his conduct
Never indulges in sex. 15

मूलमेयमहम्मस्स महादोससमुस्सयं ।
तम्हा मेहुणसंसग्गिं निग्गंथा वज्जयंति णं ॥१६॥

मूलमेतद् अधर्मस्य महादोषसमुच्छ्रयम् ।
तस्मान्मैथुनसंसर्गं निर्ग्रन्था वर्जयन्ति 'णं' ॥१६॥

"Sex-indulgence is the root of vice
It is a heap of mighty lapses
So a *nirgrantha*
Avoids the touch of sex. 16

बिडमुब्भेइमं लोणं तेल्लं सप्पिं च फाणियं ।
न ते सन्निहिमिच्छन्ति नायपुत्तवओरया ॥१७॥

बिडमुद्भेद्यं लवणं तैलं सर्पिश्च फाणितम् ।
न ते सन्निधिमिच्छन्ति ज्ञातपुत्रवचोरताः ॥१७॥

"Those who abide by the words of Mahavira
Cherish not the desire to accumulate
Black salt, sea salt, oil, *ghee* or jaggery. 17

लोभस्सेसो अणुफासो मन्ने अन्नयरामवि ।
जे सिया सन्निहीकामे गिही पव्वइए न से ॥१८॥

लोभस्यैषोऽनुस्पर्शः मन्येऽन्यतरदपि ।
यः स्यात्सन्निधिकामः गृही प्रव्रजितो न सः ॥१८॥

"Anything that is accumulated
Casts influence of greed—thus I deem.
A *śramaṇa* who desires accumulation
Is a householder, not a *śramaṇa*. 18

जं पि वत्थं व पायं वा कंबलं पायपुंछणं ।
तं पि संजमलज्जट्ठा धारंति परिहरंति य ॥१९॥

यदपि वस्त्रं वा पात्रं वा कम्बलं पादप्रोञ्छनम् ।
तदपि संयमलज्जार्थं धारयन्ति परिदधते च ॥१९॥

"Whatever cloth, vessel, rag or duster
A *muni* keeps, he does to support
Restraint and privacy
And for these he uses them. 19

न सो परिग्गहो वुत्तो नायपुत्तेण ताइणा ।
मुच्छा परिग्गहो वुत्तो इइ वुत्तं महेसिणा ॥२०॥

न स परिग्रह उक्तः ज्ञातपुत्रेण त्रायिणा ।
मूर्छा परिग्रह उक्तः इत्युक्तं महर्षिणा ॥२०॥

"Mahavira, the liberator of living beings,
Has not called cloth an item of accumulation.
Attachment is accumulation—
Convey thus the great sages. 20

सव्वत्थुवहिणा बुद्धा संरक्खणपरिग्गहे ।
अवि अप्पणो वि देहम्मि नायरंति ममाइयं ॥२१॥

सर्वत्रोपधिना बुद्धाः संरक्षणाय परिगृह्णन्ति ।
अप्यात्मनोऽपि देहे नाचरन्ति ममायितम् ॥२१॥

"At all times and in all places
The wise move with necessary clothes on.
Every enlightened person accepts cloth
For the protection of his restraint.
What to speak of cloth
They have no attachment even for the body. 21

अहो निच्चं तवोकम्मं सव्वबुद्धेहिं वण्णियं ।
जा य लज्जासमा वित्ती एगभत्तं च भोयणं ॥२२॥

अहो नित्यं तपःकर्म सर्वबुद्धैर्वर्णितम् ।
या च लज्जासमा वृत्तिः एकभक्तं च भोजनम् ॥२२॥

"Amazing it is that all the sages
Have had some say on conduct
That encourages restraint and daily penance
And suggests the taking of food but once. 22

संतिमे सुहुमा पाणा तसा अदुव थावरा ।
जाइं राओ अपासंतो कहमेसणियं चरे ॥२३॥

सन्तीमे सूक्ष्माः प्राणाः त्रसा अथवा स्थावराः ।
यान्रात्रौ अपश्यन् कथमेषणीयं चरेत् ॥२३॥

Those that are diminutive beings
Moving or without movement
Invisible are they at night
How does then a *nirgrantha* move as per rules? 23

उदउल्लं बीयसंसत्तं पाणा निवडिया महिं ।
दिया ताइं विवज्जेज्जा राओ तत्थ कहं चरे ॥२४॥

उदकार्द्रं बीजसंसक्तं प्राणाः निपतिता मह्याम् ।
दिवा तान् विवर्जयेत् रात्रौ तत्र कथं चरेत् ॥२४॥

"Food drenched with water or with seeds in
And a path infested with living beings—
These can be avoided in sun-shine
But not in the darkness of night.
Then how can a *nirgrantha* go at night? 24

एयं च दोसं दट्ठूणं नायपुत्तेण भासियं ।
सव्वाहारं न भुंजंति निग्गंथा राइभोयणं ॥२५॥

एतं च दोषं दृष्ट्वा ज्ञातपुत्रेण भाषितम् ।
सर्वाहारं न भुञ्जते निर्ग्रन्था रात्रिभोजनम् ॥२५॥

"Observing this lapse to be full of *hiṁsā*
Hath Nayaputta so ordained—
'Those that are *nirgranthas*

They take not food at night
Not even one out of the edibles four.' 25

पुढविकायं न हिंसंति मणसा वयसा कायसा ।
तिविहेस करणजोएण संजया सुसमाहिया ॥२६॥

पृथ्वीकायं न हिंसन्ति मनसा वचसा कायेन ।
त्रिविधेन करणयोगेन संयताः सुसमाहिताः ॥२६॥

"The restrained endowed with equanimity
Practises not *himsā*
Towards earth-bodies
By three instruments—mind, word and body
And by modes three—(doing, ordering, approving.) 26

पुढविकायं विहिंसंतो हिंसई उ तयस्सिए ।
तसे य विविहे पाणे चक्खुसे य अचक्खुसे ॥२७॥

पृथ्वीकायं विहिंसन् हिनस्ति तु तदाश्रितान् ।
त्रसांश्च विविधान् प्राणान् चाक्षुषांश्चाचाक्षुषान् ॥२७॥

"One practising *hiṁsā* towards earth-bodies
Does so to many others sheltered by them
Both visible and invisible, moving and immobile 27

तम्हा एयं वियाणित्ता दोसं दुग्गइवड्ढणं ।
पुढविकायसमारंभं जावज्जीवाए वज्जए ॥२८॥

तस्मादेतं विज्ञाय दोषं दुर्गति-वर्द्धनम् ।
पृथ्वीकाय-समारम्भं यावज्जीवं वर्जयेत् ॥२८॥

"Knowing it to be a sinful lapse,
That hastens the downfall, a *muni*
Discards *hiṁsā* to earth-bodies till death. 28

आउकायं न हिंसंति मणसा वयसा कायसा ।
तिविहेण करणजोएण संजया सुसमाहिया ॥२९॥

अप्-कायं न हिंसन्ति मनसा वाचा कायेन ।
त्रिविधेन करणयोगेन संयताः सुसमाहिताः ॥२९॥

"The restrained endowed with equanimity
Practises not *hiṁsā* **to water-bodies**
By three instruments and modes three. 29

आउकायं विहिंसंता हिंसई उ तयस्सिए ।
तसे य विविहे पाणे चक्खुसे य अचक्खुसे ॥३०॥

अप्-कायं विहिंसन् हिनस्ति तु तदाश्रितान् ।
त्रसांश्च विविधान् प्राणान् चाक्षुषाँश्चाचाक्षुषान् ॥३०॥

"One practising *hiṁsā* **to water-bodies**
Does so to many others sheltered by them
Visible and invisible, moving and immobile. 30

तम्हा एयं वियाणित्ता दोसं दुग्गइवड्ढणं ।
आउकायसमारंभं जावज्जीवाए वज्जए ॥३१॥

तस्मादेतं विज्ञाय दोषं दुर्गति-वर्द्धनम् ।
अप्-कायं समारम्भं यावज्जीवं वर्जयेत् ॥३१॥

"Knowing it to be a sinful lapse
That hastens the downfall
A *muni* **till death discards such injuries. 31**

जायतेयं न इच्छंति पावगं जलइत्तए ।
तिक्खमन्नयरं सत्थं सव्वओ वि दुरासयं ॥३२॥

जात-तेजसं नेच्छन्ति पावकं ज्वलयितुम् ।
तीक्ष्णमन्यतरच्छस्त्रं सर्वतोऽपि दुराश्रयम् ॥३२॥

"A *muni* **desires not to light a flame**
Which by its nature burns from the start

For, it is sharper than other weapons
And is a bad shelter by all means. 32

पाईणं पडिणं वावि उड्ढं अणुदिसामवि ।
अहे दाहिणओ वा वि दहे उत्तरओ वि य ॥३३॥

प्राच्यां प्रतीच्यां वाऽपि ऊर्ध्वमनुदिक्ष्वपि ।
अधो दक्षिणतो वापि दहेदुत्तरतोऽपि च ॥३३॥

"It burns in the east and the west
The north and the south, up and below,
And at the angular points. 33

भूयाणमेसमाघाओ हव्ववाहो न संसओ ।
तं पईवपयावट्ठा संजया किंचि नारभे ॥३४॥

भूतानामेष आघातः हव्यवाहो न संशयः ।
तं प्रदीपप्रतापार्थं संयताः किञ्चिन्नारभन्ते ॥३४॥

"Doubtless this *habbabāho* (fire)
Is a stroke to the living beings
The restrained starts it not for light or flame. 34

तम्हा एयं वियाणित्ता दोसं दुग्गइवड्ढणं ।
तेउकायसमारंभं जावज्जीवाए वज्जए ॥३५॥

तस्मादेतं विज्ञाय दोषं दुर्गति-वर्द्धनम् ।
तेजःकाय-समारम्भं यावज्जीवं वर्जयेत् ॥३५॥

"So knowing it to be a fomentor of trouble
A *muni* gives up for life
Injury to fire-bodies. 35

अनिलस्स समारंभं बुद्धा मन्नंति तारिसं ।
सावज्जबहुलं चेयं नेयं ताईहिं सेवियं ॥३६॥

अनिलस्य समारम्भं बुद्धा मन्यन्ते तादृशम् ।
सावद्य-बहुलं चैतं नैनं त्रायिभिः सेवितम् ॥३६॥

"Likewise the treatment of the air
This too is full of mighty sins
And so is not indulged in by the *muni*
Who is the liberator of living beings. 36

तालियंटेण पत्तेण साहाविहुयणेण वा ।
न ते वीइउमिच्छन्ति वीयावेऊण वा परं ॥३७॥

तालवृन्तेन पत्रेण शाखाविधुवनेन वा ।
न ते बीजितुमिच्छन्ति बीजयितुं वा परेण ॥३७॥

"It is for a concern like this
A *muni* uses not a fan, leaf, branch or feather
Nor asks another to do the same. 37

जंपि वत्थं व पायं वा कंबलं पायपुंछणं ।
न ते वायमुईरंति जयं परिहरंति य ॥३८॥

यदपि वस्त्रं वा पात्रं वा कम्बलं पादप्रोञ्छनम् ।
न ते वातमुदीरयन्ति यतं परिदधते च ॥३८॥

"Whatever cloth, vessel, rag or duster he has
He uses them not to generate wind
But uses them only with due restraint. 38

तम्हा एयं वियाणित्ता दोसं दुग्गइवड्ढणं ।
वाउकायसमारंभं जावज्जीवाए वज्जए ॥३९॥

तस्मादेतं विज्ञाय दोषं दुर्गतिवर्द्धनम् ।
वायुकायसमारम्भं यावज्जीवं वर्जयेत् ॥३९॥

Knowing it to be an augmentor of troubles
A *muni* gives up for good injury to air-bodies. 39

वणस्सइं न हिंसंति मणसा वयसा कायसा ।
तिविहेण करणजोएण संजया सुसमाहिया ॥४०॥

वनस्पतिं न हिंसन्ति मनसा वचसा कायेन ।
त्रिविधेन करण-योगेन संयताः सुसमाहिताः ॥४०॥

"The restrained endowed with equanimity
Practises not injury to plant-bodies
By three instruments and modes three. 40

वणस्सइं विहिंसंतो हिंसई उ तयस्सिए ।
तसे य विविहे पाणे चक्खुसे य अचक्खुसे ॥४१॥

वनस्पतिं विहिंसन् हिनस्ति तु तदाश्रितान् ।
त्रसांश्च विविधान् प्राणान् चाक्षुषाँश्चाचाक्षुषान् ॥४१॥

One practising injury of plant-bodies
Does so to many others sheltered by them
Visible and invisible, moving and immobile. 41

तम्हा एयं वियाणित्ता दोसं दुग्गइवड्ढणं ।
वणस्सइसमारंभं जावज्जीवाए वज्जए ॥४२॥

तस्मादेतं विज्ञाय दोषं दुर्गति-वर्द्धनम् ।
वनस्पतिसमारम्भं यावज्जीवं वर्जयेत् ॥४२॥

"Thus knowing it to be an augmentor of trouble
A *muni* gives up for life injury to plant-bodies. 42

तसकायं न हिंसंति मणसा वयसा कायसा ।
तिविहेण करणजोएण संजया सुसमाहिया ॥४३॥

त्रसकायं न हिंसन्ति मनसा वाचा कायेन ।
त्रिविधेन करण-योगेन संयताः सुसमाहिताः ॥४३॥

"The restrained endowed with equanimity
Practises not injury to moving organisms
By three instruments and modes three. 43

तसकायं विहिंसंतो हिंसई उ तयस्सिए ।
तसे य विविहे पाणे चक्खुसे य अचक्खुसे ॥४४॥

त्रसकायं विहिंसन् हिनस्ति तु तदाश्रितान् ।
त्रसांश्च विविधान् प्राणान् चाक्षुषाँश्चाचाक्षुषान् ॥४४॥

"One practising injury to moving beings
Does so to many others sheltered by them
Visible and invisible, moving and immobile. 44

तम्हा एयं वियाणित्ता दोसं दुग्गइवड्ढणं ।
तसकायसमारंभं जावज्जीवाए वज्जए ॥४५॥

तस्मादेतं विज्ञाय दोषं दुर्गति-वर्द्धनम् ।
त्रसकाय-समारम्भं यावज्जीवं वर्जयेत् ॥४५॥

"Thus knowing it to be an augmentor of trouble
The *muni* gives up for life
Injury to moving organisms. 45

जाइं चत्तारि अभोज्जाइं इसिणा हारमाईणि ।
ताइं तु विवज्जंतो संजमं अणुपालए ॥४६॥

यानि चत्वारि अभोज्यानि ऋषिणा आहारादीनि ।
तानि तु विवर्जयन् संयममनुपालयेत् ॥४६॥

Four types of non-edible food,
That are non-acceptable to a *muni*
One practising restraint avoids'em all. ‘6

पिंडं सेज्जं च वत्थं च चउत्थं पायमेव य ।
अकप्पियं न इछेज्जा पडिगाहेज्ज कप्पियं ॥४७॥

पिण्डं शय्यां च वस्त्रं च चतुर्थं पात्रमेव च ।
अकल्पिकं नेच्छेत् प्रतिगृह्णीयात् कल्पिकम् ॥४७॥

A *muni* desires not to accept *piṇḍa*
Bed, seat, cloth and vessel,
That are not acceptable
But accepts only those that are acceptable. 47

जे नियागं ममायंति कीयमुद्देसियाहडं ।
वहं ते समणुजाणंति इइ वुत्तं महेसिणा ॥४८॥

ये नित्याग्रं ममायन्ति क्रीतमौद्देशिकाहृतम् ।
वधं ते समनुजानन्ति इत्युक्तं महर्षिणा ।।४८।।

"Those who receive invitation to receive food
Or accept food bought or prepared
Or procured from a distance
Incur sin, as if they approve of slaughter—
Thus ordained the Great Saint. 48

तम्हा असणपाणाइं कोयमुद्देसियाहडं ।
वज्जयंति ठियप्पाणो निग्गंथा धम्मजीविणो ।।४९।।

तस्मादशनपानादि क्रीतमौद्देशिकाहृतम् ।
वर्जयन्ति स्थितात्मानो निर्ग्रन्था धर्मजीविनः ।।४९।।

"For this one thriving on religion,
Free from bondage and having control of mind
Avoids food bought, prepared or procured 49.

कंसेसु कंसपाएसु कुंडमोएसु वा पुणो ।
भुंजंतो असणपाणाइं आयारा परिभस्सइ ।।५०।।

कांस्येषु कांस्य-पात्रेषु 'कुण्डमोदेषु' वा पुनः ।
भुञ्जानः अशनपानादि आचारात् परिभ्रश्यति ।।५०।।

"One who eats food and drink
From bell-metal vessel, cup or tumbler
Belonging to a householder
Slips from the conduct of a *śramaṇa*. 50

सीओदगसमारंभे मत्तधोयणछड्डणे ।
जाइं छन्नंति भूयाइं दिट्ठो तत्थ असंजमो ।।५१।।

शीतोदक-समारम्भे अमत्र-धावनच्छर्दने ।
यानि क्षण्यन्ते भूतानि दृष्टस्तत्रासंयमः ।।५१।।

"It causes injury to living beings
To wash vessels with live water
And to throw that water after the wash
Has been viewed as a lack of restraint. 51

पच्छाकम्मं पुरेकम्मं सिया तत्थ न कप्पई ।
एयमट्ठं न भुंजंति निग्गंथा गिहिभायणे ॥५२॥

पश्चात्कर्म पुरःकर्म स्यात्तत्र न कल्पते ।
एतदर्थं न भुञ्जते निर्ग्रन्था गृहिभाजने ॥५२॥

"In taking food from householders' vessels
There's chance of fore-deed and after-deed
This suits not one who is a nirgrantha.
He takes not food from householders' vesssel. 52

आसंदीपलियंकेसु मंचमासालएसु वा ।
अणायरियमज्जाणं आसइत्तु सइत्तु वा ॥५३॥

आसन्दी-पर्यङ्कयोः मञ्चा-शालकयोर्वा ।
अनाचरितमार्याणां आसितुं शयितुं वा ॥५३॥

नासंदीपलियंकेसु न निसेज्जा न पीडए ।
निग्गंथाऽपडिलेहाए बुद्धवुत्तमहिट्ठगा ॥५४॥

नासन्दीपर्यङ्कयोः न निषद्यायां न पीठके ।
निर्ग्रन्थाः अप्रतिलेख्य बुद्धोक्ताधिष्ठातारः ॥५४॥

"For the Aryans, it is unlike Aryan
To sit or to lie
On plank or bed, stool or chair.
A *nirgrantha* who follows the way
Chalked out by the *tīrthankaras*
Sits not nor lies
On a wooden seat, bed, stool or chair
Before duly observing them. 53-54

गंभीरविजया एए पाणा दुप्पडिलेहगा ।
आसंदीपलियंका य एयमट्ठं विवज्जिया ॥५५॥

गम्भीरं विजया एते प्राणा दुष्प्रतिलेख्यकाः ।
आसन्दी-पर्यङ्कश्च एतदर्थं विवर्जितौ ॥५५॥

The wooden seat, etcetra, that have deep holes
And it's difficult to observe life therein
Sitting or stretching of the body
Is forbidden thereon. 55

गोयरग्गपविट्ठस्स निसेज्जा जस्स कप्पई
इमेरिसमणायारं आवज्जइ अबोहियं ॥५६॥

गोचराग्र-प्रविष्टस्य निषद्या यस्य कल्पते ।
एतादृशमनाचारं आपद्यते अबोधिकम् ॥५६॥

If a *muni* entering a house for food
Takes a seat therei n
He is a victim of lapses
That are delineated below. 56

विवत्तो बंभचेरस्स पाणाणं अवहे वहो ।
वणीमगपडिग्घाओ पडिकोहो अगारिणं ॥५७॥

विपत्तिर्ब्रह्मचर्यस्य प्राणानामवधे वधः ।
वनीपक-प्रतिघातः प्रतिक्रोधोऽगारिणाम् ॥५७॥

In sitting in the householders' abode
He runs the risk of losing celibacy
Of killing living beings premature
Of obstructing begging by other mendicants
And of generating anger in the residents. 57

अगुत्ती बंभचेरस्स इत्थीओ यावि संकणं ।
कुसीलवड्ढणं ठाणं दूरओ परिवज्जए ॥५८॥

अगुप्तिर्ब्रह्मचर्यस्य स्त्रीतश्चापि शङ्कनम् ।
कुशीलवर्धनं स्थानं दूरतः परिवर्जयेत् ॥५८॥

Where celibacy may be in jeopardy
Where attraction is created for women
Where misconduct receives a fillip
Such place needs be avoided from a distance. 58

तिण्हमन्नयरागस्स निसेज्जा जस्स कप्पई ।
जराए अभिभूयस्स वाहियस्स तवस्सिणो ॥५९॥

त्रयाणामन्यतरकस्य निषद्या यस्य कल्पते ।
जरयाऽभिभूतस्य व्याधितस्य तपस्विनः ॥५९॥

A *muni* who may be old or sick
Or emaciated with deep penance
May only seat in the householders' abode. 59

वाहिओ वा अरोगी वा सिणाणं जो उ पत्थए ।
वोक्कंतो होइ आयारो जढो हवइ संजमो ॥६०॥

व्याधितो वा अरोगी वा स्नानं यस्तु प्रार्थयते ।
व्युत्क्रान्तो भवति आचारः त्यक्तो भवति संयमः ॥६०॥

A *muni* ill or well
Desires to take ablution
He transgresses conduct proper
And violated is his restraint. 60

संतिमे सुहुमा पाणा घसासु भिलुगासु य ।
जे उ भिक्खू सिणायंतो वियडेणुप्पिलावए ॥६१॥

सन्ति इमे सूक्ष्माः प्राणाः घसासु भिलुगासु च ।
यांस्तु भिक्षुः स्नान् विकटेन उत्प्लावयति ॥६१॥

Clear it is that a soil which is loose
Or that has holes and cravices
Shelters many minute beings
A *bhikṣu* taking bath with water
Will flood them all. 61

तम्हा ते न सिणायंति सीएण उसिणेण वा ।
जावज्जीवं वयं घोरं असिणाणमहिट्ठगा ॥६२॥

तस्मात्ते न स्नान्ति शीतेन उष्णेन वा ।
यावज्जीवं व्रतं घोरं अस्नानाधिष्ठातारः ॥६२॥

A *muni* takes not bath
With water cold or hot
Till the end of his life
Pursues the terrific vow of non-ablution. 62

सिणाणं अदुवा कक्कं लोद्धं पउमगाणि य ।
गायस्सुव्वट्टणट्ठाए नायरंति कयाइ वि ॥६३॥

स्नानमथवा कल्कं लोध्रं पद्मकानि च ।
गात्रस्योद्वर्त्तनार्थं नाचरन्ति कदाचिदपि ॥६३॥

A *muni* rubs not the body
With scented powder or the toilet
Cosmetics or lotus pollen. 63

नगिणस्स वा वि मुंडस्स दीहरोमनहंसिणो ।
मेहुणा उवसंतस्स किं विभूसाए कारियं ॥६४॥

नग्नस्य वापि मुण्डस्य दीर्घरोमनखवतः ।
मैथुनाद् उपशान्तस्य किं विभूषया कार्यम् ॥६४॥

With body unclad and head tonsured
With body hair and nails overgrown

A *muni* who has discarded pleasures
What does he care for decorations ? 64

विभूसावत्तियं भिक्खू कम्मं बंधइ चिक्कणं ।
संसारसायरे घोरे जेणं पडइ दुरुत्तरे ॥६५॥

विभूषाप्रत्ययं भिक्षुः कर्म बध्नाति चिक्कणम् ।
संसार-सागरे घोरे येन पतति दुरुत्तरे ॥६५॥

With decorations a *bhikṣu*
Ties himself with bondage terrific
And slips in unfathomable worldly ocean. 65

विभूसावत्तियं चेयं बुद्धा मन्नंति तारिसं ।
सावज्जबहुलं चेयं नेयं ताईहिं सेवियं ॥६६॥

विभूषा-प्रत्ययं चेतः बुद्धा मन्यन्ते तादृशम् ।
सावद्य-बहुलं चैतत् नैतत् त्रायिभिः सेवितम् ॥६६॥

A mind attached to decorations,
A *tīrthaṅkara* deems
As serious a lapse as decoration itself,
Full of terrible sin is this.
Hence it's never entertained by the *muni*
Who is liberator of six species of beings. 66

खवेंति अप्पाणममोहदंसिणो तवे रया संजमअज्जवे गुणे ।
धुणंति पावाइं पुरेकडाइं नवाइ पावाइं न ते करेंति ॥६७॥

क्षपयन्त्यात्मानममोहदर्शिनः तपसि रताः संयमार्जवे गुणे ।
धुन्वन्ति पापानि पुराकृतानि नवानि पापानि न ते कुर्वन्ति ॥६७॥

A *muni* who sees value in non-attachment
And slims his body
By penance, restraint and plain-living
Destroys he the sinful acts of the past
And indulges not any more in sinful acts 67

सम्रोवसंता अममा अकिंचणा सविज्जविज्जाणुगया जसंसिणो ।
उउप्पसन्ने विमले व चंदिमा सिद्धिं विमाणाइ उवेंति ताइणो ॥६८॥
—त्ति बेमि ॥

सदोपशान्ता अममा अकिञ्चनाः स्वविद्यविद्यानुगता यशस्विनः ।
ऋतु-प्रसन्ने विमल इव चन्द्रमाः सिद्धिं विमानानि उपयान्ति त्रायिणः ॥६८॥
इति ब्रवीमि ॥

A *muni* who is always calm
Attachment-free and without possession
And full of knowledge of self
Who is famous and a liberator
Spotless like the autumnal moon
Attains he liberation
Or at least a seat with the Vaimanika gods. 68
So say I.

सत्तमज्झयणं (सप्तममध्ययनम्)

PRESCRIPTION SEVEN

वक्कसुद्धि (वाक्यशुद्धिः)

Purifying Speech

चउण्हं खलु भासाणं परिसंखाय पन्नवं ।
दोण्हं तु विणयं सिक्खे दो न भासेज्ज सव्वसो ॥१॥
चतसृणां खलु भाषाणां परिसंख्याय प्रज्ञावान् ।
द्वाभ्यां तु विनयं शिक्षेत द्वे न भाषेत सर्वशः ॥१॥

Knowing the speeches four
A wise *muni* learns humility by using two
And avoids the remaining two by all means. I

जा य सच्चा अवत्तव्वा सच्चामोसा य जा मुसा ।
जा य बुद्धेहिंऽणाइन्ना न तं भासेज्ज पन्नवं ॥२॥

या च सत्या अवक्तव्या सत्यामृषा च या मृषा ।
सा च बुद्धैरनाचीर्णा न तां भाषेत प्रज्ञावान् ॥२॥

Truth unwholesome
Or mixed with falsehood
Whole untruth and truth in doubt
A wise *muni* uses not. 2

असच्चमोसं सच्चं च अणवज्जमकक्कसं ।
समुप्पेहमसंदिद्धं गिरं भासेज्ज पन्नवं ॥३॥
असत्यामृषां सत्यां च अनवद्यामकर्कशाम् ।
समुत्प्रेक्षां असंदिग्धां गिरं भाषेत प्रज्ञावान् ॥३॥

A wise *muni* speaks after careful thought
Of things uncertain, even of truths,
In a manner which may be
Free from sin, mild and beyond doubt. 3

Note : *Asaccamosa* (*asatyāmṛṣa*) implies a speech whose authenticity is uncertain.

एयं च अट्ठमन्नं वा जं तु नामेइ सासयं ।
स भासं सच्चमोसं पि तं पि धीरो विवज्जए ।।४।।
एतं चार्थमन्यं वा यस्तु नामयति शाश्वतम् ।
स भाषां सत्यामृषां अपि तामपि धीरो विवर्जयेत् ।।४।।

Speaks not the wise
Something which is not known,
Or which generates confusion—
whether this or that sense is right. 4

वितहं पि तहामुत्तिं जं गिरं भासए नरो ।
तम्हा सो पुट्ठो पावेणं किं पुण जो मुसं वए ।।५।।

वितथामपि तथा मूर्त्ति यां गिरं भाषते नरः ।
तस्मात् स स्पृष्टः पापेन किं पुनर्यो मृषा वदेत् ।।५।।

A *muni* speaks of appearance
Ignoring the truth
Encounters a sin.
Then what to speak of one
who indulges in whole untruth. 5

Note: When a woman is dressed as a man and if she be called a man, it is a falsehood, though in her dress she appears like a man. This falsehood leads to sin. Obviously, the sin of one who takes full indulgence in falsehood knows no bound.

तम्हा गच्छामो वक्खामो अमुगं वा णो भविस्सई ।
अहं वा णं करिस्सामि एसो वा णं करिस्सई ।।६।।

तस्माद् गच्छामः वक्ष्यामः अमुकं वा न भविष्यति ।
अहं वा इदं करिष्यामि एष वा इदं करिष्यति ॥६॥

एवमाई उ जा भासा एसकालम्मि संकिया ।
संपयाईयमट्ठे वा तं पि धीरो विवज्जए ॥७॥

एवमादिस्तु या भाषा एष्यत्काले शङ्किता ।
साम्प्रतातीतार्थयोर्वा तामपि धीरो विवर्जयेत् ॥७॥

It is for this that a gentle soul
Says not—'I Shall go',
Or, 'say', or 'such act of mine will be done',
Or, 'I shall say this', or 'he shall say so',
Or any other speech of this nature
Based on doubt, because of link with the future,
Or of which there may be a doubtful meaning
Because of its link with the present or the past.
6-7

Note: From the standpoint of time, the speech may have a doubtful base because of its linkage with the past, present or future. Illustrations of the third are provided above. 'I shall go' is a commitment in the future which if it does not materialise becomes a falsehood. Doubt about the present may crop up if from the appearance, the true identity is not discernible. If a woman is perfectly dressed as a man or a man is perfectly dressed as a woman, one may be in doubt about the true identity, and in such circumstance, to call one a man or a woman may have its base in doubt. Likewise about the past when one remembers not whether he had seen a bull or a cow.

अईयम्मि य कालम्मी पच्चुप्पन्नमणागए ।
जमट्ठं तु न जाणेज्जा एवमेयं ति नो वए ॥८॥

अतीते च काले प्रत्युत्पन्नाऽनागते ।
यमर्थं तु न जानीयाद् एवमेतदिति नो वदेत् ।।८।।

**When one knows not true implication,
In the context of the present, past and future,
Says not one, 'Surely it's like this'. 8**

अईयम्मि य कालम्मी पच्चुप्पन्नमणागए ।
जत्थ संका भवे तं तु एवमेयं ति नो वए ॥९॥

अतीते च काले प्रत्युत्पन्नाऽनागते ।
यत्र शंका भवेत्तत्तु एवमेतदिति नो वदेत् ।।९।।

**When one is in doubt about implication,
In the context of the present, past and future,
Says not one, "Surely it's like this'. 9**

अईयम्मि य कालम्मी पच्चुप्पन्नमणागए ।
निस्संकियं भवे जं तु एवमेयं ति निद्दिसे ॥१०॥

अतीते च काले प्रत्युत्पन्नाऽनागते ।
निश्शङ्कितं भवेद्यत्तु एवमेतदिति निर्दिशेत् ।।१०।।

**'Surely it's so',—says one
When one has not an iota of doubt of implication
About the present, the past and/or the future. 10**

Note: The prohibition noted in *sūtra* 6-9 applies only when the speaker is in doubt, lest what he says should come out to be untrue. But this does not mean that he speaks it not when he is sanguine. This is clarified in *sūtra* 10. This should also dispel the criticism that the Jainas who believe in *syādvāda* never speak anything with confidence. A Jaina is required to state with conviction when there is no room for any doubt; in a contrary case, however, he does not commit himself.

तहेव फरुसा भासा गुरुभूओवघाइणी ।
सच्चा वि सा न वत्तव्वा जओ पावस्स आगमो ॥११॥

तथैव परुषा भाषा गुरुभूतोपघातिनी ।
सत्यापि सा न वक्तव्या यतः पापस्य आगमः ॥११॥

Likewise, he uses not harsh words,
Nor even truth that may cause deep hurt,
For even these generate
Bondage of sinful acts. 11

तहेव काणं काणेत्ति पंडगं पंडगे त्ति वा ।
वाहियं वा वि रोगि त्ति तेणं चोरे त्ति नो वए ॥१२॥

तथैव काणं 'काण' इति पण्डकं पण्डक इति वा ।
व्याधितं वाऽपि रोगीति स्तेनं 'चोर' इति नो वदेत् ॥१२॥

He calls not an one-eyed as one-eyed
An impotent as impotent
An ailing man as ill
A thief a thief. 12

एएणन्नेण वट्ठेण परो जेणुवहम्मई ।
आयारभावदोसन्नू न तं भासेज्ज पन्नवं ॥१३॥

एतेनाऽन्येन वाऽर्थेन परो येनोपहन्यते ।
आचार-भाव-दोषज्ञः न तं भाषेत प्रज्ञावान् ॥१३॥

A wise soul conscious of sinful thought
Speaks not words as prohibited above
Or any other that may cause hurt. 13

तहेव होले गोलेत्ति साणे वा वसुलेत्ति य ।
दमए दुहए वा वि नेवं भासेज्ज पन्नवं ॥१४॥

तथैव 'होलः' 'गोल' इति 'श्वा' वा, 'वृषल' इति च ।
'द्रमको' 'दुर्भग'श्चाऽपि नैवं भाषेत प्रज्ञावान् ॥१४॥

Utters not a wise *muni*—
'Oh, ye damned soul', 'ye rascal',
'dog', '*Śūdra*' or 'bastard'
Or says he not, 'Ye a wretch'. 14

अज्जिए पज्जिए वा वि अम्मो माउस्सिय त्ति य ।
पिउस्सिए भाइणेज्ज त्ति धुए नत्तुणिए त्ति य ॥१५॥

आर्यिके प्रार्यिके वाऽपि अम्ब मातृष्वसः इति च ।
पितृष्वसः भागिनेयि इति दुहितः नप्तृके इति च ॥१५॥

हले हले त्ति अन्ने त्ति भट्टे सामिणि गोमिणि ।
होले गोले वसुले त्ति इत्थियं नेवमालवे ॥१६॥

हले हला इति 'अन्ने' इति भट्टे स्वामिनि गोमिनि ।
होले गोले वृषले इति स्त्रियं नैवमालपेत् ॥१६॥

नामधिज्जेण णं बूया इत्थीगोत्तेण वा पुणो ।
जहारिहमभिगिज्झ आलवेज्ज लवेज्ज वा ॥१७॥

नामधेयेन तां ब्रुयात् स्त्रीन्गोत्रेण वा पुनः ।
यथार्हमभिगृह्य आलपेत् लपेत् वा ॥१७॥

Likewise, he addresses not a lady
As 'grandma', 'great-gran'-ma' or 'mother',
'Aunty', 'niece','daughter, or 'grand-daughter'
Or with sounds of endearment—
'*Hale*', '*gole*', '*anne*', '*bhaṭṭe*',
Or 'madam' or any other,
But addresses her duly,
Keeping in view, proper and improper,

Either once or more than once,
By her name or surname. 15-17

अज्जए पज्जए वा वि बप्पो चुल्लपिउ त्ति य ।
माउला भाइणेज्ज त्ति पुत्ते नत्तुणिय त्ति य ।।१८।।

आर्यक प्रार्यक वाऽपि वप्तः क्षुल्लपितः इति च ।
मातुल भागिनेय इति पुत्र नप्तः इति च ।।१८।।

हे हो हले त्ति अन्ने त्ति भट्टा सामिय गोमिए ।
होल गोल वसुले त्ति पुरिसं नेवमालवे ।।१९।।

हे भो हल इतिं 'अन्न' इति भट्ट स्वामिक गोमिक ।
'होल' 'गोल' 'वृषल' इति पुरुषं नैवमालपेत् ।।१९।।

नामधेज्जेण णं बूया पुरिसगोत्तेण वा पुणो ।
जहारिहमभिगिज्झ आलवेज्ज लवेज्ज वा ।।२०।।

नामधेयेन तं ब्रूयात् पुरुष-गोत्रेण वा पुनः ।
यथार्हमभिगृह्य आलपेत् लपेत् वा ।।२०।।

Nor does he address a man
As 'gran-'pa, 'great-gran-'pa, or 'daddy'
'Uncle', 'nephew', 'son' or 'grandson'
'Hala', 'gola', 'anna' bhaṭṭa'
Or 'master' or any other
But addresses him duly
Keeping in view proper and improper
Either once or more than once
By his name or surname. 18-20

पंचिंदियाण पाणाणं एस इत्थी अयं पुमं ।
जाव णं न विजाणेज्जा ताव जाइ त्तिआलवे ।।२१।।

पञ्चेन्द्रियाणां प्राणानां एषा स्त्री अयं पुमान् ।
यावत्तां न विजानीयात् तावत् 'जातिः' इत्यालपेत् ।।२१।।

Of living animals with senses five
So long as it is not known
Whether one is male or female
It's better to mention by specie name. 21

तहेव मणुस्सं पसुं पक्खिं वा वि सरीसिवं ।
थूले पमेइले वज्झे पाइमे त्ति य नो वए ॥२२॥

तथैव मनुष्यं पशुं पक्षिणं वाऽपि सरीसृपम् ।
स्थूलः प्रमेदुरो वध्यं पाक्य इति च नो वदेत् ॥२२॥

परिवुड्ढे त्ति णं बूया बूया उवचिए त्ति य ।
संजाए पीणिए वा वि महाकाए त्ति आलवे ॥२३॥

परिवृद्ध इत्येनं ब्रूयात् ब्रूयादुपचित इति च ।
संजातः प्रीणितो वाऽपि महाकाय इत्यालपेत् ॥२३॥

Likewise, with men, birds, beasts, or reptiles
Says he not: 'It's thick, fatty, killable'
Though he may mention these to be:
Paribuḍḍha, uvaciye, saṁjāye, pāṇiye, mahākā'e. 22-23

Note : The words '*paribuddha*', etc., convey the sense of thick, fatty, etc. Their use is not forbidden in right context.

तहेव गाओ दुज्झाओ दम्मा गोरहग त्ति य ।
वाहिमा रहजोग त्ति नेवं भासेज्ज पन्नवं ॥२४॥

तथैव गावो दोह्या दम्या 'गोरहगा' इति च ।
वाह्या रथयोग्या इति नैवं भाषेत प्रज्ञावान् ॥२४॥

जुवं गवे त्ति णं बूया धेणुं रसदय त्ति य ।
रहस्से महल्लए वा वि वए संवहणे त्ति य ॥२५॥

युवा गौरित्येनं ब्रूयात् धेनुं रसदा इति च ।
ह्रस्वो वा महान् वाऽपि वदेत् संवहन इति च ॥२५॥

In the same manner, a *muni* who is wise,
Says not—'This cow is fit for being milked',
Or 'this ox is castigable'
Or 'capable of drawing a plough or carrying a load'
Or 'of drawing a chariot'.
(But if need be)
Permissible is the following vocabulary:
'This is a milch cow'
'The ox is young,
'The bull is thick or short'
Or 'this is worthy of a chariot.' 24-25

तहेव गंतुमुज्जाणं पव्वयाणि वणाणि य ।
रुक्खा महल्ल पेहाए नेवं भासेज्ज पन्नवं ॥२६॥

तथैव गत्वोद्यानं पर्वतान् वनानि च ।
रुक्षान् महतः प्रेक्ष्य नैवं भाषेत प्रज्ञावान् ॥२६॥

अलं पासायखंभाणं तोरणाणं गिहाण य ।
फलिहग्गलनावाणं अलं उदगदोणिणं ॥२७॥

अलं प्रासादस्तम्भाभ्यां तोरणेभ्यो गृहेभ्यश्च ।
परिघार्गलनौभ्यः अलं उदकद्रोण्यै ॥२७॥

On seeing a park, a mountain, or a forest
A *muni* who is wise says not :
'This (tree) is fit to build a palace,
'A pillar, a gate or a house,
'A latch, a bolt, a boat, or a water-pot' 26-27

पीढए चंगबेरे य नंगले मइयं सिया ।
जंतलट्ठी व नाभी वा गंडिया व अलं सिया ॥२८॥

पीठकाय 'चंगबेराय' च लाङ्गलाय 'मयिकाय' स्यात् ।
यन्त्रयष्टयै वा नाभये वा गंडिकायै वा अलं स्यात् ॥२८॥

Or 'to make a platform, or a vessel,
'A plough, a staircase, handle of tool,
'Centre-piece of wheel, or a water-tub ! 28.

आसणं सयणं जाणं होज्जा वा किंचुवस्सए ।
भुओवघाइणिं भासं नेवं भासेज्ज पन्नवं ॥२६॥

आसनं शयनं यानं भवेद्वा किञ्चिदुपाश्रये ।
भूतोपघातिनीं भाषां नैवं भाषेत प्रज्ञावान् ॥२६॥

'Or (these trees contain) some (wood)
'That is useful for a stool or bed,
'A cart or a house of religion'.
The above a wise *bhikṣu* utters not
That may be of hurt to living beings. 29

तहेव गंतुमुज्जाणं पव्वयाणि वणाणि य ।
रुक्खा महल्ल पेहाए एवं भासेज्ज पन्नवं ॥३०॥

तथैव गत्वोद्यानं पर्वतान् वनानि च ।
रुक्षान् महतः प्रेक्ष्य एवं भाषेत प्रज्ञावान् ॥३०॥

जाइमंता इमे रुक्खा दीहवट्टा महालया ।
पयायसाला विडिमा वए दरिसणि त्ति य ॥३१॥

जातिमन्त इमे रुक्षा दीर्घवृत्ता महान्तः ।
प्रजातशाला विटपिनो वदेद् दर्शनीया इति च ॥३१॥

But going to a park, forest or mountain
Or seeing grown up trees therein,
(If need be), says he :
'These trees are of high specie,
'They are long and round,
'Their twigs and branches are many
'And they are worthy to be seen.' 30-31

तहा फलाइं पक्काइं पायखज्जाइं नो वए ।
वेलोइयाइं टालाइं वेहिमाइ त्ति नो वए ॥३२॥

तथा फलानि पक्वानि पाकखाद्यानि नो वदेत् ।
वेलोचितानि 'टालाइं' वेध्यानि इति नो वदेत् ॥३२॥

And says not he :
'These fruits are ripe,
'They are worthy of ripening,
'They are to be plucked soon,
'They have not yet taken seed,
'They are fit to be sliced.' 32

असंथडा इमे अंबा बहुनिवट्टिमा फला ।
वएज्ज बहुसंभूया भूयरूव त्ति वा पुणो ॥३३॥

असंस्कृता इमे आम्रा बहुनिर्वर्तित-फलाः ।
वदेद् बहुसंभूता भूतरूपा इति वा पुनः ॥३३॥

If need be, says he :
'These mango-trees are no more fruit-yielding,
'These are fruit-yielding,
'These yield many fruits at a time',
Or, 'these are soft.' 33

तहेवोसहीओ पक्काओ नीलियाओ छवीइय ।
लाइमा भज्जिमाओ त्ति पिहुखज्ज त्ति नो वए ॥३४॥

तथैवोषधयः पक्वा नीलिकाः छविमत्यः ।
लवनीया भर्जनीया इति पृथु-खाद्या इति नो वदेत् ॥३४॥

Says he not, 'The herbs are ripe'
'They are unripe', 'have beans on',
'Fit to be cut', 'to be fried',
Or, 'they are edible after being parched'. 34

रूढा बहुसंभूया थिरा ऊसढा वि य ।
गब्भियाओ पसूयाओ ससाराओ त्ति आलवे ॥३५॥

रूढा बहुसम्भूताः स्थिरा उच्छ्रता अपि च ।
गर्भिताः प्रसृताः ससारा इत्यालपेत् ॥३५॥

(If needs be), says he thus :
'The herbs have germinated,
'Their first leaves have come out,
'Their roots have grown,
'Their trunks are steady,
'Their growth is full,
'They are now fruit-yielding,
'The stalks are covered with corn.' 35

Note : The above seven sentences signify the seven stages in the life of a herb, viz., *rūḍhā*, *bahusaṁbhūyā* (*bahusambhūtā*), *thirā* (*sthirā*), *ūsaḍhā* (*ucchṛtā*), *gabbhiyā* (*garbhitā*), *pasūā* (*prasṛtā*), and *sasārā*.

तहेव संखडिं नच्चा किच्चं कज्जं ति नो वए ।
तेणगं वा वि वज्झे त्ति सुतित्थ त्ति य आवगा ॥३६॥

तथैव संस्कृतिं ज्ञात्वा कृत्यं कार्यमिति नो वदेत् ।
स्तेनकं वाऽपि वध्य इति सुतीर्था इति चापगाः ॥३६॥

Says he not :
'The feast is to be organized,
'The offering is to be made to departed parents,
'The thief deserves to be beaten,
'The river has fine embankments.' 36

संखडिं संखडिं बूया पणियट्ठ त्ति तेणगं ।
बहुसमाणि तित्थाणि आवगाणं वियागरे ॥३७॥

संस्कृतिं संस्कृतिं ब्रूयात् पणितार्थं इति स्तेनकम् ।
बहुसमानि तीर्थानि आपगानां व्यागृणीयात् ॥३७॥

(If need be), says he :
'This is a feast,
'This is one who risks life for another's wealth,
'The river bank is almost flat.' 37

तहा नईओ पुण्णाओ कायतिज्ज त्ति नो वए ।
नावाहिं तारिमाओ त्ति पाणिपेज्ज त्ति नो वए ॥३८॥

तथा नद्यः पूर्णाः कायतार्या इति नो वदेत् ।
नौभिस्तार्या इति प्राणिपेया इति नो वदेत् ॥३८॥

Says he not :
'The rivers are full,
'One may cross them by swimming,
'By boat, or animals seated on the bank
'May drink water from them.' 38

बहुवाहडा अगाहा बहुसलिलुप्पिलोदगा ।
बहुवित्थडोदगा यावि एवं भासेज्ज पन्नवं ॥३९॥

बहुप्रभृता अगाधा बहुसलिलोत्पीडोदकाः ।
बहुविस्तृतोदकाश्चापि एवं भाषेत प्रज्ञावान् ॥३९॥

(If need be), says he:
'These rivers are near full,
'Very deep, full of water,
'Their current is growing from feeder rivers,
'They have a wide expanse.' 39

तहेव सावज्जं जोगं परस्सट्ठाए निट्ठियं ।
कीरमाणं ति वा नच्चा सावज्जं न लवे मुणी ॥४०॥

तथैव सावद्यं योगं परस्यार्थाय निष्ठितम् ।
क्रियमाणमिति वा ज्ञात्वा सावद्यं न लपेत् मुनिः ॥४०॥

सुकडे त्ति सुपक्के त्ति सुछिन्ने सुहडे मडे ।
सुनिट्ठिए सुलट्ठे त्ति सावज्जं वज्जए मुणी ॥४१॥

सुकृतमिति सुपक्वमिति सुच्छिन्नं सुहृतं मृतम् ।
सुनिष्ठितं सुलष्टमिति सावद्यं वर्जयेत् मुनिः ॥४१॥

Even knowing it to be a sin-free affair,
That has been done or is being done for another
A *muni* utters not, though sin-free, words as follows:
'Well-done,' 'well-cooked', 'well-cut',
'Well-spiced', 'well-juiced', 'well-seasoned',
'A tasty food indeed'. 40-41

पयत्तपक्के त्ति पक्कमालवे पयत्तछिन्न त्ति व छिन्नमालवे ।
पयत्तलट्ठ त्ति व कम्महेउयं पहारगाढ त्ति व गाढमालवे ॥४२॥

प्रयत्नपक्वमिति वा पक्वमालपेत्
प्रयत्नच्छिन्नमिति वा छिन्नमालपेत् ।
प्रयत्नलष्टमिति वा कर्महेतुकं
गाढप्रहारमिति वा गाढमालपेत् ॥४२॥

(But if need be), he calls
A ripe thing as *payatta-pakka*
A thing plucked as *payatta-chinna*
A thing done with expert hands as *payatta-laṭṭha*
And a deep cut as *pahāra-gāḍha*. 42

सव्वुक्कसं परग्घं वा अउलं नत्थि एरिसं ।
अविक्कयमवत्तव्वं अचियत्तं चेव नो वए ॥४३॥

सर्वोत्कर्षं परार्घं वा अतुलं नास्ति ईदृशम् ।
अविक्रेयमवक्तव्यम् 'अचियत्तं' चैव नो वदेत् ॥४३॥

(In the affairs of purchase and sale), says he not:
'This thing is the best', 'most costly',

'Beyond comparison', 'not now salable',
'Indescribable', 'unthinkable'. 43

सव्वमेयं वइस्सामि सव्वमेयं त्ति नो वए।
अणुवीइ सव्वं सव्वत्थ एवं भासेज्ज पन्नवं ॥४४॥

सर्वमेतद् वदिष्यामि सर्वमेतदिति नो वदेत्।
अनुविविच्य सर्वं सर्वत्र एवं भाषेत प्रज्ञावान् ॥४४॥

(If one sends a message), says he not :
'I shall say all this', or 'this is just so',
But says, after keeping in view,
All the aforesaid rules
(So that no *karma* bondage grows.) 44

सुक्कीयं वा सुविक्कीयं अकेज्जं केज्जमेव वा।
इमं गेण्ह इमं मुंच पणियं नो वियागरे ॥४५॥

सुक्रीतं वा सुविक्रीतम् अक्रेयं क्रेयमेव वा।
इदं गृहाण इदं मुञ्च पण्यं नो व्यागृणीयात् ॥४५॥

And as to merchandise, says he not :
'Bought well,' 'sold well',
'This is not worthy of sale, this is so worthy',
'Buy this,' or 'sell that'. 45

अप्पग्घे वा महग्घे वा कए वा विक्कए वि वा।
पणियट्ठे समुपन्ने अणवज्जं वियागरे ॥४६॥

अल्पार्घे वा महार्घे वा क्रये वा विक्रयेऽपि वा।
पण्यार्थे समुत्पन्ने अनवद्यं व्यागृणीयात् ॥४६॥

As to purchase or sale of wares,
Costly or cheap, says a *muni* words sin-free
(In other words, in such affairs, says a *muni*,
He has no right to say anything.) 46

तहेवासंजयं धीरो ग्रास एहि करेहि वा ।
सय चिट्ठ वयाहि त्ति नेवं भासेज्ज पन्नवं ।।४७।।

तथैवाऽसंयतं धीरः आस्व एहि कुरु वा ।
शेष्व तिष्ठ व्रज इति नैवं भाषेत प्रज्ञावान् ।।४७।।

Likewise a *muni* wise and balanced,
Asks not a householder to come, sit or do,
To lie, wait, stand or go away. 47

बहवे इमे ग्रसाहू लोए वुच्चंति साहुणो ।
न लवे ग्रसाहुं साहु त्ति साहुं साहु त्ति ग्रालवे ।।४८।।

बहव इमे असाधवः लोके उच्यन्ते साधवः ।
न लपेदसाधुं साधुरिति साधुं साधुरित्यालपेत् ।।४८।।

Many a dishonest pass in the world as honest.
(But a *sādhu*) calls not him honest
Only one who is honest he calls honest. 48

नाणदंसणसंपन्नं संजमे य तवे रयं ।
एवंगुणसमाउत्तं संजयं साहुमालवे ।।४९।।

ज्ञानदर्शनसंपन्नं संयमे च तपसि रतम् ।
एवं गुणसमायुक्तं संयतं साधुमालपेत् ।।४९।।

A *sādhu* is one who is rich in knowledge and faith
And is devoted to penance and restraint. 49

देवाणं मणुयाणं च तिरियाणं च वुग्गहे ।
ग्रमुयाणं जग्रो होउ मा वा होउ त्ति नो वए ।।५०।।

देवानां मनुजानाञ्च तिरश्चां च व्युदग्रहे ।
ग्रमुकानां जयो भवतु मा वा भवतु इति नो वदेत् ।।५०।।

When men, gods, birds or beasts fight,
Says he not, 'This shall win and not that'. 50

वाश्रो वुट्ठं व सीउण्ह खेमं धायं सिवं ति वा ।
कया णु होज्ज एयाणि मा वा होउ त्ति नो वए ॥५१॥

वातो वृष्टं वा शीतोष्णं क्षेमं 'धायं' शिवमिति वा ।
कदा नु भवेयुरेतानि मा वा भवेयुरिति नो वदेत् ॥५१॥

And utters he not a forecast
About wind or rain, winter or summer,
Plenty, prosperity and epidemic,
When these will exist and when these will not. 51

तहेव मेहं व नहं व माणवं न देव देव त्ति गिरं वएज्जा ।
सम्मुच्छिए उन्नए वा पश्रोए वएज्ज वा वुट्ठ बलाहए त्ति ॥५२॥

तथैव मेघं वा नभो वा मानवं न देव देव इति गिरं वदेत् ।
संमूर्छितः उन्नतो वा पयोदः वदेद् वा वृष्टो बलाहक इति ॥५२॥

About clouds, sky or men,
Says he not, these are gods,
But says, the clouds are gathering,
Spreading, rising, or just started raining. 52

श्रंतलिक्खे त्ति णं बूया गुज्भाणुचरिय त्ति य ।
रिद्धिमंतं नरं दिस्स रिद्धिमंतं ति श्रालवे ॥५३॥

श्रन्तरिक्षमिति तद् ब्रूयात् गुह्यानुचरितमिति च ।
ऋद्धिमन्तं नरं दृष्ट्वा ऋद्धिमान् इत्यालपेत् ॥५३॥

The sky and the clouds are to be called
Antalikkha **or** *guhyāṇucariya.*
On seeing an affluent man, says he,
'This man is endowed with *ṛddhi.*' 53

तहेव सावज्जणुमोयणी गिरा ओहारिणी जा य परोवघाइणी ।
से कोह लोह भयसा व माणवो न हासमाणो वि गिरं वएज्जा
॥५४॥

तथैव सावद्यानुमोदिनी गीः अवधारिणी या च परोपघातिनी ।
स क्रोध-लोभ-भयेन वा मानवो न हसन्नपि गिरं वदेत् ॥५४॥

Likewise he makes not a speech
That supports sin, or that is based on doubt,
Or that may cause hurt or injury to living beings
A *muni* speaks not in anger or with attachment
Or under fear, nor speaks he
Jokingly of others. 54

सवक्कसुद्धि समुपेहिया मुणी गिरं च दुट्ठं परिवज्जए सया ।
मियं अदुट्ठं अणुवीइ भासए सयाण मज्झे लहई पसंसणं ॥५५॥

सवाक्यशुद्धि समुत्प्रेक्ष्य मुनिः गिरं च दुष्टां परिवर्जयेत् सदा ।
मितामदुष्टाम् अनुविविच्य भाषकः सतां मध्ये लभते प्रशंसनम् ॥५५॥

Knowing well the mode of purifying speech
He utters not words of blemish;
Measured and blemish-free words he speaks
And that after careful thought.
A *muni* practising this
Attains fame in the group of righteous men. 55

भासाए दोसे य गुणे य जाणिया तीसे य दुट्ठे परिवज्जए सया ।
छसु संजए सामणिए सया जए वएज्ज बुद्धे हियमाणुलोमियं ॥५६॥

भाषायाः दोषांश्च गुणांश्च ज्ञात्वा तस्याश्च दुष्टायाः परिवर्जकः सदा ।
षट्सु संयतः श्रामण्ये सदा यतः वदेद्बुद्धः हितामानुलोमिकीम् ॥५६॥

Knowing the virtues and vices of speech
One who discards the words of blemish,

Who is restrained towards six species of beings,
Careful about a *śramaṇa's* conduct,
Enlightened, a *bhikṣu*,
Speaks he what is good and favourable. 56

परिक्खभासी सुसमाहिइंदिए चउक्कसायावगए अरिणस्सिए ।
स निद्धुणे धन्नमलं पुरेकडं आराहए लोगमिणं तहा परं ॥५७॥
त्ति बेमि ॥

परीक्ष्यभाषी सुसमाहितेन्द्रियः अपगतचतुष्कषायः अनिश्रितः ।
स निर्धूय धुन्नमलं पुराकृतम् आराधयेल्लोकमिमं तथा परम् ॥५७॥
इति ब्रवीमि ।

A *bhikṣu* who speaks
After measuring the virtue and vice of words,
Has full control of senses,
Free from *kaṣāyas*, and *aṇissiya*,
Uproots he the dirt of past sins
And worships he the present and future *logas*. 57
So say I.

अट्ठमज्झयणं (अष्टममध्ययनम्)

PRESCRIPTION EIGHT

आयारपणिही (आचार-प्रणिधिः)

Code of Conduct

आयारप्पणिहिं लद्धुं जहा कायव्व भिक्खुणा ।
तं भे उदाहरिस्सामि आणुपुव्विं सुणेह मे ॥१॥

आचार-प्रणिधिं लब्ध्वा यथा कर्तव्यं भिक्षुणा ।
तं भवद्भ्य उदाहरिष्यामि आनुपूर्व्या शृणुत मे ॥१॥

I shall now tell you how,
On receiving the Code of Conduct,
A *sādhu* should behave.
Listen from me in order. 1

पुढवि दग अगणि मारुय तणरुक्ख सबीयगा ।
तसा य पाणा जीव त्ति इइ वुत्तं महेसिणा ॥२॥

पृथिव्युदकाग्निमारुताः तृणरुक्षाः सबीजकाः ।
त्रसाश्च प्राणाः जीवा इति इति उक्तं महर्षिणा ॥२॥

Ordains thus the *Maharṣi*:
Earth, water, fire, air and flora upto seeds
And all moving beings are *jīvas*. 2

तेसिं अच्छणजोएण निच्चं होयव्वयं सिया ।
मणसा कायवक्केण एवं भवइ संजए ॥३॥

तेषामक्षरण-योगेन नित्यं भवितव्यं स्यात् ।
मनसा काय-वाक्येन एवं भवति संयतः ॥३॥

A *bhikṣu* **should entertain non-injury to these**
By mind, word and deed.
Thus lodged in non-injury
One is restrained. 3

पुढविं भित्तिं सिलं लेलुं नेव भिंदे न संलिहे ।
तिविहेण करणजोएण संजए सुसमाहिए ॥४॥

पृथिवीं भित्तिं शिलां लेष्टुं नैव भिन्द्यात् न संलिखेत् ।
त्रिविधेन करण-योगेन संयतः सुसमाहितः ॥४॥

The restrained lodged in equanimity
Neither divides nor digs
By three instruments and modes three
Earth, river-bank, rock or stone. 4

सुद्धपुढवीए न निसिए ससरक्खम्मि य आसणे ।
पमज्जित्तु निसीएज्जा जाइत्ता जस्स ओग्गहं ॥५॥

शुद्धपृथिव्यां न निषीदेत् ससरक्षे च आसने ।
प्रमृज्य तु निषीदेत् याचित्वा यस्यावग्रहम् ॥५॥

A *muni* **sits not on bare earth**
Nor on a cushion with live-dust;
Sits he on clean soil after wiping
And with the permission from the owner. 5

सोओदगं न सेवेज्जा सिलावुट्ठं हिमाणि य ।
उसिणोदगं तत्तफासुयं पडिगाहेज्ज संजए ॥६॥

शीतोदकं न सेवेत शिलावृष्टं हिमानि च ।
उष्णोदकं तप्तप्रासुकं प्रतिगृह्णीयात् संयतः ॥६॥

The restrained takes not water which is cold
Nor hail-stones, rain-water or dew;
Accepts he such water only
As may be life-free after boiling. 6

उदउल्लं अप्पणो कायं नेव पुंछे न संलिहे ।
समुप्पेह तहाभूयं नो णं संघट्टए मुणी ॥७॥

उदआर्द्रमात्मनः कायं नैव प्रोञ्छेत न संलिखेत् ।
समुत्प्रेक्ष्य तथाभूतं नैनं संघट्टयेत् मुनिः ॥७॥

A *muni* dries not his body
Nor drenches it with a shower,
And seeing a body drenched
He touches it not. 7

इंगालं अगणिं अच्चिं अलायं वा सजोइयं ।
न उंजेज्जा न घट्टेज्जा नो णं निव्वावए मुणी ॥८॥

अङ्गारमग्निमर्चिः अलातं वा सज्योतिः ।
नोत्सिञ्चेत् न घट्टयेत् नैनं निर्वापयेद् मुनिः ॥८॥

A *muni* neither enkindles
Nor touches nor puts out
Burning ashes, fire or a burning log
Or even a portion thereof. 8

तालियंटेण पत्तेण साहाविहुयणेण वा ।
न वीएज्ज अप्पणो कायं बाहिरं वा वि पोग्गलं ॥९॥

तालवृन्तेन पत्रेण शाखा-विधुवनेन वा ।
न व्यजेदात्मनः कायं बाह्यं वाऽपि पुद्गलम् ॥९॥

A *muni* fans not
His own self or an external *pudgala*
With *camara*, leaf, twig or a fan. 9

तणरुक्खं न छिंदेज्जा फलं मूलं व कस्सई ।
आमगं विविहं बीयं मणसा वि न पत्थए ॥१०॥

तृणरुक्षं न छिन्द्यात् फलं मूलं वा कस्यचित् ।
आमकं विविधं बीजं मनसापि न प्रार्थयेत् ॥१०॥

A *muni* cuts not grass, tree, fruit or root
Nor desires in mind various live-seeds. 10

गहणेसु न चिट्ठेज्जा बीएसु हरिएसु वा ।
उदगम्मि तहा निच्चं उत्तिगपणगेसु वा ॥११॥

गहनेषु न तिष्ठेत् बीजेषु हरितेषु वा ।
उदके तथा नित्यम् 'उत्तिङ्गपनकेषु' वा ॥११॥

A *muni* stands not in a forest
On seed, or greenery or ever-multiplying flora
On rain-sprouts or even on fresh moss. 11

तसे पाणे न हिंसेज्जा वाया अदुव कम्मुणा ।
उवरओ सव्वभूएसु पासेज्ज विविहं जगं ॥१२॥

त्रसान् प्राणान् न हिंस्यात् वाचा अथवा कर्मणा ।
उपरतः सर्वभूतेषु पश्येद् विविधं जगत् ॥१२॥

A *muni* injures not
Moving animal by word or deed.
Desisting from injury to all animals
Views he the diversity of the universe. 12

अट्ठ सुहुमाइं पेहाए जाइं जाणित्तु संजए ।
दयाहिगारी भूएसु आस चिट्ठ सएहि वा ॥१३॥

अष्टौ सूक्ष्माणि प्रेक्ष्य यानि ज्ञात्वा संयतः ।
दयाधिकारी भूतेषु आस्व उत्तिष्ठ शेष्व वा ॥१३॥

A restrained ***muni*** **sits, stands or lies**
After observing eight species of minute beings
And only with a knowledge of these eight
One can extend compassion to them all. 13

कयराइं अट्ठ सुहुमाइं जाइं पुच्छेज्ज संजए।
इमाइं ताइं मेहावी आइक्खेज्ज वियक्खणो ॥१४॥

कतराणि अष्टौ सूक्ष्माणि यानि पृच्छेत् संयतः।
इमानि तानि मेधावी आचक्षीत विचक्षणः ॥१४॥

What are these eight ?—
When thus the disciple asks,
Replies thus the ***guru***
Who is learned and wise. 14

सिणेहं पुप्फसुहुमं च पाणुत्तिगं तहेव य।
पणगं बीय हरियं च अंडसुहुमं च अट्ठमं ॥१५॥

स्नेहं पुष्प-सूक्ष्मं च 'प्राणोत्तिङ्गं' तथैव च।
'पनकं' बीज-हरितं च 'अण्डसूक्ष्मं' च अष्टमम् ॥१५॥

As follows are these eight :
Dews, flowers, organisms, ants,
Moss, seeds, greenery and eggs. 15

एवमेयाणि जाणित्ता सव्वभावेण संजए।
अप्पमत्तो जए निच्चं सव्विंदियसमाहिए ॥१६॥

एवमेतानि ज्ञात्वा सर्वभावेन संयतः।
अप्रमत्तो यतेत नित्यं सर्वेन्द्रिय-समाहितः ॥१६॥

A ***sādhu*** **with his senses restrained**
Knowing these minute beings in all respects
Behaves in a very steadfast way. 16

धुवं च पडिलेहेज्जा जोगसा पायकंबलं ।
सेज्जमुच्चारभूमिं च संथारं अदुवासणं ।।१७।।

ध्रुवं च प्रतिलेखयेत् योगेन पात्र-कम्बलम् ।
शय्यामुच्चारभूमिं च संस्तारमथवासनम् ।।१७।।

In time and as per prescription
Checks a *muni* a vessel, a rag,
The residence, the place for taking out excreta,
The cloth on which to lie,
And one on which to sit. 17

उच्चारं पासवणं खेलं सिंघाणजल्लियं ।
फासुयं पडिलेहित्ता परिट्ठावेज्ज संजए ।।१८।।

उच्चारं प्रस्रवणं 'खेलं' सिंघाणं 'जल्लियम्' ।
प्रासुकं प्रतिलेख्य परिष्ठापयेत् संयतः ।।१८।।

A restrained *muni* carefully observes
A plot free from living beings
Before depositing stool and urine,
Phlegm, saliva and dirt from nose. 18

पविसित्तु परागारं पाणट्ठा भोयणस्स वा ।
जयं चिट्ठे मियं भासे ण य रूवेसु मणं करे ।।१९।।

प्रविश्य परागारं पानार्थं भोजनाय वा ।
यतं तिष्ठेत् मितं भाषेत न च रूपेषु मनः कुर्यात् ।।१९।।

Entering a house for food and drink
A *muni* stands in right place,
Speaks measured words,
And diverts not his mind to beauty. 19

बहुं सुणेइ कण्णेहिं बहुं अच्छीहिं पेच्छइ ।
न य दिट्ठं सुयं सव्वं भिक्खू अक्खाउमरिहइ ॥२०॥

बहु शृणोति कर्णैः बह्वक्षीभिः प्रेक्षते ।
न च दृष्टं श्रुतं सर्वं भिक्षुराख्यातुमर्हति ॥२०॥

He hears much by the ears,
He sees much by the eyes,
But it is not proper for a *bhikṣu*
To repeat all that he has heard or seen. 20

सुयं वा जइ वा दिट्ठं न लवेज्जोवघाइयं ।
न य केणइ उवाएणं गिहिजोगं समायरे ॥२१॥

श्रुतं वा यदि वा दृष्टं न लपेद् औपघातिकम् ।
न च केनचिदुपायेन गृहियोगं समाचरेत् ॥२१॥

A *sādhu* **says not anything**
That may cause hurt
Nor does he participate in activity
That may befit a householder. 21

निट्ठाणं रसनिज्जूढं भद्दगं पावगं ति वा ।
पुट्ठो वा वि अपुट्ठो वा लाभालाभं न निद्दिसे ॥२२॥

निष्ठानं निर्यूढरसम् भद्रकं पापकमिति वा ।
पृष्टो वाप्यपृष्टो वा लाभालाभं न निर्दिशेत् ॥२२॥

Asked or unasked, says he not,
'This is juicy and this is without juice',
Or 'this is good and this is bad'.
Nor does he mention whether
The meal he got is dainty or coarse. 22

न य भोयणम्मि गिद्धो चरे उंछं अयंपिरो ।
अफासुयं न भुंजेज्जा कीयमुद्देसियाहडं ॥२३॥

न च भोजने गृद्धः चरेदुञ्छमजल्पिता ।
अप्रासुकं न भुञ्जीत क्रीतमौद्देशिकाहृतम् ॥२३॥

Being attracted by rich food
Goes he not to affluent households
And without being covetous
He takes a morsel from many houses.
He eats not, even when taken by mistake,
A food that is live or brought,
Prepared or bought,
From a distance for his sake. 23

Note : The remnants of grains lying scattered on the farm after the harvest is reaped is called *uncha* whence the word *uncha-vṛtti*, which signifies one who lives on remnants. The idea is extended here to begging when a person collects food in morsels from many households.

सन्निहिं च न कुव्वेज्जा अणुमायं पि संजए ।
मुहाजीवी असंबद्धे हवेज्ज जगनिस्सिए ॥२४॥

सन्निधिं च न कुर्याद् अणुमात्रमपि संयतः ।
मुधाजीवी असंबद्धः भवे 'ज्जग' निश्रितः ॥२४॥

The restrained accumulates not
Even a small quantity of food.
Lives he on begging
Perfectly non-attached,
And depending in full on households. 24

Note : The *muni* depends on the householder for his food. This dependence is one-sided and total, without giving anything or any service in return. Sometimes a monk may be found performing a *pūjā* or offering a talisman to householder for his worldly happiness and affluence. But such a thing is totally prohibited for a *muni*.

लूहवित्ती सुसंतुट्ठे अप्पिच्छे सुहरे सिया ।
आसुरत्तं न गच्छेज्जा सोच्चाणं जिणसासणं ॥२५॥

रूक्षवृत्तिः सुसन्तुष्टः अल्पेच्छः सुभरः स्यात् ।
आसुरत्वं न गच्छेत् श्रुत्वा जिन-शासनम् ॥२५॥

A *muni* should live on coarse food
Be contented and with limited desires
And gratified with a scanty meal.
Hearing the rules of the Jaina Order
Bursts he not in wrath. 25

कण्णसोक्खेहिं सद्देहिं पेमं नाभिनिवेसए ।
दारुणं कक्कसं फासं काएण अहियासए ॥२६॥

कर्णसौख्येषु शब्देषु प्रेम नाभिनिवेशयेत् ।
दारुणं कर्कशं स्पर्शं कायेन अध्यासीत ॥२६॥

Loves not words
That are pleasing to the ears,
Bears he with pleasure a touch
That may be terrific and harsh. 26

खुहं पिवासं दुस्सेज्जं सीउण्हं अरई भयं ।
अहियासे अव्वहिओ देहे दुक्खं महाफलं ॥२७॥

क्षुधां पिपासां दुश्शय्यां शीतोष्णमरतिं भयम् ।
अध्यासीताऽव्यथितः देहे दुःखं महाफलम् ॥२७॥

Bears he with unperturbed mind
Hunger, thirst, and lying on uneven ground
Cold, heat, fear or mental pain.
For, toleration of suffering in the body
Becomes the source of results great. 27

अत्थंगयम्मि आइच्चे पुरत्था य अणुग्गए ।
आहारमइयं सव्वं मणसा वि न पत्थए ॥२८॥

अस्तङ्गते आदित्ये पुरस्तात् चानुद्गते ।
आहारमयं सर्वं मनसापि न प्रार्थयेत् ॥२८॥

Desires not food of any kind
From sun-down till it rises again. 28

अतितिणे अचवले अप्पभासी मियासणे ।
हवेज्ज उयरे दंते थोवं लद्धुं न खिसए ॥२९॥

'अतितिणः' अचपलः अल्पभाषी मिताशनः ।
भवेदुदरे दान्तः स्तोकं लब्ध्वा न खिसयेत् ॥२९॥

In not getting food at all
Or in getting what is coarse
He grumbles not nor gets restless
But stays with measured speech and food
With full control over the stomach.
Speaks he not ill of the donor
Even when offered a scanty food. 29

न बाहिरं परिभवे अत्ताणं न समुक्कसे ।
सुयलाभे न मज्जेज्जा जच्चा तवस्सिबुद्धिए ॥३०॥

न बाह्यं परिभवेत् आत्मानं न समुत्कर्षयेत् ।
श्रुतलाभे न माद्येत जात्या तपस्वि-बुद्ध्या ॥३०॥

Abuses not he another
Nor sings in praise of self,
Takes no pride in his *śruta* knowledge,
Gain, caste, intellect or his own monkhood. 30.

से जाणमजाणं वा कट्टु आहम्मियं पयं ।
संवरे खिप्पमप्पाणं बीयं तं न समायरे ॥३१॥

अथ जानन्न जानन्वा कृत्वा अधार्मिकं पदम् ।
संवृणुयात् क्षिप्रमात्मानं द्वितीयं तं न समाचरेत् ॥३१॥

Knowingly or without knowledge
If he indulges in a sinful act,
Then immediately he desists from that
And repeats it not any more. 31

अणायारं परक्कम नेव गूहे न निण्हवे ।
सुई सया वियडभावे असंसत्ते जिइंदिए ॥३२॥

अनाचारं पराक्रम्य नैव गूहेत न निह्नुवीत ।
शुचिः सदा विकटभावः असंसक्तो जितेन्द्रियः ॥३२॥

If perchance indulges in acts not prescribed
Suppresses them not nor denies,
But always remains pure and frank,
Unattached, and in full control of senses 32

अमोहं वयणं कुज्जा आयरियस्स महप्पणो ।
तं परिगिज्झ वायाए कम्मुणा उववायए ॥३३॥

अमोघं वचनं कुर्यात् आचार्यस्य महात्मनः ।
तत्परिगृह्य वाचा कर्मणोपपादयेत् ॥३३॥

Makes fruitful the words of great *ācāryas*
Accepts by word what they say
And then practises them in deeds. 33

अधुवं जीवियं नच्चा सिद्धिमग्गं वियाणिया ।
विणियट्टेज्ज भोगेसु आउं परिमियमप्पणो ॥३४॥

अध्रुवं जीवितं ज्ञात्वा सिद्धिमार्गं विज्ञाय ।
विनिवर्त्तेत भोगेभ्यः आयुः परिमितमात्मनः ॥३४॥

One desirous of liberation
Should know life to be transient
And life-span with a limit,
And attaining the way of liberation
Desists he from enjoyments. 34

(बलं थामं च पेहाए सद्धामारोगमप्पणो ।
खेत्तं कालं च विन्नाय तहप्पाणं निजुंजए ॥)*

(बलं स्थाम च प्रेक्ष्य श्रद्धामारोग्यमात्मनः ।
क्षेत्रं कालं च विज्ञाय तथात्मानं नियुञ्जीत ॥)

(Knowing his strength and prowess,
Devotion and health,
And with knowledge of time and place,
Employs he his soul,
And practises penance as per capability.)

जरा जाव न पीलेइ वाही जाव न वड्ढई ।
जाविंदिया न हायंति ताव धम्मं समायरे ॥३५॥

जरा यावन्न पीडयति व्याधिर्यावन्न वर्धते ।
यावदिन्द्रियाणि न हीयन्ते तावद्धर्मं समाचरेत् ॥३५॥

Practises religion
Till age afflicts him,
Ailment overpowers him
And senses lose their sharpness. 35

*These lines occur in a few texts, not in all.

कोहं माणं च मायं च लोभं च पाववड्ढणं ।
वमे चत्तारि दोसे उ इच्छंतो हियमप्पणो ॥३६॥

क्रोधं मानं च मायां च लोभं च पापवर्धनम् ।
वमेच्चतुरो दोषांस्तु इच्छन् हितमात्मनः ॥३६॥

Anger, pride, attachment, greed
These magnify sin
One desiring weal of self
Gives up these lapses four. 36

कोहो पीइं पणासेइ माणो विणयनासणो ।
माया मित्ताणि नासेइ लोहो सव्वविणासणो ॥३७॥

क्रोधः प्रीतिं प्रणाशयति मानो विनयनाशनः ।
माया मित्राणि नाशयति लोभः सर्वविनाशनः ॥३७॥

Anger spoils good relation
Pride destroys humility
Attachment is the killer of friendship
And greed destroys all. 37

उवसमेण हणे कोहं माणं मद्दवया जिणे ।
मायं चज्जवभावेण लोभं संतोसम्रो जिणे ॥३८॥

उपशमेन हन्यात् क्रोधं मानं मार्दवेन जयेत् ।
मायां च ऋजुभावेन लोभं सन्तोषतो जयेत् ॥३८॥

Kills he anger by forgiveness
Pride by humility
Attachment by simplicity
And greed by contentment. 38

काहो य माणो य अणिग्गहीया माया य लोभो य पवड्ढमाणा ।
चत्वारि ए ए कसिणा कसाया सिंचंति मूलाइं पुणब्भवस्स ॥३९॥

क्रोधश्च मानश्चानिगृहीतौ माया च लोभश्च प्रवर्धमानौ ।
चत्वार एते कृत्स्नाः कषायाः सिंचन्ति मूलानि पुनर्भवस्य ।।३९।।

Anger and pride not under control
Attachment and greed on the wax
These four black *kaṣāyas*
Water the roots of Re-birth tree. 39

Note : Anything that turns the soul from the path of liberation and directs it to the worldly life is *kaṣāya*. Just as a piece of cloth placed in the *kaṣāya* juice takes a permanent stain, so the soul gets besmeared with anger, greed, etc., because of which these are held as *kaṣāyas*.

राइणिएसु विणयं पउंजे धुवसीलयं सययं न हावएज्जा ।
कुम्भो व्व अल्लीणपलीणगुत्तो परक्कमेज्जा तवसंजमम्मि ।।४०।।

रात्निकेषु विनयं प्रयुञ्जीत ध्रुवशीलतां सततं न हापयेत् ।
कूर्म इवालीनप्रलीनगुप्तः पराक्रामेत् तपस्संयमे ।।४०।।

Respects the seniors in initiation
Transgresses not the rules of conduct
Takes to penance and restraint
With senses controlled, tortoise-like,
Asserts in restraint and penance. 40

निद्दं च न बहुमन्नेज्जा संपहासं विवज्जए ।
मिहोकहाहिं न रमे सज्झायम्मि रओ सया ।।४१।।

निद्रां च न बहु मन्येत संप्रहासं विवर्जयेत् ।
मिथः कथासु न रमेत स्वाध्याये रतः सदा ।।४१।।

Attaches not much value to slumber
Indulges not in vigorous laughter
Takes no interest in sex talks,
Remains immersed always in *svādhyāya.* 41

जोगं च समणधम्मम्मि जुंजे अणलसो धुवं ।
जुत्तो य समणधम्मम्मि अट्ठं लहइ अणुत्तरं ॥४२॥

योगं च श्रमणधर्मे युञ्जीतानलसो ध्रुवम् ।
युक्तश्च श्रमणधर्मे अर्थं लभतेऽनुत्तरम् ॥४२॥

Overcoming idleness, with full concentration
To a *śramaṇa's* **conduct in proper manner**
Performs his duties in time
A *muni* **thus attached to the** *śramaṇa* **cult**
Attains he the highest of results. 42

इहलोगपारत्तहियं जेणं गच्छइ सोग्गइं ।
बहुस्सुयं पज्जुवासेज्जा पुच्छेज्जत्थविणिच्छयं ॥४३॥

इहलोकपरत्रहितं येन गच्छति सुगतिम् ।
बहुश्रुतं पर्युपासीत पृच्छेदर्थविनिश्चयम् ॥४३॥

To attain that which gives the highest weal
In this life as also hereafter
And to attain a better status after death
Worships he those well-versed in the *śrutas*
And asks for the clarification of their import. 43

हत्थं पायं च कायं च पणिहाय जिइंदिए ।
अल्लीणगुत्तो निसिए सगासे गुरुणो मुणी ॥४४॥

हस्तं पादं च कायं च प्रणिधाय जितेन्द्रियः ।
आलीनगुप्तो निषीदेत् सकाशे गुरोर्मुनिः ॥४४॥

A *muni* **whose senses are conquered**
Restrains his hands and feet and body
Before he sits near the *guru*
Neither very near nor very far
With his mind and body duly restrained. 44

न पक्खग्रो न पुरग्रो नेव किच्चाएा पिट्ठग्रो ।
न य ऊरुं समासेज्जा चिट्ठेज्जा गुरुएांतिए ॥४५॥

न पक्षतः न पुरतः नैव कृत्यानां पृष्ठतः ।
न च ऊरुं समाश्रित्य तिष्ठेद् गुर्वन्तिके ॥४५॥

Sits not at the same level with the *ācārya*
Neither sits in front nor in the rear
Though near the *guru*, he never allows
His knee to touch that of the *guru*. 45

ग्रपुच्छिग्रो न भासेज्जा भासमाएस्स ग्रंतरा ।
पिट्ठिमंसं न खाएज्जा मायामोसं विवज्जए ॥४६॥

ग्रपृष्टो न भाषेत भाषमाएस्यान्तरा ।
पृष्ठमांसं न खादेत् मायामृषा विवर्जयेत् ॥४६॥

Speaks not unasked
Interferes not when another is speaking
Speaks not about somebody in his absence
And avoids deceitful untruth. 46

ग्रप्पत्तियं जेएा सिया ग्रासु कुप्पेज्ज वा परो ।
सव्वसो तं न भासेज्जा भासं ग्रहियगामिरिंग ॥४७॥

ग्रप्रीतिर्येन स्यात् आशु कुप्येद्वा परः ।
सर्वशस्तां न भाषेत भाषामहितगामिनीम् ॥४७॥

Never uses speech that may be harmful
Or that may cause displeasure
Or that may put another out of form. 47

दिट्ठं मियं ग्रसंदिद्धं पडिपुन्नं वियंजियं ।
ग्रयंपिरमणुव्विग्गं भासं निसिर ग्रत्तवं ॥४८॥

दृष्टां मितामसंदिग्धां प्रतिपूर्णां व्यक्तां जिताम् ।
अजल्पाकीमनुद्विग्नां भाषां निसृजेदात्मवान् ॥४८॥

He uses a language that is wise,
About a seen object, measured and doubt-free,
Correct, distinct and familiar,
Without exaggeration or fear. 48

आयारपन्नत्तिधरं दिट्ठिवायमहिज्जगं ।
वइविक्खलियं नच्चा न तं उवहसे मुणी ॥४९॥

आचार-प्रज्ञप्ति-धरं दृष्टिवादाभिज्ञम् ।
वाग्विस्खलितं ज्ञात्वा न तमुपहसेन्मुनिः ॥४९॥

A *muni* **laughs not at another's lapse**
Though he may be well-versed in the *nayavāda*
And well aware of the rules of syntax. 49

नक्खत्तं सुमिणं जोगं निमित्तं मंतं भेसजं ।
गिहिणो तं न आइक्खे भूयाहिगरणं पयं ॥५०॥

नक्षत्रं स्वप्नं योगं निमित्तं मंत्र-भेषजम् ।
गृहिणस्तन्नाचक्षीत भूताधिकरणं पदम् ॥५०॥

The stars, the outcome of a dream, mysmerism,
Astrology, *mantra,* **and herbs,**
These may be instruments of injury to *jīva.*
So a *muni* **never tells a householder**
The outcome of any one of them. 50

अन्नट्ठं पगडं लयणं भएज्ज सयणासणं ।
उच्चारभूमिसंपन्नं इत्थीपसुविवज्जियं ॥५१॥

अन्यार्थं प्रकृतं लयनं भजेत शयनासनम् ।
उच्चारभूमिसम्पन्नं स्त्रीपशुविवर्जितम् ॥५१॥

A *muni* uses not a bed or cushion
That may have been prepared for another
Nor a room attached to a latrine
Or haunted by women or living beings. 51

विवित्ता य भवे सेज्जा नारीणं न लवे कहं ।
गिहिसंथवं न कुज्जा कुज्जा साहूहिं संथवं ॥५२॥

विविक्ता च भवेच्छय्या नारीणां न लपेत् कथाम् ।
गृहि-संस्तवं न कुर्यात् कुर्यात् साधुभिः संस्तवम् ॥५२॥

A *muni* offers not sermon
In a women's gathering in an isolated place
Nor does he ask identity of householder
Courts acquaintance only of the *sādhus*. 52

जहा कुक्कुडपोयस्स निच्चं कुललओ भयं ।
एवं खु बंभयारिस्स इत्थीविग्गहओ भयं ॥५३॥

यथा कुक्कुटपोतस्य नित्यं कुललतो भयम् ।
एवं खलु ब्रह्मचारिणं स्त्रीविग्रहतो भयम् ॥५३॥

Like a chicken always afraid of the cat
A *brahmacāri* is afraid of a woman's frame. 53

चित्तभित्तिं न निज्झाए नारिं वा सुअलंकियं ।
भक्खरंपिव दट्ठूणं दिट्ठिं पडिसमाहरे ॥५४॥

चित्रभित्तिं न निध्यायेत् नारीं वा स्वलङ्कृताम् ।
भास्करमिव दृष्ट्वा दृष्टिं प्रतिसमाहरेत् ॥५४॥

Never casts a wistful glance
At a fresco (that depicts women)
Nor looks at one with decorations
If perchance his gaze falls on a woman
It needs rebound as from the midday sun. 54

हत्थपायपडिच्छिन्नं कण्णनासविगप्पियं ।
अवि वाससइं नारिं बंभयारी विवज्जए ॥५५॥

प्रतिच्छिन्न-हस्तपादां विकल्पित-कर्णनासाम् ।
अपि वर्षशतां नारीं ब्रह्मचारी विवर्जयेत् ॥५५॥

A *brahmacārī* remains at a distance
From a lady even a hundred years old
Whose hands and feet may be cut
And nose and ears may be out of order. 55

विभूसा इत्थिसंसग्गी पणीयरसभोयणं ।
नरस्सत्तगवेसिस्स विसं तालउडं जहा ॥५६॥

विभूषा स्त्री-संसर्गः प्रणीत-रसभोजनम् ।
नरस्यात्मगवेषिणः विषं तालपुटं यथा ॥५६॥

For one desirous of the soul's liberation
Dress rich and company of women
And the taking of rich food
Are as harmful as the *tālpuṭ* poison. 56

अंगपच्चंगसंठाणं चारुल्लवियपेहियं ।
इत्थीण तं न निज्झाए कामरागविवड्ढणं ॥५७॥

अङ्ग-प्रत्यङ्ग-संस्थानं चारुलपितप्रेक्षितम् ।
स्त्रीणां तन्न निध्यायेत कामरागविवर्धनम् ॥५७॥

Looks he not at a woman's frame,
Her limbs, her shape, her overtures and glance
Never cares he for these,
For, they inflame the lust. 57

विसएसु मणुन्नेसु पेमं नाभिनिवेसए ।
अणिच्चं तेसिं विन्नाय परिणामं पोग्गलाण उ ॥५८॥

विषयेषु मनोज्ञेषु प्रेम नाभिनिवेशयेत् ।
अनित्यं तेषां विज्ञाय परिणामं पुद्गलानां तु ॥५८॥

Sound shape, smell, taste and touch—
Knowing these *pudgala*–outcomes to be transient
Develops not a *brahmacārī*
Attachment to attractive things. 58

पोग्गलाण परीणामं तेसिं नच्चा जहा तहा ।
विणीयतण्हो विहरे सीईभूएण अप्पणा ॥५९॥

पुद्गलानां परिणामं तेषां ज्ञात्वा यथा तथा ।
विनीततृष्णो विहरेत् शीतीभूतेनात्मना ॥५९॥

Knowing the outcome of *pudgala*
That may be the objects of senses,
Wanders he, thirst-less,
With soul pinned in detachment. 59

जाए सद्धाए निक्खंतो परियायट्ठाणमुत्तमं ।
तमेव अणुपालेज्जा गुणे आयरियसम्मए ॥६०॥

यया श्रद्धया निष्क्रान्तः पर्यायस्थानमुत्तमम् ।
तामेवाऽनुपालयेत् गुणेषु आचार्यसम्मतेषु ॥६०॥

The devotion for which he exchanges home
In favour of a place of penance,
Pursues he, devoted as before,
To the pursuit of virtues
As indicated by the *ācāryas*. 60

तवं चिमं संजमजोगयं च सज्झायजोगं च सया अहिट्ठए ।
सूरे व सेणाए समत्तमाउहे अलमप्पणो होइ अलं परेसिं ॥६१॥

तपश्चेदं संयमयोगं च स्वाध्याययोगं च सदाऽधितिष्ठेत् ।
शूर इव सेनया समाप्तायुधः अलमात्मने भवत्यलं परेभ्यः ॥६१॥

Like a hero armed
Saving himself though surrounded
One devoted to penance
Saṁjama-yoga and *svādhyāya-yoga*
Is able to save his self
As those of others. 61

सज्झायज्झाणरयस्स ताइणो अपावभावस्स तवे रयस्स ।
विसुज्झई जं सि मलं पुरेकडं समीरियं रुप्पमलं व जोइणा ॥६२॥

स्वाध्याय-सद्ध्यानरतस्य त्रायिणं अपापभावस्य तपसि रतस्य ।
विशुद्ध्यते यत् तस्य मलं पुराकृतं समीरितं रूप्यमलमिव ज्योतिषा ॥६२॥

Like a piece of gold
Which is purified in fire,
The accumulated dirt of a *muni*
Devoted to *svādhyāya* and honest meditation
Saviour and sinless
Immersed in penance
Gets cleansed. 62

से तारिसे दुक्खसहे जिइंदिए सुएण जुत्ते अममे अकिंचणे ।
विरायई कम्मघणम्मि अवगए कसिणब्भपुडावगमे व चंदिमा ॥६३॥
त्ति बेमि ॥

स तादृशो दुःखसहो जितेन्द्रियः श्रुतेन युक्तोऽममोऽकिञ्चनः ।
विराजते कर्मघनेऽपगते कृत्स्नाभ्रपुटापगमे इव चन्द्रमाः ॥६३॥

इति ब्रवीमि ॥

He who is wrapped in aforesaid virtues
And capable enough to bear suffering
Conquers senses, masters scriptures,
Is devoid of attachment and possession,
Shines, on the cessation of *karma*–clouds,
As a moon does in a cloud-free sky. 63

So say I

नवमं अज्झयणं (नवममध्ययनम्)

PRESCRIPTION NINE

विणयसमाही (विनय-समाधिः)

On Humility

Part I—On mental health that humility imparts

थंभा व कोहा व मयप्पमाया गुरुस्सगासे विणयं न सिक्खे ।
सो चेव उ तस्स अभूइभावो फलं व कीयस्स वहाय होइ ॥१॥

स्तम्भाद्वा क्रोधाद्वा मायाप्रमादात् गुरु-सकाशे विनयं न शिक्षेत ।
स चैव तु तस्याऽभूतिभावः फलमिव कीचकस्य वधाय भवति ॥१॥

A *muni* who out of pride,
Anger, attachment or illusion,
Learns not humility from his *guru*
Causes his own ruin
Like bamboo-flowers killing the bamboo-tree. 1

जे यावि मंदि त्ति गुरुं विइत्ता डहरे इमे अप्पसुएत्ति नच्चा ।
हीलंति मिच्छं पडिवज्जमाणा करेंति आसायण ते गुरूणं ॥२॥

ये चापि 'मन्द' इति गुरुं विदित्वा 'डहरो' ऽयं 'अल्पश्रुत' इति ज्ञात्वा ।
हीलयन्ति मिथ्या प्रतिपद्यमानाः कुर्वन्त्याशातनां ते गुरूणाम् ॥२॥

When, deeming him dull,
Junior in age and inferior in knowledge
A *muni* considers his words wrong
Disrespects he his *guru*. 2

पगईए मंदा वि भवंति एगे डहरा वि य जे सुयबुद्धोववेया ।
आयारमंता गुण सुट्ठिअप्पा जे होलिया सिहिरिव भास कुज्जा ॥३॥

प्रकृत्या मन्दा अपि भवन्ति एके डहरा अपि च ये श्रुत-बुद्ध्युपेताः ।
आचारवन्तो गुणसुस्थितात्मानः ये हीलिताः शिखीव भस्म कुर्युः ॥३॥

Some *ācāryas* though old
Are by nature dull
Some though young are intelligent
And masters of the *śruta*
An *ācārya* who follows rules of conduct,
And whose soul is fixed in virtue
He may be dull or wise,
But in showing contempt
A *muni* destroys his merit
As fire destroys wood. 3

जे यावि नागं डहरं ति नच्चा आसायए से अहियाय होइ ।
एवायरियं पि हु हीलयंतो नियच्छई जाइपहं खु मंदे ॥४॥

ये चापि नागं डहर इति ज्ञात्वा आशातयेयुः तस्याहिताय भवति ।
एवमाचार्यमपि खलु हीलयन् निर्गच्छति जातिपथं खलु मन्दः ॥४॥

Suffers he who neglects a snake
On the ground of its being small
So one who neglects an *ācārya*
That may be young
Roams in cycles of inferior births. 4

आसीविसो यावि परं सुरुट्ठो किं जीवनासाओ परं नु कुज्जा ।
आयरियपाया पुण अप्पसन्ना अबोहिआसायण नत्थि मोक्खो ॥५॥

आशीविषश्चापि परं सुरुष्टः किं जीवनाशात् परं न कुर्यात् ।
आचार्यपादाः पुनरप्रसन्नाः अबोधिमाशातनया नास्ति मोक्षः ॥५॥

A poisonous snake fired with anger
Can at the most deprive one of life
But an *ācārya*, if displeased,
Debars enlightenment
So disrespect to him deprives one of *mokṣa*. 5

जो पावगं जलियमवक्कमेज्जा आसोविसं वा वि हु कोवएज्जा ।
जो वा विसं खायइ जोवियट्ठी एसोवमासायणया गुरूणं ॥६॥

यः पावकं ज्वलितमपक्रामेत् आशीविषं वाऽपि खलु कोपयेत् ।
यो वा विषं खादति जीवितार्थी एषोपमाऽशातनया गुरूणाम् ॥६॥

Some may go across a burning flame,
Some enrage a poisonous snake,
Some take poison. At par with these
Is disrespect to *guru*.
All these lead not to good.
So disrespect not the *guru*. 6

सिया हु से पावय नो डहेज्जा आसोविसो वा कुविओ न भक्खे ।
सिया विसं हालहलं न मारे न यावि मोक्खो गुरुहीलणाए ॥७॥

स्यात् खलु स पावको नो दहेत् आशीविषो वा कुपितो न भक्षेत् ।
स्याद्विषं हलाहलं न मारयेत् न चापि मोक्षो गुरुहीलनया ॥७॥

Maybe one escapes from the burning flame
Maybe a snake though enraged bites not
And poison may perchance fail to kill
But *mokṣa* is never attained by disrespecting the *guru*. 7

जो पव्वयं सिरसा भेत्तुमिच्छे सुत्तं व सीहं पडिबोहएज्जा ।
जो वा दए सत्तिअग्गे पहारं एसोवमासायणया गुरूणं ॥८॥

यः पर्वतं शिरसा भेत्तुमिच्छेत् सुप्तं वा सिंहं प्रतिबोधयेत् ।
यो वा ददीत शक्त्यग्रे प्रहारं एषोपमाशातनया गुरूणाम् ॥८॥

Some wish to pierce a rock by the head
Some may wake up a sleeping lion
Some strike their person with a spear
Disrespect to *guru* is at par with these. 8

सिया हु सीसेण गिरिं पि भिंदे सिया हु सीहो कुविश्रो न भक्खे ।
सिया न भिंदेज्ज व सत्तिश्रग्गं न यावि मोक्खो गुरुहीलणाए ॥६॥

स्यात् खलु शीर्षेण गिरिमपि भिन्द्यात् स्यात् खलु सिंहः कुपितो न भक्षेत् ।
स्यान्न भिन्द्याद्वा शक्त्यग्रं न चापि मोक्षो गुरुहीलनया ॥६॥

Maybe one pierces the rock with his head
Maybe a lion though enraged devours not
Maybe the spear-head fails to pierce
But one neglecting the *guru* never attains *mokṣa*. 9

श्रायरिय पाया पुण श्रप्पसन्ना श्रबोहिं श्रासायण नत्थि मोक्खो ।
तम्हाश्रणाबाह सुहाभिकंखी गुरुप्पसायाभिमुहो रमेज्जा ॥१०॥

श्राचार्यपादाः पुनरप्रसन्नाः श्रबोधिमाशातनया नास्ति मोक्षः ।
तस्मादनाबाधसुखाभिकांक्षी गुरुप्रसादाभिमुखो रमेत ॥१०॥

With *ācārya* displeased, attains not enlightenment
By disrespecting him, attains not *mokṣa*.
So a *muni* desirous of bliss eternal
Is ever careful about the *guru's* grace. 10

जहाहियग्गी जलणं नमंसे नाणाहुईमंतपयाभिसित्तं ।
एवायरियं उवचिट्ठएज्जा श्रणंतनाणोवगश्रो वि संतो ॥११॥

यथाऽहिताग्निर्ज्वलनं नमस्येद् नानाहुतिमन्त्रपदाभिषिक्तम् ।
एवमाचार्यमुपतिष्ठेत श्रनन्तज्ञानोपगतोऽपि सन् ॥११॥

Just as a fire-worshipper adores fire
By various offerings and *mantras*

And bows before it
Though possessing knowledge infinite,
A muni **seeks** *ācārya's* **grace with devotion. 11**

जस्संतिए धम्मपयाइ सिक्खे तस्संतिए वेणइयं पउंजे ।
सक्कारए सिरसा पंजलीओ कायग्गिरा भो मणसा य निच्चं ॥१२॥

यस्यान्तिके धर्मपदानि शिक्षेत तस्यान्तिके वैनयिकं प्रयुञ्जीत ।
सत्कुर्वीत शिरसा प्राञ्जलिकः कायेन गिरा भो मनसा च नित्यम् ॥१२॥

Shows he the greatest respect to one
From whom he receives spiritual knowledge
With head bowed and folded palms
Adores he with body, word and mind. I2

लज्जा दया संजम बंभचेरं कल्लाणभागिस्स विसोहिठाणं ।
जे मे गुरू सययमणुसासयंति ते हं गुरू सययं पूययामि ॥१३॥

लज्जा दया संयमब्रह्मचर्यं कल्याणभागिनः विशोधिस्थानम् ।
ये मां गुरवः सततमनुशासति तानहं गुरून् सततं पूजयामि ॥१३॥

Dishonour, compassion, restraint and celibacy
Fear of these purifies one covetous of bliss
'Always worship I the *guru*
Who always teaches me these.' 13

जहा निसंते तवणच्चिमाली पभासई केवलभारहं तु ।
एवायरिओ सुयसीलबुद्धिए विरायई सुरमज्झे व इंदो ॥१४॥

यथा निशान्ते तपन्नर्चिर्माली प्रभासते केवलभारतं तु ।
एवमाचार्यः श्रुत-शील-बुद्ध्या विराजते सुरमध्य इव इन्द्रः ॥१४॥

As the sun lightens the entire land of Bharata
So does *guru* **endowed with** *śruta*, **conduct and intellect**
Enlightens the whole world.
As Indra shines in the company of gods,
So does *guru* **in the company of monks. 14**

जहा ससी कोमुइजोगजुत्तो नक्खत्ततारागणपरिवुडप्पा ।
खे सोहई विमले अब्भमुक्के एवं गणी सोहइ भिक्खुमज्झे ॥१५॥

यथा शशी कौमुदीयोगयुक्तः नक्षत्रतारागणपरिवृतात्मा ।
खे शोभते विमलेऽभ्रमुक्ते एवं गणी शोभते भिक्षुमध्ये ॥१५॥

Just as the full moon appears
In a clean and cloud-free firmament
Surrounded by stars and other luminaries,
So shines the *ācārya* **in the group of** *bhikṣus*. **15**

महागरा आयरिया महेसी समाहिजोगे सुयसीलबुद्धिए ।
संपाविउकामे अणुत्तराइं आराहए तोसए धम्मकामी ॥१६॥

महाकरान् आचार्यान् महैषिणः समाधियोगस्य श्रुतशीलबुद्ध्याः ।
सम्प्राप्तुकामोऽनुत्तराणि आराधयेत् तोषयेत् धर्मकामी ॥१६॥

A *muni* **desirous of attaining supreme knowledge,**
And seeker of *nirjarā*, **worships the** *guru*,
And seeks his grace, who aids liberation,
And who himself is the greatest fountain-head
Of *samādhi*, *śruta*, **conduct and intellect. 16**

सोच्चाण मेहावी सुभासियाइं सुस्सूसए आयरियप्पमत्तो ।
आराहइत्ताण गुणे अणेगे से पावई सिद्धिमणुत्तरं ॥१७॥

—त्ति बेमि ॥

श्रुत्वा मेधावी सुभाषितानि शुश्रूषयेत् आचार्यमप्रमत्तः ।
आराध्य गुणाननेकान् स प्राप्नोति सिद्धिमनुत्तराम् ॥१७॥

इति ब्रवीमि ॥

On listening these admonitions
A *muni* **endowed with intellect**
Listens with attention the *ācārya's* **words,**
And by acquiring multifarious virtues
Attains he the never-surpassed perfection. 17

So say I

नवमं अज्झयणं (नवममध्ययनम्)

PRESCRIPTION NINE

विणयसमाही (विनय-समाधिः)

On Humility

Part II—(uddessa or Uddeśaka)

Merits of one with Humility & the Reverse

मुलाओ खंधप्पभवो दुमस्स खंधाओ पच्छा समुवेंति साहा ।
साहप्पसाहा विरुहंति पत्ता तओ से पुप्फं च फलं रसो य ॥१॥

मूलात् स्कन्धप्रभवो द्रुमस्य स्कन्धात् पश्चात्समुपयन्ति शाखाः ।
शाखाभ्यः प्रशाखा विरोहन्ति पत्राणि ततस्तस्य पुष्पं च फलं च रसश्च॥१॥

In a tree, the trunk stems from the root
After the trunk branches, and after the branches twigs
And after the twigs leaves, flowers, fruits and juice. 1

एवं धम्मस्य विणओ मूलं परमो से मोक्खो ।
जेण कित्ति सुयं सिग्घं निस्सेसं चाभिगच्छई ॥२॥

एवं धर्मस्य विनयो मूलं परमस्तस्य मोक्षः ।
येन कीर्ति श्रुतं श्लाघ्यं निःशेषं चाधिगच्छति ॥२॥

Likewise, humility is the root of *dharma*
Of which the juice is *mokṣa*
With humility acquires he quick
The knowledge of *śruta*, **which brings him fame,**
And ultimately attains he *mokṣa*. 2

जे य चंडे मिए थद्धे दुव्वाई नियडो सढे ।
वुज्झइ से अविणीयप्पा कट्ठं सोयगयं जहा ॥३॥

यश्च चण्डो मृगस्तब्धः दुर्वादी निकृतिः शठः ।
उह्यते सोऽविनीतात्मा काष्ठं स्त्रोतोगतं यथा ॥३॥

One who is haughty, ignorant, stagnant,
Harsh, hypocritical and deceitful,
Such a soul unsaturated with humility
Floats at random in the world-current
As a piece of log in the flow of the river. 3

विणयं पि जो उवाएणं चोइम्रो कुप्पई नरो ।
दिव्वं सो सिरिमेज्जंतिं दंडेण पडिसेहए ॥४॥

विनयमपि यः उपायेन चोदितः कुप्यति नरः ।
दिव्यां स श्रियमायान्तीं दण्डेन प्रतिषेधति ॥४॥

When one is inducted into humility
And yet rebounds with rage
Debars he, as if with a club,
The approaching goddess of wealth
(His own chance of attaining *mokṣa*). 4

तहेव अविणीयप्पा उववज्झा हया गया ।
दीसंति दुहमेहंता आभिओगमुवट्ठिया ॥५॥

तथैवाऽविनीतात्मानः उपवाह्या हया गजाः ।
दृश्यन्ते दुःखमेधमानाः आभियोग्यमुपस्थिताः ॥५॥

When a riding horse or an elephant is untame
He is found suffering while on service. 5

तहेव सुविणीयप्पा उववज्झा हया गया ।
दीसंति सुहमेहंता इड्ढिं पत्ता महायसा ॥६॥

तथैव सुविनीतात्मानः उपवाह्या हया गजाः ।
दृश्यन्ते सुखमेधमानाः ऋद्धिं प्राप्ता महायशसः ॥६॥

When a riding horse or an elephant is tame
He is seen receiving all care,
And attains he fame and happiness. 6

तहेव अविणीयप्पा लोगंसि नरनारिओ ।
दीसंति दुहमेहंता छाया विगलितेंदिया ॥७॥

तथैवाऽविनीतात्मानः लोके नरनार्यः ।
दृश्यन्ते दुःखमेधमानाः छाता विकलितेन्द्रियाः ॥७॥

दंडसत्थपरिजुण्णा असब्भवयणेहि य ।
कलुणा विवन्नछंदा खुप्पिवासाए परिगया ॥८॥

दण्डशस्त्राभ्यां परिजीर्णाः असभ्यवचनैश्च ।
करुणा विपन्नच्छन्दसः क्षुत्पिपासया परिगताः ॥८॥

So in this world, a man or woman,
Whoever is devoid of humility,
Becomes wounded or weak,
With senses in disorder, overpowered
With cane and weapon,
Chastised with abusive speech,
Pitiable, dependent, in hunger and thirst,
Is seen suffering from pain. 7-8

तहेव सुविणीयप्पा लोगंसि नरनारिओ ।
दीसंति सुहमेहंता इड्ढि पत्ता महायसा ॥९॥

तथैव सुविनीतात्मानः लोके नरनार्यः ।
दृश्यन्ते सुखमेधमानाः ऋद्धिं प्राप्ता महायशसः ॥९॥

A man or woman graced with humility
Is seen attaining happiness and a great name. 9

तहेव अविणीयप्पा देवा जक्खा य गुज्झगा ।
दीसंति दुहमेहंता आभिओगमुवट्ठिया ॥१०॥

तथैवाऽविनीतात्मानः देवा यक्षाश्च गुह्यकाः ।
दृश्यन्ते दुःखमेधमानाः आभियोग्यमुपस्थिताः ॥१०॥

A god, a *yakṣa* **or a denizen of** *bhavanas*,
If he has no humility in him,
Is seen suffering from pain. 10

तहेव सुविणीयप्पा देवा जक्खा च गुज्झगा ।
दीसंति सुहमेहंता इड्ढि पत्ता महायसा ॥११॥

तथैव सुविनीतात्मानः देवा यक्षाश्च गुह्यकाः ।
दृश्यन्ते सुखमेधमानाः ऋद्धिं प्राप्ता महायशसः ॥११॥

A god, a *yakṣa*, a denizen of *bhavanas*,
If he has humility in him,
Is seen to attain happiness and fame. 11

जे आयरियउवज्झायाणं सुस्सूसावयणंकरा ।
तेसिं सिक्खा पवड्ढंति जलसित्ता इव पायवा ॥१२॥

ये आचार्योपाध्याययोः शुश्रूषावचनकराः ।
तेषां शिक्षाः प्रवर्धन्ते जलसिक्ता इव पादपाः ॥१२॥

A *muni* who carefully listens
And obeys the words of *ācaryas* and *upādhyāyas*
Grows in learning, like a tree duly watered. 12

अप्पणट्ठा परट्ठा वा सिप्पा णेउणियाणि य ।
गिहिणो उवभोगट्ठा इहलोगस्स कारणा ॥१३॥

आत्मार्थं परार्थं वा शिल्पानि नैपुण्यानि च ।
गृहिण उपभोगार्थम् इहलोकस्य कारणाय ॥१३॥

जेण बंधं वहं घोरं परियावं च दारुणं ।
सिक्खमाणा नियच्छंति जुत्ता ते ललिइंदिया ॥१४॥

येन बन्धं वधं घोरं परितापं च दारुणम् ।
शिक्षमाणा नियच्छन्ति युक्तास्ते ललितेन्द्रियाः ॥१४॥

Those householders who for self and others
For enjoying the pleasures of the world,
Learn crafts and acquire skills,
These busy with acquiring them,
Though with carefully reared senses,
Attain slavery, death and suffering great
Even in the process of learning. 13-14

ते वि तं गुरुं पूयंति तस्स सिप्पस्स कारणा ।
सक्कारेंति नमंसंति तुट्ठा निद्देसवत्तिणो ॥१५॥

तेऽपि तं गुरुं पूजयन्ति तस्य शिल्पस्य कारणाय ।
सत्कुर्वन्ति नमस्यन्ति तुष्टा निर्देशवर्तिनः ॥१५॥

Even these, to acquire the skills,
Adore the *guru*, worship him, salute him,
And with pleasure carry his orders. 15

किं पुण जे सुयग्गाही अणंतहियकामए ।
आयरिया जं वए भिक्खू तम्हा तं नाइवत्तए ॥१६॥

किं पुनर्यः श्रुतग्राही अनन्तहितकामकः ।
आचार्या यद् वदेयुः भिक्षुः तस्मात्तन्नाति वर्त्तयेत् ॥१६॥

Then what to speak of one who cares for
The knowledge of scriptures and the highest bliss
So the *bhikṣu* never transgresses
The words of the *ācārya*. 16

नीयं सेज्जं गइं ठाणं नीयं च आसणाणि य ।
नीयं च पाए वंदेज्जा नीयं कुज्जा य अंजलिं ॥१७॥

नीचां शय्यां गतिं स्थानं नीचं चासनानि च ।
नीचं च पादौ वन्देत नीचं कुर्याच्चाञ्जलिम् ॥१७॥

A *bhikṣu* places his bed below the *ācārya's*,
Walks and stands behind and sits below,
Bows to touch the *ācārya's* feet,
And bows with folded palms. 17

संघट्टइत्ता काएणं तहा उवहिणामवि ।
खमेह अवराहं मे वएज्ज न पुणो त्ति य ॥१८॥

संघट्य कायेन तथोपधिनापि ।
क्षमस्वापराधं मे वदेन्न पुनरिति च ॥१८॥

If perchance he touches the *ācārya*
By his person, personal effect or in any other way,
Says he, 'Forgive me, sir,
This shall not happen again.' 18

दुग्गश्रो वा पश्रोएणं चोइश्रो वहई रहं ।
एवं दुबुद्धि किच्चाणं वुत्तो वुत्तो पकुव्वई ॥१६॥

दुर्गवो वा प्रतोदेन चोदितो वहति रथम् ।
एवं दुर्बुद्धिः कृत्यानाम् उक्त उक्तः प्रकरोति ॥१६॥

A wicked bull draws a chariot
Only when forced by a whip,
So an evil-minded disciple works
Only when goaded by the *ācārya*. 19

(श्रालवंते लवंते वा न निसेज्जाए पडिस्सुणे ।
मोत्तूणं श्रासणं धीरो सुस्सूसाए पडिस्सुणे ॥)

(श्रालपन्तं लपन्तं वा न निषिद्यायां प्रतिशृणुयात् ।
मुक्त्वा श्रासनं धीरः शुश्रूषया प्रतिशृणुयात् ॥)

कालं छंदोवयारं च पडिलेहित्ताण हेउहिं ।
तेण तेण उवाएण तं तं संपडिवायए ॥२०॥

कालं छन्दोपचारं च प्रतिलेख्य हेतुभिः ।
तेन तेनोपायेन तत्तत्संप्रतिपादयेत् ॥२०॥

(An intelligent disciple, on being called,
Once, or time and again,
Remains not on his seat,
But relinquishes it,

And listens to his *guru's* words.)*
Knowing the time, desire and mode of summon
He attends the *ācārya's* call in a befitting way. 20

विवत्ती अविणीयस्स संपत्ती विणियस्स य ।
जस्सेयं दुहओ नायं सिक्खं से अभिगच्छइ ॥२१॥

विपत्तिरविनीतस्य सम्पत्तिर्विनीतस्य च ।
यस्यैतद्द्विधा ज्ञातं शिक्षां सोऽभिगच्छति ॥२१॥

Without humility one attains demerit.
With humility, one attains merit.
Knowing this, one knows what learning is. 21

जे यावि चंडे मइइड्ढिगारवे पिसुणे नरे साहसहीणपेसणे ।
अदिट्ठधम्मे विणए अकोविए असंविभागी न हु तस्स मोक्खो ॥२२॥

यश्चापि चण्डो मतिऋद्धिगौरवः पिशुनो नरः साहसहीनप्रेषणः ।
अदृष्टधर्मा विनयेऽकोविदः असंविभागी न खलु तस्य मोक्षः ॥२२॥

A man who is haughty
Who is proud of his intellect and fortune,
Who talks ill of others in their absence,
Who is discourteous and obeys not the *guru's* order
Who is a fatalist,
Who is not equipped with humility,
Who is selfish (and shares not his food
With brothers-in-faith), never attains *mokṣa*. 22

निद्देसवत्ती पुण जे गुरूणं सुयत्थधम्मा विणयम्मि कोविया ।
तरित्तु ते ओहमिणं दुरुत्तरं खवित्तु कम्मं गइमुत्तमं गय ॥२३॥
—त्ति बेमि ।

* These lines occur in a few texts, not in all.

निर्देशवर्तिनः पुनर्ये गुरूणां श्रुतार्थधर्माणो विनये कोविदाः
तीर्त्वा ते ओघमिमं दुरुत्तरं क्षपयित्वा कर्म गतिमुत्तमां गताः ॥२३॥

इति ब्रवीमि ।

He who is obedient to the *guru*
Has heard the significance of religion,
And is equipped with humility,
Crosses this worldly ocean so difficult to cross,
Exhausts *karma* **and attains** *mokṣa*. 23

So say I.

नवमं अज्झयणं (नवममध्ययनम्)

PRESCRIPTION NINE

(विणयसमाही विनय-समाधिः)

On Humility

Part III—(Uddessa or Uddeśaka)

One who is revered, his attributes, and advice on his being an arhat

आयरियं अग्गिमिवाहियग्गी सुस्सूसमाणो पडिजागरेज्जा ।
आलोइयं इंगियमेव नच्चा जो छन्दमाराहयइ स पुज्जो ॥१॥

आचार्यमग्निमिवाहिताग्निः शुश्रूषमाणः प्रतिजागृयात् ।
आलोकितम् इङ्गितमेव ज्ञात्वा यश्छन्दमाराधयति स पूज्यः ॥१॥

Just as a man who worships the sacred flame
Remains ever alert,
So one is to remain ever alert
To the *ācārya's* word, gesture and mood
And be worthy of reverence. 1

आयारमट्ठा विणयं पउंजे सुस्सूसमाणो परिगिज्झ वक्कं ।
जहोवइट्ठं अभिकंखमाणो गुरुं तु नासाययई स पुज्जो ॥२॥

आचारार्थं विनयं प्रयुञ्जीत शुश्रूषमाणः परिगृह्य वाक्यम् ।
यथोपदिष्टमभिकाङ्क्षन् गुरुं तु नाशातयति स पूज्यः ॥२॥

Worthy of reverence is he,
Who practises humility to build up conduct
Who, desirous of listening to the *ācārya*,
Accepts his words and acts favourably,
And disobeys him not at any time. 2

राइणिएसु विणयं पउंजे डहरा वि य जे परियायजेट्ठा ।
नियत्तणे वट्टइ सच्चवाई ओवायवं वक्ककरे स पुज्जो ॥३॥

रात्निकेषु विनयं प्रयुञ्जीत डहरा अपि ये पर्यायज्येष्ठाः ।
नीचत्वे वर्तते सत्यवादी अवपातवान् वाक्यकरः स पूज्यः ॥३॥

Revered is he who shows humility to *sādhus*
Junior in age, but senior in initiation
Who is polite in behaviour and speaks the truth,
Who stays with the *ācārya* and obeys his orders. 3

अन्नायउंछं चरई विसुद्धं जवणट्ठया समुयाणं च निच्च ।
अलद्धयं नो परिदेवएज्जा लद्धुं न विकत्थयई स पुज्जो ।।४।।

अज्ञातोञ्छं चरति विशुद्धं यापनार्थं समुदानं च नित्यम् ।
अलब्ध्वा न परिदेवयेत् लब्ध्वा न विकत्थते स पूज्यः ।।४।।

Revered is he who reveals not his own identity
But always subsists on begging from many,
Who is not sad if he gets not alms,
And who is not jubilant when he obtains it. 4

संथारसेज्जासणभत्तपाणे अप्पिच्छया अइलाभे वि संते ।
जो एवमप्पाणभितोसएज्जा संतोसपाहन्नरए स पुज्जो ।।५।।

संस्तार-शय्यासन-भक्तपाने अल्पेच्छताऽतिलाभेपि सति ।
य एवमात्मानमभितोषयेत् सन्तोषप्राधान्यरतः स पूज्यः ।।५।।

Revered is he who despite plentiful offer
Of bed, abode, seat, food and drink,
Be of restricted needs, accepts not in excess,
Takes as little as he can
And leads a life of contentment. 5

सक्का सहेउं आसाए कंटया अओमया उच्छहया नरेणं ।
अणासए जो उ सहेज्ज कंटए वईमए कण्णसरे स पुज्जो ।।६।।

शक्याः सोढुमाशया कण्टकाः अयोमया उत्सहमानेन नरेण ।
अनाशया यस्तु सहेत कण्टकान् वाङ्मयान् कर्णशरान् स पूज्यः ।।६।।

Men hopeful of acquiring riches
Bear the pain of iron nails,
But revered is he who without expectation
Bears thorn-like harsh words with his ears. 6

मुहुत्तदुक्खा हु हवंति कंटया अग्रोमया तेवि तग्रो सुउद्धरा ।
वायादुरुत्ताणि दुरुद्धराणि वेराणुबंधीणि महब्भयाणि ॥७॥

मुहूर्तंदुःखास्तु भवन्ति कण्टकाः अयोमयास्तेऽपि ततः सूद्धराः
वाग्-दुरुक्तानि दुरुद्धराणि वैरानुबन्धीनि महाभयानि ॥७॥

Iron-nails cause a temporary pain
And these are removable from the body
But thorn-like harsh words are not easy to go,
Dangerous, these augment the legacy of hatred. 7

समावयंता वयणाभिघाया कण्णंगया दुम्मणियं जणंति ।
धम्मो त्ति किच्चा परमग्गसूरे जिइंदिए जो सहई स पुज्जो ॥८॥

समापतन्तो वचनाभिघाताः कर्णंगता दौर्मनस्यं जनयन्ति ।
धर्मेति कृत्वा परमाग्रशूरः जितेन्द्रियो यः सहते स पूज्यः ॥८॥

Lashes of words reach the ears
And generate restlessness in the mind
Revered is he who, foremost among the heroes,
And conqueror of senses, bears them thinking
'It' s my duty to bear them'. 8

अवण्णवायं च परम्मुहस्स पच्चक्खग्रो पडिणीयं च भासं ।
ओहारिणिं अप्पियकारिणिं च भासं न भासेज्ज सया स पुज्जो ॥९॥

अवर्णवादञ्च पराङ्मुखस्य प्रत्यक्षतः प्रत्यनीकाञ्च भाषाम् ।
अवधारिणीमप्रियकारिणीञ्च भाषां न भाषेत सदा स पूज्यः ॥९॥

Revered is he who speaks not ill in one's absence
Who uses not a sharp tongue in one's presence

Who speaks not with assertion
Nor uses words that are harsh. 9

अलोलुए अक्कुहए अमाई अपिसुणे यावि अदीणवित्ती ।
नो भावए नो वि य भावियप्पा अकोउहल्ले य सया स पुज्जो ॥१०॥

अलोलुपः अकुहकः अमायी अपिशुनश्चापि अदीनवृत्तिः ।
नो भावयेत् नो अपि च भावितात्मा अकौतूहलश्च सदा स पूज्यः ॥१०॥

Revered is he who is not greedy of ***rasa*****,**
Who displays not occult powers,
Who has no deceit,
Who blames not another in his absence,
Who humbles not self in seeking
Who entertains not flattery of self
Who extols not self nor evinces curiosity. 10

गुणेहि साहू अगुणेहिऽसाहू गिण्हाहि साहूगुण मुंचऽसाहू ।
वियाणिया अप्पगमप्पएणं जो रागदोसेहिं समो स पुज्जो ॥११॥

गुणैः साधुरगुणैरसाधुः गृहाण साधुगुणान् मुञ्चाऽसाधून् ।
विज्ञाय आत्मकमात्मकेन यो रागद्वेषयोः समः स पूज्यः ॥११॥

With merit one becomes a ***sādhu*****,**
Just the reverse of it with demerit.
Embrace ye the merits of a ***sādhu***
And drop demerits of one who is not a ***sādhu*****.**
Revered is he who knowing self by self
Maintains equanimity to attachment and deceit. 11

तहेव डहरं व महल्लगं वा इत्थीपुमं पव्वइयं गिहिं वा ।
नो हीलए नो वि य खिंसएज्जा थंभं च कोहं च चए स पुज्जो ॥१२॥

तथैव डहरं च 'महान्तं' वा स्त्रियं पुमांसं प्रव्रजितं गृहिणं वा ।
नो हीलयेन्नो अपि च खिंसयेत् स्तम्भञ्च क्रोधञ्च त्यजेत् स पूज्यः ॥१२॥

Revered is he who puts not to shame
Young or aged, man or woman,
Either one in domestic or in spiritual order,
By reminding him of his misconduct,
Who speaks not ill of them,
And forsakes pride and anger. 12

जे माणिया सययं माणयंति जत्तेण कन्नं व निवेसयंति ।
ते माणए माणरिहे तवस्सी जिइंदिए सच्चरए स पुज्जो ॥१३॥

ये मानिताः सततं मानयन्ति यत्नेन कन्यामिव निवेशयन्ति ।
तान्मानयेन्मानार्हांस्तपस्विनः जितेन्द्रियान् सत्यरतान् स पूज्यः ॥१३॥

Revered himself, pays he due attention to disciples,
Settles them as a father does his daughter.
Revered is he (disciple) to adore such *ācārya*
Who is worthy of reverence, immersed in penance,
Whose senses are controlled and who is rooted in truth. 13

तेसिं गुरूणं गुणसागराणं सोच्चाण मेहावि सुभासियाइं ।
चरे मुणी पंचरए तिगुत्तो चउक्कसायावगए स पुज्जो ॥१४॥

तेषां गुरूणां गुणसागराणां श्रुत्वा मेधावी सुभाषितानि ।
चरेन्मुनिः पञ्चरतस्त्रिगुप्तः अपगत-चतुष्कषायः स पूज्यः ॥१४॥

Revered is that gifted *muni*
Who practises the well-said words of the *guru*
Who himself is an ocean of merit,
Who is devoted to the five *mahāvratas*
Who withholds mind, word and body
(So as to be *tri-gupta*, the withholder of the three)
And who discards anger, pride, attachment and greed. 14

गुरुमिह सययं पडियरिय मुणी जिणमयनिउणे अभिगमकुसले ।
धुणिय रयमलं पुरेकडं भासुरमउलं गइं गय ॥१५॥

—त्ति बेमि ॥

गुरुमिह सततं प्रतिचर्य मुनिः जिनमतनिपुणोऽभिगमकुशलः ।
धूत्वा रजोमलं पुरा कृतं भास्वरामतुलां गतिं गतः ॥१५॥

इति ब्रवीमि ।

Always serve the *guru* in this world
A *muni* versed in the words of the *jinas*
And seasoned with the practice of humility
Shakes off the dust of accumulated *karma*
And attains effulgent state of liberation. 15

So say I

नवमं अज्झयणं (नवममध्ययनम्)

PRESCRIPTION NINE

विणयसमाही (विनय-समाधिः)

On Humility

Part IV—Uddessa or (Uddesaka)– Classification of humility

सुयं मे आउसं तेणं भगवया एवमक्खायं—इह खलु थेरेहिं भगवंतेहिं चत्तारि विणयसमाहिट्ठाणा पन्नत्ता ।।सू० १।।

श्रुतं मया आयुष्मन् तेन भगवतैवमाख्यातम्—इह खलु स्थविरैर्भगवद्भिश्चत्वारि विनय-समाधि-स्थानानि प्रज्ञप्तानि ।।१।।

Oh the long-lived one, have I heard
The Lord hath said thus. In this *nirgrantha* **discourse**
The revered Lord has assigned four places to
vinaya samāhi. Sū. 1

कयरे खलु ते थेरेहिं भगवंतेहिं चत्वारि विणयसमाहिट्ठाणा पन्नत्ता ।। सू० २।।

कतराणि खलु तानि स्थविरैर्भगवद्भिश्चत्वारि विनय-समाधि-स्थानानि प्रज्ञप्तानि ।।२।।

What are these four classifications of *vinaya samāhi*
that have been ordained by the revered Lord. 2

इमे खलु ते थेरेहिं भगवंतेहिं चत्वारि विणयसमाहिट्ठाणा पन्नत्ता तं जहा—

१. विणयसमाही　　२. सुयसमाही
३. तवसमाही　　४. आयारसमाही ।

इमानि खलु तानि स्थविरैर्भगवद्भिश्चत्वारि
विनय-समाधि-स्थानानि प्रज्ञप्तानि । तद्यथा—

१. विनयसमाधिः । २. श्रुतसमाधिः ।
३. तपःसमाधिः । ४. आचारसमाधिः ।

These four classifications of *vinaya samāhi* as follows
Have been ordained by the revered Lord :
Concentration on humility is *vinaya samāhi*
Concentration on scriptures is *suya samāhi*
Concentration on penance is *taba samāhi*
Concentration on conduct is *āyāra samāhi*.

विणए सुए अ तवे आयारे निच्चं पंडिया ।
अभिरामयंति अप्पाणं जे भवंति जिइंदिया ॥१॥ सू० ३

विनये श्रुते च तपसि आचारे नित्यं पण्डिताः ।
अभिरामयन्त्यात्मानं ये भवन्ति जितेन्द्रियाः ॥१॥

1. Those wise people who are self-possessed—
Who have their organs of senses under control
Keep their soul always concentrated
On humility, scriptures, penance and conduct. *Sū*. 3

चउव्विहा खलु विणयसमाही भवइ तं जहा—
१. अणुसासिज्जंतो सुस्सूसइ २. सम्मं संपडिवज्जइ
३. वेयमाराहयइ ४. न य भवइ अत्तसंपग्गहिए । चउत्थं पयं भवइ ।

चतुर्विधः खलु विनय-समाधिर्भवति । तद्यथा—
१. अनुशास्यमानः शुश्रूषते २. सम्यक् सम्प्रतिपद्यते ३. वेदमाराधयति
४. न च भवति सम्प्रगृहीतात्मा । चतुर्थं पदं भवति ।

Vinaya samāhi **has four sub-classes :**
1. The disciple desires to listen to the *guru's* prescriptions
2. He duly accepts the prescriptions
3. He Adores the *śruta;*

4. **He never extols his attainment—this is the fourth sub-class.**

And here is a *śloka* :

भवइ य इत्थ सिलोगो—
पेहेइ हियाणुसासणं सुस्सूसइ तं च पुणो अहिट्ठए ।
न य माणमएण मज्जइ विणयसमाही आययट्ठिए ॥२॥ सू० ४

भवति चाऽत्र श्लोकः—
स्पृहयति हितानुशासनं शुश्रूषते तच्च पुनरधितिष्ठति ।
न च मान-मदेन माद्यति विनयसमाधावायतार्थिकः ॥२॥

2. **A** *muni* **covetous of liberation desires prescription for liberation, duly accepts the prescription, acts according to the prescription, never gets mad with the pride that he is an adept in** *vinaya samāhi*...*Sū*. **4**

चउव्विहा खलु सुयसमाही भवइ तं जहा—
१. सुयं मे भविस्सइ त्ति अज्झाइयव्वं भवइ । २. एगग्गचित्तो भविस्सामि त्ति अज्झाइयव्वं भवइ । ३. अप्पाणं ठावइस्सामि त्ति अज्झाइयव्वं भवइ । ४. ठिओ परं ठावइस्सामि त्ति अज्झाइयव्वं भवइ ।

चउत्थं पयं भवइ ।

चतुर्विधः खलु श्रुतसमाधिर्भवति । तद्यथा—
१. श्रुतं मे भविष्यतीत्यध्येतव्यं भवति ।
२. एकाग्रचित्तो भविष्यामीत्यध्येतव्यं भवति ।
३. आत्मानं स्थापयिष्यामीत्यध्येतव्यं भवति ।
४. स्थितः परं स्थापयिष्यामीत्यध्येतव्यं भवति ।
चतुर्थं पदं भवति ।

Suya samāhi **has four sub-classes. They are :**

1. **I shall attain** *śruta;* **so should I read.**
2. **I shall have a concentrated mind; so should I read.**
3. **I shall tie my soul to religion; so should I read.**
4. **I shall fix myself in spiritual pursuit**

and help others to do the same; so should I read—this is the fourth sub-class.

And here is a *śloka* :

भवइ य इत्थ सिलोगो—
नाणमेगग्गचित्तो य ठिओ ठावयई परं ।
सुयाणि य अहिज्जित्ता रओ सुयसमाहिए ॥३॥ सू० ५

भवति चाऽत्र श्लोकः—
ज्ञानमेकाग्रचित्तश्च स्थितः स्थापयति परम् ।
श्रुतानि चाधीत्य रतः श्रुतसमाधौ ॥३॥

3. By study one acquires knowledge, has concentration of mind, is fixed in religion and helps others to be so fixed. Then by studying multifarious *śrutas* **he becomes absorbed in** *suya samāhi. Sū.* **5**

चउव्विहा खलु तवसमाही भवइ तं जहा—
१. नो इहलोगट्ठयाए तवमहिट्ठेज्जा २. नो परलोगट्ठयाए तवमहिट्ठेज्जा ३. नो कित्तिवण्णसद्दसिलोगट्ठयाए तवमहिट्ठेज्जा ४. नन्नत्थ निज्जरट्ठयाए तवमहिट्ठेज्जा ।
चउत्थं पयं भवइ ।

चतुर्विधः खलु तपःसमाधिर्भवति । तद्यथा—
१. नो इहलोकार्थं तपोधितिष्ठेत् २. नो परलोकार्थं तपोधितिष्ठेत् ३. नो कीर्तिवर्णशब्दश्लोकार्थं तपोधितिष्ठेत् ४. नान्यत्र निर्जरार्थात् तपोधितिष्ठेत् ।
चतुर्थं पदं भवति ।

Taba samāhi **has four sub-classes. These are :**

1. Not to practise penance for this world.

2. Not to practise penance for the next world.

3. Not to practise penance for praise, status, fame or renown.

4. Not to practise penance for any other purpose except *nirjarā*--this is the fourth sub-class.

And here is a *śloka* :

भवइ य इत्थ सिलोगो—
विविहगुणतवोरए य निच्चं भवइ निरासए निज्जरट्ठिए ।
तवसा धुणइ पुराणपावगं जुत्तो सया तवसमाहिए ।।४।। सू० ६

भवति चाऽत्र श्लोकः—
विविधगुणतपोरतश्च नित्यं भवति निराशकः निर्जरार्थिकः ।
तपसा धुनोति पुराण-पापकं युक्तः सदा तपः-समाधिना ।।४।।

4. **A *muni* given to the practice of diverse penances is devoid of a desire for acquisition in *paudgalic* terms. He is only covetous of *nirjarā*, destroys past *karma*-accumulations by penance and always becomes absorbed in *taba samāhi*. *Sū*. 6**

चउव्विहा खलु आयारसमाही भवइ तं जहा—
१. नो इहलोगट्ठयाए आयारमहिट्ठेज्जा २. नो परलोगट्ठयाए आयारमहिट्ठेज्जा ३. नो कित्तिवण्णसद्दसिलोगट्ठयाए आयारमहिट्ठेज्जा ४. नन्नत्थ आरहंतेहिं हेऊहिं आयारमहिट्ठेज्जा ।
चउत्थं पयं भवइ ।

चतुर्विधः खल्वाचारसमाधिर्भवति । तद्यथा—
१. नो इहलोकार्थमाचारमधितिष्ठेत् २. नो परलोकार्थमाचारमधितिष्ठेत् ३. नो कीर्तिवर्णशब्दश्लोकार्थमाचारमधितिष्ठेत् ४. नान्यत्राऽर्हतेभ्यो हेतुभ्य आचारमधितिष्ठेत् ।
चतुर्थं पदं भवति ।

***Āyāra samāhi* has four sub-classes. These are :**

1. Not to practise *ācāra* for this world.

2. Not to practise *ācāra* for the next world.

3. **Not to practise** *ācāra* **for praise, status, fame or renown.**
4. **Not to practise** *ācāra* **for any other purpose except for attaining the state of an** *arhat*—**this is the fourth sub-class.**

And here is a *śloka* **:**

भवइ य इत्थ सिलोगो—
जिणवयणरए अंतितिणे पडिपुण्णाययमायट्ठिए ।
आयारसमाहिसंवुडे भवइ य दंते भावसंधए ।।५।। सू० ७

भवति चाऽत्र श्लोकः—
जिनवचनरतोऽतिन्तिणः प्रतिपूर्णं आयतमायतार्थिकः ।
आचारसमाधिसंवृतः भवति च दान्तो भावसंधकः ।।५।।

5. **He who is devoted to the words of a** *Jina*, **who argues not, who is filled with the significance of the** *sūtras*, **who is keen to attain liberation, is, equipped as he is with** *ācāra samādhi*, **able to control senses and mind and brings himself nearer to liberation.** *Sū*. 7

अभिगम चउरो समाहिओ सुविसुद्धो सुसमाहियप्पओ ।
विउलहियसुहावहं पुणो कुव्वइ सो पयखेममप्पणो ।।६।।

अभिगम्य चतुरः समाधीन् सुविशुद्धः सुसमाहितात्मकः ।
विपुलहितसुखावहं पुनः करोति स पदं क्षेममात्मनः ।।६।।

6. **He who knowing the** *samādhis* **becomes well-purified and self-possessed attains the state of** *mokṣa* **which is all bliss.**

जाइमरणाओ मुच्चई इत्थंथं च चयइ सव्वसो ।
सिद्धे वा भवइ सासए देवे वा अप्परए महिड्ढिए ।।७।।

—त्ति बेमि ।

जातिमरणात् मुच्यते इत्थंस्थं च त्यजति सर्वशः ।
सिद्धो वा भवति शाश्वतः देवो वाऽल्परजा महर्द्धिकः ॥७॥

इति ब्रवीमि

Freed is he of rebirth and avoids he the hell and similar other states. Thus he either becomes a *siddha* (perfected) or (at least) a *deva* (a celestial being) in the highest heaven with a few *karma* 7

So say I

दसममज्झयणं (दशममध्ययनम्)

PRESCRIPTION TEN

स-भिक्खु (सभिक्षुः)

Sa-bhikshu

(*On the traits of a bhikṣu : Discourse on his being an arhat*)

निक्खम्ममाणाए बुद्धवयणे निच्चं चित्तसमाहिओ हवेज्जा ।
इत्थीण वसं न यावि गच्छे वंतं नो पडियायई जे स भिक्खू ॥१॥

निष्क्रम्याज्ञया बुद्धवचने नित्यं समाहितचित्तो भवेत् ।
स्त्रीणां वशं न चापि गच्छेत् वान्तं न प्रत्यापिबति यः स भिक्षुः ॥१॥

A *bhikṣu* renounces on the words of the enlightened
He has his mind fixed and firm in the *śruta*;
Who is not distracted by women
And who resumes not things once discarded. 1

पुढविं न खणे न खणावए सीओदगं न पिए न पियावए ।
अगणिसत्थं जहां सुनिसियं तं न जले जलावए जे स भिक्खू ॥२॥

पृथ्वीं न खनेन्न खानयेत् शीतोदकं न पिबेन्न पाययेत् ।
अग्निशस्त्रं यथा सुनिशितं तन्न ज्वलेन्न ज्वलयेद्यः स भिक्षुः ॥२॥

A *bhikṣu* is one who digs not the earth nor gets it done
Who drinks not nor offers unboiled water
Who lights not fire, sharp as weapon,
Nor orders another to do so. 2

अनिलेण न वीए न वीयावए हरियाणि न छिंदे न छिंदावए ।
बीयाणि सया विवज्जयंतो सच्चित्तं नाहारए जे स भिक्खू ॥३॥

अनिलेन न व्यजेन्न व्यजयेत् हरितानि न छिन्द्यान्न छेदयेत् ।
बीजानि सदा विवर्जयन् सचित्तं नाहरेत् यः स भिक्षुः ॥३॥

A *bhikṣu* is one who fans not nor orders another to do so
Who cuts not green objects nor orders another to do so
Who keeps himself off from seeds
And who eats not live objects. 3

वहणं तसथावराण होइ पुढवितणकट्ठनिस्सियाणं ।
तम्हा उद्देसियं न भुंजे नो विपए न पयावए जे स भिक्ख ॥४॥

हननं त्रसस्थावराणां भवति पृथ्वीतृणकाष्ठनिःश्रितानाम् ।
तस्मादौद्देशिकं न भुञ्जीत नो अपि पचेन्न पाचयेत् यः स भिक्षुः ॥४॥

In cooking food are killed living beings, mobile or static,
Sheltered in the earth, hay or wood
A *bhikṣu* is one who accepts not food cooked for him
Nor cooks nor orders another to do so. 4

रोइय नायपुत्तवयणे अत्तसमे मन्नेज्ज छप्पि काए ।
पंच य फासे महव्वयाइं पंचासवसंवरे जे स भिक्खू ॥५॥

रोचयित्वा ज्ञातपुत्रवचनम् आत्मसमान्मन्येत षडपि कायान् ।
पञ्च च स्पृशेन्महाव्रतानि पंचाश्रवान् संवृणुयात् यः स भिक्षुः ॥५॥

A *bhikṣu* is one who respecting the words of the Lord
Looks on all living beings as his own self,
Practises the five *mahāvratas*
And withdraws from five *āśravas*. 5

चत्तारि वमे सया कसाए धुवयोगी य हवेज्ज बुद्धवयणे ।
अहणे निज्जायरूवरयए गिहिजोगं परिवज्जए जे स भिक्खू ॥६॥

चतुरो वमेत् सदा कषायान् ध्रुवयोगी च भवेद् बुद्धवचने ।
अधनो निर्जातरूपरजतः गृहियोगं परिवर्जयेद् यः स भिक्षुः ॥६॥

A *bhikṣu* is one who gives up the four *kaṣāyas*
Who is steadfast in the words of the *nirgranthas*
Who is without wealth, gold and silver
Who indulges not in the householder's way. 6

सम्मद्दिट्ठी सया अमूढे अत्थि हु नाणे तवे संजमे य ।
तवसा धुणइ पुराणपावगं मणवयकायसुसंवुडे जे स भिक्खू ॥७॥

सम्यग्दृष्टिः सदाऽमूढः अस्ति खलु ज्ञानं तपः संयमश्च ।
तपसा धुनोति पुराणपापकं सुसंवृत-मनोवाक्-कायः यः स भिक्षुः ॥७॥

A *bhikṣu* is one who has equanimity
Who believes in knowledge, penance and restraint,
Who shakes the past sins by penance
And is in full command of mind, word and body. 7

तहेव असणं पाणगं वा विविहं खाइमसाइमं लभित्ता ।
होही अट्ठो सुए परे वा तं न निहे न निहावए जे स भिक्खू ॥८॥

तथैवाशनं पानकं वा विविधं खाद्यं स्वाद्यं लब्ध्वा ।
भविष्यत्यर्थः श्वः परस्मिन्वा तं न निदध्यान्न निधापयेद् यः स भिक्षुः ॥८॥

A *bhikṣu* is one who obtains food,
Drink in above manner
Who accumulates not saying : 'I shall use it to-morrow,
'Or the day following.'
Nor causes accumulation by others. 8

तहेव असणं पाणयं वा विविहं खाइमसाइमं लभित्ता ।
छंदिय साहम्मियाण भुंजे भोच्चा सज्झायरए य जे स भिक्खू ॥९॥

तथैवाशनं पानकं वा विविधं खाद्यं स्वाध्यं लब्ध्वा ।
छन्दयित्वा सार्धमिकान् भुञ्जीत भुक्त्वा स्वाध्यायरतश्च यः स भिक्षुः ॥९॥

A *bhikṣu* is one who obtains food, drink in above manner
And shares 'em with his fellow monks,
And thereafter having taken his meal
Devotes to the reading of sacred texts. 9

न य वुग्गहियं कहं कहेज्जा न य कुप्पे निहुइंदिए पसंते ।
संजमधुवजोगजुत्ते उवसंते अविहेडए जे स भिक्खू ॥१०॥

न च वैग्रहिकीं कथां कथयेत् न च कुप्येन्निभृतेन्द्रियः प्रशान्तः ।
संयम-ध्रुवयोगयुक्तः उपशान्तो ऽविहेठको यः स भिक्षुः ॥१०॥

**A *bhikṣu* is one who utters not quarrelsome words,
Who is not angry, allows not excitement of senses,
Who is calm, and steadfast in restraint,
Perfect in control and abuses not others. 10**

जो सहइ हु गामकंटए अक्कोसपहारतज्जणाओ य ।
भयभैरवसद्दसंपहासे समसुहदुक्खसहे य जे स भिक्खू ॥११॥

यः सहते खलु ग्रामकण्टकान् आक्रोशप्रहारतर्जनाश्च ।
भयभैरवशब्दसंप्रहासान् समसुखदुःखसहश्च यः स भिक्षुः ॥११॥

**A *bhikṣu* is one who tolerates thorn-like objects of senses,
Words of anger, lashes, and threats
Or even dreadful laughter,
And who bears with equanimity pleasures and pains. 11**

पडिमं पडिवज्जिया मसाणे नोभायए भयभेरवाइं दिस्स ।
विविहगुणतवोरए य निच्चं न सरीरं चाभिकंखई जे स भिक्खू ॥१२॥

प्रतिमां प्रतिपद्य श्मशाने नो बिभेति भयभैरवाणि दृष्ट्वा ।
विविधगुणतपोरतश्च नित्यं न शरीरं चाभिकांक्षति यः स भिक्षुः ॥१२॥

**A *bhikṣu* is one who is not afraid of terrific sights
When practising penance in a cremation ground,
Who is immersed in diverse virtues and penances,
And who has no attachment for the body. 12**

असइं वोसट्ठचत्तदेहे अक्कुट्ठे व हए व लूसिए वा ।
पुढवि समे मुणी हवेज्जा अनियाणे अकोउहल्ले य जे स भिक्खू ॥१३॥

असकृद् व्युत्सृष्टत्यक्तदेहः आक्रुष्टो वा हतो वा लूषितो वा ।
पृथ्वीसमो मुनिर्भवेत् अनिदानोऽकौतूहलो यः स भिक्षुः ॥१३॥

A *bhikṣu* is one who often stands in meditation
And gives up care of the body, remains earth-like
Forgiving all harshness, lashes or injury,
Who practises not penance for material wealth;
Who desires not to see an opera. 13

अभिभूय काएण परीसहाइं समुद्धरे जाइपहाओ अप्पयं ।
विइत्तु जाईमरणं महब्भयं तवे रए सामणिए जे स भिक्खू ॥१४॥

अभिभूय कायेन परिषहान् समुद्धरेज्जातिपथादात्मकम् ।
विदित्वा जातिमरणं महाभयं तपसि रतः श्रामण्ये यः स भिक्षुः ॥१४॥

A *bhikṣu* is one who bears all hardships
And rescues himself from birth and death,
Who is immersed in the penance of a *śramaṇa*
Knowing well the great fear of rebirth. 14

हत्थसंजए पायसंजए वायसंजए संजइंदिए ।
अज्झप्परए सुसमाहियप्पा सुत्तत्थं च वियाणई जे स भिक्खू ॥१५

हस्तसंयतः पादसंयतः वाक्संयतः संयतेन्द्रियः ।
अध्यात्मरतः सुसंमाहितात्मा सूत्रार्थं च विजानाति यः स भिक्षुः ॥१५॥

A *bhikṣu* is one who is restrained in his hands,
Restrained in feet, in words and senses,
Who is immersed in things of the spirit,
Who spends much time in meditation,
And who knows well the *sūtras* and their imports. 15

उवहिम्मि अमुच्छिए अगिद्धे अन्नायउंछं पुलनिप्पुलाए ।
कयविक्कयसन्निहिओ विरए सव्वसंगावगए य जे स भिक्खू ॥१६॥

उपधौ अम्मूर्च्छितोऽगृद्धः अज्ञातोञ्छं पुलोनिष्पुलाकः ।
क्रयविक्रयसन्निधितो विरतः सर्वसङ्गापगतो यः स भिक्षुः ॥१६॥

A *bhikṣu* is one who is not overwhelmed with objects
Nor is in bondage with them,
Who is a seeker of alms from unknown households,
Who is free from demerits that stain restraint,
Who keeps off from purchase, sale and stock,
And who is above all attachments. 16

अलोलभिक्खू न रसेसु गिद्धे उंछं चरे जीविय नाभिकंखे ।
इड्ढिं च सक्कारण पूयणं च चए ठियप्पा अणिहे जे स भिक्खू ॥१७॥

अलोलो भिक्षुर्न रसेषु गृद्धः उञ्छं चरेज्जीवितं नाभिकांक्षेत् ।
ऋद्धिं च सत्कारणं पूजनञ्च त्यजति स्थितात्मा अनिभो यः स भिक्षुः ॥१७॥

A *bhikṣu* is one who is not greedy of objects,
Nor is in bondage with them.
Who takes morsels of food from unknown households,
Who covets not a reckless living,
Who discards desire for affluence, adoration and respect,
Who is fixed in self and is above deceit. 17

न परं वएज्जासि अयं कुसीले जेणऽन्नो कुप्पेज्ज न तं वएज्जा ।
जाणिय पत्तेयं पुण्णपावं अत्ताणं न समुक्कसे जे स भिक्खू ॥१८॥

न परं वदेदयं कुशीलः येनान्यः कुप्येन्न तद् वदेत् ।
ज्ञात्वा प्रत्येकं पुण्यपापं आत्मानं न समुत्कर्षयेद्यः स भिक्षुः ॥१८॥

A *bhikṣu* is one who on knowing
That virtues and vices vary from person to person
Calls not another as indulgent in vices
So that another may get irritated
Nor is he proud of his own attainments. 18

न जाइमत्ते न य रूवमत्ते न लाभमत्ते न सुएणमत्ते ।
मयाणि सव्वाणि विवज्जइत्ता धम्मज्झाणरए जे स भिक्खू ॥१९॥

न जातिमत्तो न च रूपमत्तः न लाभमत्तो न श्रुतेन मत्तः ।
मदान् सर्वान् विवर्ज्य धर्मध्यानरतो यः स भिक्षुः ॥१९॥

A ***bhikṣu*** **is one who is not proud of his own lineage,**
Nor of beauty, nor of the acquisition of ***śruta,***
Who discards all pride.
And is deeply immersed in spiritual meditation. 19

पवेयए अज्जपयं महामुणी धम्मे ठिओ ठावयई परं पि ।
निक्खम्मं वज्जेज्ज कुसीलर्लिगं न यावि हस्सकुहए जे स भिक्खू ॥२०॥

प्रवेदयेदार्यपदं महामुनिः धर्मे स्थितः स्थापयति परमपि ।
निष्क्रम्य वर्जयेत् कुशीललिङ्गं न चापि हास्यकुहको यः स भिक्षुः ॥२०॥

A ***bhikṣu,*** **a great** ***muni,*** **preaches the learning of the Arya**
Is himself fixed in religion and does so to others,
Never indulges after renunciation in acts not befitting,
And makes not curious ventures to make others laugh. 20

तं देहवासं असुइं असासयं सया चए निच्चं हियट्ठियप्पा ।
छिंदित्तु जाईमरणस्स बंधणं उवेइ भिक्खू अपुणागमं गइं ॥२१॥
—त्ति बेमि ।

तं देहवासमशुचिमशाश्वतं सदा त्यजेन्नित्यहितः स्थितात्मा ।
छित्वा जातिमरणस्य बन्धनम् उपैति भिक्षुरपुनरागमां गतिम् ॥२१॥
इति ब्रवीमि ।

Knowing the body to be impure and of short-span
Discards attachment for it,—all the time
By devoting the soul to spiritual well-being
And by cutting the bondage of births and deaths,
Attains he a state wherefrom there is no return. 21
So say I.

पढमा चुलिया (प्रथमा चूलिका)

CHULIKA ONE

रइवक्का (रतिवाक्या)

Rati-vākyā

इह खलु भो पव्वइएणं उप्पन्नदुक्खेणं संजमे अरइसमावन्नचित्तेणं ओहाणुप्पेहिणा अणोहाइएणं चेव हयरस्सि-गयंकुसं-पोयपडागाभूयाइं इमाइं अट्ठारस ठाणाइं सम्मं संपडिलेहियव्वाइं भवंति। तं जहा—

इह खलु भोः प्रव्रजितेन उत्पन्नदुःखेन संयमेऽरतिसमापन्नचित्तेन अवधावनोत्प्रेक्षिणा अनवधावितेन चैव हयरश्मिगजांकुशपोतपताकाभूतानि इमान्यष्टादशस्थानानि सम्यक् संप्रतिलेखितव्यानि भवन्ति। तद्यथा--

Oh ye desirous of liberation, those who have embraced renunciation by the words of the *nirgranthas*, if such, out of illusion, be overpowered by sorrow, if their minds have slackened from restraint, if they desire to give up restraint and return to the life of a householder, they would, before renouncing renunciation, be well advised to consider the following eighteen items. For one with unstable mind, these have the same use, as a bridle for a horse, a hook for an elephant and a flag for a ship. Such are they :

हं भो दुस्समाए दुप्पजीवी ॥१॥

हं हो दुष्षमायां दुष्प्रजीविनः ॥१॥

Oh, in this *dussama* phase of the time-cycle, people earn their livelihood with the greatest hardship. 1

लहुस्सगा इत्तरिया गिहीणं कामभोगा ॥२॥

लघुस्वका इत्वरिका गृहिणां कामभोगाः ॥२॥

2. The enjoyment of pleasures by the householders is of little substance and of limited span.

भुज्जो य साइबहुला मणुस्सा ॥३॥

भूयश्च सातिबहुला मनुष्याः ॥३॥

3. Men are crooks.

इमे य मे दुक्खे न चिरकालोवट्ठाई भविस्सइ ॥४॥

इदं च मे दुःखं न चिरकालोपस्थायि भविष्यति ॥४॥

4. This my hardship will not last for ever.

ओमजणपुरक्कारे ॥५॥

अवमजनपुरस्कारः ॥५॥

5. A householder has to adore even inferior people.

वंतस्स य पडियाइयणं ॥६॥

वान्तस्य च प्रत्यापानम् ॥६॥

6. To give up restraint and to return to domestic life are like taking back things vomited.

अहरगइवासोवसंपया ॥७॥

अधरगतिवासोपसंपदा ॥७॥

7. To give up restraint and return to domestic life are like embracing the life of hell.

दुल्लभे खलु भो गिहीणं धम्मे गिहिवासमज्झे वसंताणं ॥८॥

दुर्लभः खलु भो गृहिणां धर्मो गृहवासमध्ये वसताम् ॥८॥

8. Oh, for householders immersed in worldly living, rare must be the touch of religion.

आयंके से वहाय होइ ॥९॥

आतङ्कस्तस्य वधाय भवति ॥९॥

9. In this living, terrors lead to death.

संकप्पे से वहाय होइ ॥१०॥

संकल्पस्तस्य वधाय भवति ॥१०॥

10. In this living, shocks lead to death.

सोवक्केसे गिहवासे ।
निरुवक्केसे परियाए ॥११॥

सोपक्लेशो गृहवासः ।
निरुपक्लेशः पर्यायः ॥११॥

11. Residence in household is painful; joining the holy order is pain-free.

बंधे गिहवासे ।
मोक्खे परियाए ॥१२॥

बन्धो गृहवासः ।
मोक्षः पर्यायः ॥१२॥

12. Residence in household is bondage; spiritual order is ***mokṣa.***

सावज्जे गिहवासे ।
अणवज्जे परियाए ॥१३॥

सावद्यो गृहवासः ।
अनवद्यः पर्यायः ॥१३॥

13. Residence in household is sinful; spiritual order is sinfree.

बहुसाहारणा गिहीणं कामभोगा ॥१४॥

बहुसाधारणा गृहिणां काम-भोगाः ॥१४॥

14. For a householder, the pursuit of pleasures is well within reach.

पत्तेयं पण्णपावं ॥१५॥

प्रत्येकं पुण्यपापम् ।१५॥

15. Virtues and vices go with each person.

अणिच्चे खलु भो मणुयाण
जीविए कुसग्गजलबिन्दुचंचले ॥१६॥

अनित्यं खलु भो मनुजानां
जीवितं कुशाग्रजलविन्दुचञ्चलम् ॥१६॥

16. Oh, human life is so transient, like a drop of water placed at the tip of a blade of *Kuśa* grass.

बहुं च खलु पावं कम्मं पगडं ॥१७॥

बहु च खलु भोः पापं कर्म प्रकृतम् ।१७॥

17. Oh, before this have I indulged in many a sinful act.

पावाणं च खलु भो कडाणं कम्माणं पुव्विं
दुच्चिण्णाणं दुप्पडिक्कंताणं वेयइत्ता मोक्खो
नत्थि अवेयइत्ता तवसा वा झोसइत्ता ।
अट्ठारसमं पयं भवइ ॥१८॥

पापानां च खलु भोः कृतानां कर्मणां पूर्वं
दुश्चीर्णानां दुष्प्रतिक्रान्तानां वेदयित्वा मोक्षः—
नास्त्यवेदयित्वा तपसा वा शोषयित्वा ।
अष्टादशपदं भवति ॥१८॥

18. Oh, *mokṣa* is attained only when sinful acts accumulated in the past by evil conduct and evil effort are either suffered till exhaustion or get withered through penance. There is no *mokṣa* till they are exhausted or withered.

Such are the eighteen items.

Follow the *ślokas:*

भवइ य इत्थ सिलोगो—
जया य चयई धम्मं अणज्जो भोगकारणा ।
से तत्थ मुच्छिए बाले आयइं नावबुज्झइ ॥१॥

भवति चाऽत्र श्लोकः—
यदा च त्यजति धर्मम् अनार्यो भोगकारणात् ।
स तत्र मूर्च्छितो बालः आयतिं नावबुध्यते ॥१॥

1. When a *sādhu*, fallen from the path of the *Ārya*, gives up spiritual endeavour and courts enjoyment, then he, the ignoramous, blinded by desires, understands not his own future.

जया ओहाविओ होइ इंदो वा पडिओ छमं ।
सव्वधम्मपरिब्भट्ठो स पच्छा परितप्पइ ॥२॥

यदाऽवधावितो भवति इन्द्रो वा पतितः क्षमाम् ।
सर्वधर्मपरिभ्रष्टः सः पश्चात्परितप्यते ॥२॥

2. When a *sādhu* returns to the household order, then, deprived of all disciplines, repents he, as Indra fallen from heaven.

जया य वंदिमो होइ पच्छा होइ अवंदिमो ।
देवया व चुया ठाणा स पच्छा परितप्पइ ॥३॥

यदा च वन्द्यो भवति पश्चाद् भवत्यवन्द्यः ।
देवतेव च्युता स्थानात् स पश्चात् परितप्यते ॥३॥

3. **When a *sādhu* is in spiritual order, he is worthy of adoration; but when he slips away from it, he ceases to be so and repents like a god fallen from his station.**

जया य पूइमो होइ पच्छा होइ अपूइमो ।
राया व रज्जपब्भट्ठो स पच्छा परितप्पइ ॥४॥

यदा च पूज्यो भवति पश्चात् भवत्यपूज्यः ।
राजेव राज्यप्रभ्रष्टः स पश्चात्परितप्यते ॥४॥

4. **When a *sādhu* is in spiritual order, he is worthy of respect; but when he slips away from it, he ceases to be so and repents like a king who has lost his kingdom.**

जया य माणिमो होइ पच्छा होइ अमाणिमो ।
सेट्ठि व्व कब्बडे छूढो स पच्छा परितप्पइ ॥५॥

यदा च मान्यो भवति पश्चाद् भवत्यमान्यः ।
श्रेष्ठी कर्बटे क्षिप्तः स पश्चात्परितप्यते ॥५॥

5. **When a *sādhu* is in spiritual order, he is worthy of honour; but when he slips away from it, he ceases to be so and repents as a merchant would do when he is confined to a small place (where there is no trade).**

जया य थेरओ होइ समइक्कंतजोव्वणो ।
मच्छो व्व गलं गिलित्ता स पच्छा परितप्पइ ॥६॥

यदा च स्थविरो भवति समतिक्रान्तयौवनः ।
मत्स्य इव गलं गिलित्वा स पश्चात्परितप्यते ॥६॥

6. When, after the passage of youth, the fallen *sādhu* grows old, he repents like a fish that has swallowed a hook.

जया य कुकुडंबस्स कुतत्तीहिं विहम्मइ ।
हत्थी व बंधणे बद्धो स पच्छा परितप्पइ ॥७॥

यदा च कुकुटुम्बस्य कुतप्तिभिर्विहन्यते ।
हस्तीव बन्धने बद्धः स पश्चात् परितप्यते ॥७॥

7. When the fallen *sādhu* is overwhelmed with worry about his kith and kin, then he repents like an elephant tied to a pole.

पुत्तदारपरिकिण्णो मोहसंताणसंतओ ।
पंकोसन्नो जहा नागो स पच्छा परितप्पइ ॥८॥

पुत्रदारपरिकीर्णः मोहसन्तानसन्ततः ।
पङ्कावसन्नो यथा नागः स पश्चात्परितप्यते ॥८॥

8. Surrounded by progeny and wife and enveloped by attachment, he repents like an elephant who has fallen in the mud.

अज्ज आहं गणी हुंतो भावियप्पा बहुस्सुओ ।
जइ हं रमंतो परियाए सामण्णे जिणदेसिए ॥९॥

अद्य तावदहं गणी अभविष्यं भावितात्मा बहुश्रुतः ।
यद्यहमरंस्ये पर्याये श्रामण्ये जिनदेशिते ॥९॥

9. Had I remained in the *śramaṇa* order as organised by the *Jinas*, I would have been an enlightened soul well-versed in the *śrutas*, and even an *ācārya*.

देवलोगसमाणो उ परिआओ महेसिणं ।
रयाणं अरयाणं तु महानिरयसारिसो ॥१०॥

देवलोकसमानस्तु पर्यायो महर्षीणाम् ।
रतानामरतानां च महानरकसदृशः ॥१०॥

10. For a *muni* immersed in restraint, the monks' order is as pleasant as the abode in heaven; but for one who is not so immersed, the holy order is as painful as an abode in the great hell.

अमरोवमं जाणिय सोक्खमुत्तमं रयाण परियाए तहारयाणं ।
निरओवमं जाणिय दुक्खमुत्तमं रमेज्ज तम्हा परियाय पंडिए ॥११॥

अमरोपमं ज्ञात्वा सौख्यमुत्तमं रतानां पर्याये तथाऽरतानाम् ।
निरयोपमं ज्ञात्वा दुःखमुत्तमं रमेत तस्मात्पर्याये पण्डितः ॥११॥

11. Knowing that a *sādhu* immersed in restraint has pleasures as good as those of the gods, and that one not so immersed has all the pains of hell, a learned *muni* relishes in restraint.

धम्माउ भट्ठं सिरिओ ववेयं जन्नग्गि विज्झायमिवप्पतेयं ।
हीलंति णं दुव्विहियं कुसीलं दाढुद्धियं घोरविसं व नागं ॥१२॥

धर्माद् भ्रष्टं श्रियो व्यपेतं यज्ञाग्नि विध्यातमिवाल्पतेजसम् ।
हीलयन्ति एनं दुर्विहितं कुशीलाः उद्धतदंष्ट्रं घोरविषमिव नागम् ॥१२॥

12. Just as even ordinary folks care not for poisonous snakes whose teeth are uprooted, so even men of debatable conduct speak ill of a *sādhu* who is fallen from the spiritual path, who is devoid of the grandeur of conduct, who is as lustreless as the exhausted sacrificial fire and and who pursues an undesirable course.

इहेव धम्मो अयसो अकित्ती दुन्नामधेज्जं च पिहुज्जणम्मि ।
चुयस्स धम्माउ अहम्मसेविणो संभिन्नवित्तस्स य हेट्ठओ गई ॥१३॥

इहैव अधर्मोऽयशोऽकीर्तिः दुर्नामधेयं च पृथग्जने ।
च्युतस्य धर्मादधर्मसेविनः संभिन्नवृत्तस्य चाधस्ताद् गतिः ॥१३॥

13. A *sādhu* who is fallen, who serves *adharma* and transgresses the rules of conduct, practises *adharma* in the earthly life. He attains ill-fame and ill-reputation. Even ordinary folks speak ill of him and he goes down.

भुंजित्तु भोगाइ पसज्झ चेयसा तहाविहं कट्टु असंजमं बहुं ।
गइं च गच्छे अणभिज्झियं दुहं बोही य से नो सुलभा पुणो पुणो ।१४।

भुक्त्वा भोगान् प्रसह्य चेतसा तथाविधं कृत्वाऽसंयमं बहुम् ।
गतिं च गच्छेदनभिध्यातां दुःखां बोधिश्च तस्य नो सुलभा पुनः पुनः ॥१४॥

14. A *sādhu* fallen from restraint enjoys with his heart full of emotion and undergoes much laxity and then reaches a state full of misery and pain; and even though he is born and dies several times, the attainment of enlightenment, does not become easy.

इमस्स ता नेरइयस्स जंतुणो दुहोवणीयस्स किलेसवत्तिणो ।
पलिओवमं झिज्जइ सागरोवमं किमंग पुण मज्झ इमं मणोदुहं ॥१५॥

अस्य तावन्नारकस्य जन्तोः उपनीतदुःखस्य क्लेशवृत्तेः ।
पल्योपमं क्षीयते सागरोपमं किमङ्ग पुनर्ममेदं मनोदुःखम् ॥१५॥

15. Even very long life-span of the denizens of hells, which figures cannot express, and which is full of misery and pain, ends; then what to bother about (the span of) my mental misery ?

न मे चिरं दुक्खमिणं भविस्सई असासया भोगपिवास जंतुणो ।
न चे सरीरेण इमेण वेस्सई अविस्सई जीवियपज्जवेण मे ॥१६॥

न मे चिरं दुःखमिदं भविष्यति अशाश्वती भोगपिपासा जन्तोः ।
न चेच्छरीरेणानेनापैष्यति अपैष्यति जीवित-पर्यवेण मे ॥१६॥

16. This my misery won't last for good. The enjoyment of pleasures by the *jīvas* is transient. Even though this ends not in my mortal frame, then it must surely end at the end of my life.

जस्सेवमप्पा उ हवेज्ज निच्छिश्रो चएज्ज देहं न उ धम्मसासणं ।
तं तारिसं नो पयलेंति इंदिया उवेंतवाया व सुदंसणं गिरिं ॥१७॥

यस्यैवमात्मा तु भवेन्निश्चितः त्यजेद्देहं न खलु धर्मशासनम् ।
तं तादृशं न प्रचालयन्तीन्द्रियाणि उपयद्वाता इव सुदर्शनं गिरिम् ॥१७॥

17. He, whose soul is steadfast enough to say, "Better give up this body than the prescriptions," is never shaken by the drive of desires, as Mount Sudarshana is never shaken by the gust of hurricane.

इच्चेव संपस्सिय बुद्धिमं नरो श्रायं उवायं विविहं वियाणिया ।
काएण वाया श्रदु माणसेणं तिगुत्तिगुत्तो जिणवयणमहिट्ठि जासि ।१८।
—त्ति बेमि ॥

इत्येवं संदृश्य बुद्धिमान्नरः श्रायमुपायं विविधं विज्ञाय ।
कायेन वाचाऽथ मानसेन त्रिगुप्तिगुप्तो जिनवचनमधितिष्ठेत् ॥१८॥
इति ब्रवीमि ।

18. A wise person considering this properly, and knowing the diverse gains, and their instruments, becomes a '*gupta*' in the three *guptis* (body, word and mind) and takes shelter in the words of a *Jina*.

So say I.

बिवित्तचरिया (विविक्तचर्या)

CHULIKA TWO

Vivikta-charyā

चूलियं तु पवक्खामि सुयं केवलिभासियं ।
जं सुणित्तु सपुन्नाणं धम्मे उप्पज्जए मई ॥१॥

चूलिकां तु प्रवक्ष्यामि श्रुतां केवलिभाषिताम् ।
यां श्रुत्वा स पुण्यानां धर्मे उत्पद्यते मतिः ॥१॥

1. I shall speak out the *cūlikā* which is stated to have been delivered by the *Kevalins* and on hearing which the pious souls have their mind fixed in religion.

अणुसोयपट्ठिए बहुजणम्मि पडिसोयलद्धलक्खेणं ।
पडिसोयमेव अप्पा दायव्वो होउ कामेणं ॥२॥

अनुस्रोतः प्रस्थिते बहुजने प्रतिस्रोतो लब्धलक्ष्येण ।
प्रतिस्रोत एवात्मा दातव्यो भवितुकामेन ॥२॥

2. Most people move with the current (of enjoying earthly pleasures). But he, who is desirous of liberation, who is tired of the enjoyment of objects and is keen to court restraint, should direct the soul against the current.

अणुसोयसुहो लोगो पडिसोओ आसवो सुविहियाणं ।
अणुसोओ संसारो पडिसोओ तस्स उत्तारो ॥३॥

अनुस्रोतः सुखो लोकः प्रतिस्रोत आश्रवः सुविहितानाम् ।
अनुस्रोतः संसारः प्रतिस्रोतस्तस्योत्तारः ॥३॥

3. People find pleasure in moving with the current. But one who is an enlightened *sādhu*—his self-control takes him against it. The world feeds the current; movement against the current takes one out.

तम्हा आयारपरक्कमेण संवरसमाहिबहुलेणं ।
चरिया गुणा य नियमा य होंति साहूण दट्ठव्वा ॥४॥

तस्मादाचारपराक्रमेण संवरसमाधिबहुलेन ।
चर्या गुणाश्च नियमाश्च भवन्ति साधूनां द्रष्टव्याः ॥४॥

4. So the *sādhus*, who are steadfast in conduct, who have courted *saṁvara*, should adhere to rules, regulations and sanctions pertaining to conduct.

अणिएयवासो समुयाणचरिया अन्नायउंछं पइरिक्कया य ।
अप्पोवही कलहविवज्जणा य विहारचरिया इसिणं पसत्था ॥५॥

अनिकेतवासः समुदानचर्या अज्ञातोञ्छं प्रतिरिक्तता च ।
अल्पोपधिः कलहविवर्जना च विहारचर्या ऋषीणां प्रशस्ताः ॥५॥

5. Renunciation of residence in one's own house, begging food from many households, begging food from unknown households, living alone, possession of few things and avoidance of quarrel—these are the essentials for *ṛṣis* devoted to *vihāra-charyā*.

आइण्णओमाणविवज्जणा य ओसन्नदिट्ठाहडभत्तपाणे ।
संसट्ठकप्पेण चरेज्ज भिक्खू तज्जायसंसट्ठ जई जएज्जा ॥६॥

आकीर्णावमानविवर्जना च उत्सन्नदृष्टाहृतभक्तपानम् ।
संसृष्टकल्पेन चरेद् भिक्षुः तज्जातसंसृष्टे यतिर्यतेत ॥६॥

6. Non-acceptance of food from a place where there is a crowd of seekers, non-acceptance of food when it is apprehended to be inadequate, acceptance of food

and drink from a spot which is near-visible—these are wholesome for a *ṛṣi.* A *bhikṣu* accepts food from a vessel and by the hand that are tainted with food particles. Effort should be made to take food from a vessel and the hand that are so tainted.

अमज्जमंसासि अमच्छरी या अभिक्खणं निव्विगइं गया य ।
अभिक्खणं काउसग्गकारी सज्झायजोगे पयओ हवेज्जा ॥७॥

अमद्यमांसाशी अमत्सरी च अभीक्ष्णं निर्विकृतिं गतश्च ।
अभीक्ष्णं कायोत्सर्गकारी स्वाध्याययोगे प्रयतो भवेत् ॥७॥

7. A *sādhu* takes not liquor or meat; he is free from external show; he takes not things that are often transformed; practises *kāyotsarga*; and is immersed in *svādhyāya* as ordained.

न पडिन्नवेज्जा सयणासणाइं सेज्जं निसेज्जं तहे भत्तपाणं ।
गामे कुले वा नगरे व देसे ममत्वभावं न कहिं चि कुज्जा ॥८॥

न प्रतिज्ञापयेत् शयनासनानि शय्यां निषद्यां तथा भक्तपानम् ।
ग्रामे कुले वा नगरे वा देशे ममत्वभावं न क्वचित् कुर्यात् ॥८॥

8. At the time of departure, a *sādhu* makes not a householder promise that a particular bed, seat, residence or place of *svādhyāya* is to be given to him when he comes back again or even food and drink. He never develops attachment to a village, a family, a town or a country.

गिहिणो वेयावडियं न कुज्जा अभिवायणं वंदण पूयणं च ।
असंकिलिट्ठेहिं समं वसेज्जा मुणी चरित्तस्य जओ न हाणी ॥९॥

गृहिणो वयापृत्यं न कुर्यात् अभिवादनं पूजनं च ।
असंक्लिष्टैः समं वसेत मुनिश्चारित्रस्य यतो न हानिः ॥९॥

9. A *sādhu* serves not a householder, nor salutes, adores or worships him. A *muni* lives with such other

sādhus **as are non-attached to house-holders so that they incur not a stain on their character.**

न या लभेज्जा निउणं सहायं गुणाहियं वा गुणग्रो समं वा ।
एक्को वि पावाइं विवज्जयंतो विहरेज्ज कामेसु ग्रसज्जमाणो ॥१०॥

न वा लभेत निपुणं सहायं गुणाधिकं वा गुणतः समं वा ।
एकोऽपि पापानि विवर्जयन् विहरेत् कामेष्वसज्जन् ॥१०॥

10. If by chance he gets not a companion superior in merit or even his equal, then he wanders alone avoiding sinful acts and remaining detached to the enjoyment of desires.

संवच्छरं चावि परं पमाणं बीयं च वासं न तहिं वसेज्जा ।
सुत्तस्स मग्गेण चरेज्ज भिक्खू सुत्तस्स ग्रत्थो जह ग्राणवेइ ॥११॥

संवत्सरं वाऽपि परं प्रमाणं द्वितीयं च वर्षं न तत्र वसेत् ।
सूत्रस्य मार्गेण चरेद् भिक्षुः सूत्रस्यार्थो यथाज्ञापयति ॥११॥

11. If a *muni* **has lived in a village upto the maximum period prescribed, he stays not there again without giving a gap of two years. A** *bhikṣu* **follows the way prescribed in the** *sūtras* **and follows it in the same manner as the implication of the** *sūtra* **permits.**

जो पुव्वरत्तावररत्तकाले संपिक्खई ग्रप्पगमप्पएणं ।
किं मे कडं किं च मे किच्च सेसं किं सक्कणिज्जं न समायरामि ॥१२॥

यः पूर्वरात्रापररात्रकाले संप्रेक्षते ग्रात्मकमात्मकेन ।
किं मया कृतं किं च मे कृत्यशेषं किं शकनीयं न समाचरामि ॥१२॥

12. A *sādhu* **should introspect as follows in the first and last quarters of the night—'What have I done? What work needs be completed by me? What is that act which out of illusion I do not do?**

किं मे परो पासइ किं व अप्पा किं वाहं खलियं न विवज्जयामि ।
इच्चेव सम्मं अणुपासमाणो अणागयं नो पडिबंध कुज्जा ॥१३॥

किं मम परः पश्यति किं वात्मा किं वाऽहं स्खलितं न विवर्जयामि ।
इत्येवं सम्यगनुपश्यन् अनागतं नो प्रतिबन्धं कुर्यात् ॥१३॥

13. 'Is my carelessness observed by others or do I myself observe my own carelessness? What are these lapses that I have not discarded?'—thus by introspecting self in due manner, a *muni* entraps not himself in (*karma*) not yet arrived.

जत्थेव पासे कइ दुप्पउत्तं काएण वाया अदु माणसेणं ।
तत्थेव धीरो पडिसाहरेज्जा आइन्नओ खिप्पमिव क्खलीणं ॥१४॥

यत्रैव पश्येत् क्वचिद् दुष्प्रयुक्तं कायेन वाचाऽथ मानसेन ।
तत्रैव धीरः प्रतिसंहरेत् आकीर्णकः क्षिप्रमिव खलीनम् ॥१४॥

14. A restrained *sādhu* wakes up when he notices his mind, word or body going wayward, in the same manner as a pedigree horse becomes cautious at a pull of the bridle.

जस्सेरिसा जोग जिइंदियस्स धिइमओ सप्पुरिसस्स निच्चं ।
तमाहु लोए पडिबुद्धजीवी सो जीवइ संजमजीविएणं ॥१५॥

यस्येदृशा योगा जितेन्द्रियस्य धृतिमतः सत्पुरुषस्य नित्यम् ।
तमाहुर्लोके प्रतिबुद्धजीविनं स जीवति संयमजीवितेन ॥१५॥

15. When the acquisition of one, with senses controlled, intelligence acquired and saintliness possessed, is like this, he is called a *padibuddha-jīvī* in the world. He, who is like this, leads a life of restraint.

अप्पा खलु सययं रक्खियव्वो सव्विंदिएहिं सुसमाहिएहिं ।
अरक्खिओ जाइपहं उवेइ सुरक्खिओ सव्वदुहाण मुच्चइ ॥१६॥

—त्ति बेमि ।

आत्मा खलु सततं रक्षितव्यः सर्वेन्द्रियैः सुसमाहितैः ।
अरक्षितो जातिपथमुपैति सुरक्षितः सर्वदुःखेभ्यो मुच्यते ॥१६॥

इति ब्रवीमि ।

16. One should always protect the soul by restraining the senses. A soul that is unprotected moves in the path of birth and death. A protected soul is liberated from all misery.

So say I.

INDEX OF TERMS*

अ (9.4.3.1) and.
अइउक्कस (5.2.42) (one who has attained) a high level.
अइक्कमित्तु, अइक्कम्म (5.2.11) cross, to cross.
अइदूर (5.1.23) very far.
अइभूमि (5.1.24) sector prohibited to, and not usually traversed by, outsiders.
अइयार (5.1.89) transgress, violate rules of conduct
अइलाभ (9.3.5) great gain.
अवइत्त (ए) (9.1.16) transgress.
अइवायते, अइवाएज्जा, अइवायावेज्जा, अइवायंत, अइवाय (4.1.11) injury, slaughter.
अइहील (5.1.99) despise, overlook.
अईअ (7.8) past.
अउल (7.43) beyond comparison.
अओमय (ा) (9.3.6) made of iron.
अंकुस (2.10) hook (for controlling elephant).
अंग (8.57) limb.
अंग (किम्) (chu 1.15) what length.
अंगपच्चंगसंठाणं (8.57) arrangement of limbs, body structure.
अंतलिक्ख (7.53) sky.
अंधगवण्हि (2.8) of the line of Yadu.
अकप्प, अकप्पिय (5.1.27) forbidden for acceptance, prohibited object.
अकामेणं, अकाम (5.1.80) with reluctance.
अकिंचण (6.68) without possession.
अकेज्ज (7.45) not purchasable.
अकोउहल्ल (9.3.10) one who evinces not curiosity.
अकोविए (य) (9.2.22) unequipped.

*Figures within brackets indicate the *Sūtra* where the word first occurs.

अक्कम	(5.1.7) cross.
अक्कुट्ठ	(10.13) chastised with harsh words.
अक्कुह्य	(9.3.10) one who displays not magical power.
अक्कोस-पहार-तज्जणाओ	(10.11) अक्कोस words of anger; पहार lashes तज्जणा threats
अक्खाउमरिहइ	(8.20) behoves not to repeat.
अक्खाय	(4.1) said.
अक्खोडंत, अक्खोड	(4.19) lashing of wet cloth.
अखंडफुडिय	(6.6) transgress neither the part not the whole.
अगंधण	(2.6) a species of poisonous snake.
अगणि	(4.20) fire; अग्गि : (9.3.1) fire.
अगारिणा, अगारि	(6:57) resident, householder.
अगाहा, अगाह	(7.39) very deep.
अगिद्धे, अगिद्ध	(10.16) unattached.
अगुणप्पेही (हि)	(5.2.41) one who views other's misdeeds; अगुणा demerits.
अगुत्ती (त्ति)	(6.58) danger, jeopardy.
अग्ग	(5.1.12) leader; (9.1.8) sprout.
अग्गबीज	(4.8) where the tip of the plant serves as seedling.
अचक्खुविसअ	(95.1.20) not an object of vision.
अचक्खुस	(6.27) invisible.
अचवल	(8.29) fixed, static.
अचित्तमंत, अचित्तं (त्त)	(4.13) without living object, non-life.
अचियत्तकुलं	(5.1.17) unpleasant household; अचियत्त (7.43) indescribable, beyond words, unthinkable
अच्चंबिल	(5.1.78) too sour; अंबिल (5.1.97) sour.
अच्चि	(4.20) tip of a burning lamp.
अच्चिमालि	(9.1.14) the sun.
अच्छणणजोएण (जोय)	(8.3) by non-injury, one who slaughters not; छणण injury; अच्छणण non-injury.
अच्छंदा, अच्छंद	(2.2) dependent.
अजाइया	(5.1.18) without seeking. जाय, जाइअ : seek, request for.
अजीवं, अजीव	(5.1.77) free from living object, non-life.
अज्ज	(6.53) Aryan; (chu.9) to-day.

अज्जपयं, अज्जपय	(10.20) the way of the Aryan.
अज्जय	(7.18) grand parent (male).
अज्जव	(6.67), अज्जवभाव (8.38) simplicity.
अज्जिया	7.15) grand parent (female).
अज्झपरय	(10.15) immersed in things of the spirit.
अज्झयण	(4.1) chapter, section.
अज्झाइयव्व	(9.4.5) to be acquired or studied.
अज्झोयर	(5.1.55) to increase the quantity (of food prepared for self in order to oblige a monk) in the middle of the cooking process.
अट्ठ	(3.4), अत्थ (10.15) meaning, import, purpose, object.
अट्ठ	(6.7) eight; अट्ठम (8.15) eight.
अट्ठया	(9.4.6) purpose, object
अट्ठसुहुमाइ	(8.13) eight minute living beings.
अट्ठारस, अट्ठारसम	(chu 1.1) eighteen, eighteenth.
अट्ठावए (य)	(3.4) gambling, dice, economics.
अट्ठिय	(5.1.84) with a seed.
अट्ठियप्प (।)	(2.9) restless in the soul; अट्ठिय : restless.
अणंतनाणोवगओ	(9.1.11) master of infinite knowledge.
अणंतहियकामय	(9.2.16) desirous of liberation; अणंतहिय liberation.
अणगारिया	(4.S18) state of homelessness, mendicancy.
अणवज्ज	(chu 1.1) non-Aryan.
अणभिज्झिय	(chu 1.14) full of misery, evil.
अणज्ज	(7.3) free from sin.
अणाइण्ण (न्न)	(3.1) never indulged in, not fit for indulgence.
अणाउल	(5.1.13) not sullen; आउलि, आउलिअ : sullenness.
अणागय	(7.8) not come, future.
अणाबाह सुहाभिकंखि	(9.1.10) desirous of limitless happiness/liberation अणाबाहसुह : liberation.
अणायण, अणायतण,	
अणाययण	(5.1.10) harlot's abode.
अणायरियमज्जाणं	(6.53) not performed by the Aryans.
अणायार	(6.56) licence, non-observance (of sanctions).
अणासए, अणासा	(9.3.6) without hope.

अणिएयवास	(chu 2.5) homeless state, mendicancy.
अणिग्गहीय	(8.39) not brought under control.
अणिच्च	(8.58) transcient.
अणिमिस	(5.1.73) pine apple.
अणिस्सिय (-या)	(1.5) unsheltered, wholly independent.
अणिह	(10.17) frank.
अणु	(4.13) particle.
अणुग्ग (ए) य	(8.28) (the sun) having risen.
अणुचिट्ठ	(5.2.30) stay.
अणुजाणा	(6.14) approve.
अणुत्तराइं, अणुत्तर	(4.s19) unsurpassed, highest.
अणुदिसा	(6.33) angular points between directions.
अणुन्न (ण्ण) य	(5.1.13) bend low, not look up.
अणुण्ण (वेत्तु) विय	(5.1.19) seek/obtain permission.
अणुपाल	(6.40) bring up, rear.
अणुपासमाण	(chu2.13) introspecting.
अणुप्पत्त	(3.15) obtained.
अणुफास	(6.18) touch, influence.
अणुबंधि	(9.3.7) binding, augmenting.
अणुमाय	(5.2.49) even a little.
अणुमोयणी	(7.54) approving.
अणुवीइ	(7.44) having considered.
अणुविग्ग	(5.1.2) calm, at ease, without anxiety.
अणुसासिज्जंत, अणुसास (ण)	(9.1.13) guide; (9.4.4.2) prescribe.
अणुसोय	(chu2.2) following the stream.
अणुसिन्न	(5.2.21) not properly boiled/cooked.
अणोग-साहु-पुइय	(5.2.43) worshipped by many monks.
अणोहाइय	(chu1.1) one who has not transgressed restraint.
अंतिंतिण	(8.29) not garrulous, not murmuring.
अत्त	(4.17) soul; अत्तव (8.48) self-contained.
अत्तट्ठा-गुरुअ	(5.2.32) one who values one's own soul, one who gives greater importance to self.
अत्तसंपग्गहिय	(9.4.4) extolling one's achievement.
अत्त-हियट्ठाए	(4.17) for the well-being of self.
अत्थंगय	(8.28) (the sun) having set.
अत्थविणिच्छय	(8.43) determining correct import.
अत्थसंजुत्त	(5.2.43) one endowed with purified self.

अत्थिय	(5.1.73) name of a fruit
अदिट्ठधम्म	(9.2.22) fatalist.
अदिन्ना (ण्णा) दाण	(4.13) usurpation, taking something not duly bestowed, अदिन्न (ण्ण) not bestowed.
अदीणवित्ति	(9.3.10) one who humbles not self in his profession; अदीण (5.2.26) not feeling humble/small
अदेंत	(5.2.28) not giving.
अनियाण	(10.13) one who hankers not after result.
अनिव्वुड	(3.7) with living objects, wherein life has not ceased to exist, unripe.
अन्नट्ठं पगडं	(8.51) made for others.
अन्नयर	(4.23), अन्नयराग (6.59) some one. अन्नयरामवि, अण्णयर : (6.18) either.
अन्नाणि	(4.10) without knowledge, ignorant.
अन्नायउंछ	(9.3.4) begging without revealing identity. अन्ना (ण्णा) य; unknown.
अपडिलेहाए	(6.55) without observing.
अपरिसाडय	(5.1.96) without dropping.
अपावभाव	(8.63) sinless in mind/thought.
अपासंत	(6.23) without observing.
अपिसुण	(9.3 ;10) one who speaks not ill of another in one's absence.
अपुणागम	(10.21) never-to-return
अपूइय	(chu 1) not worthy of worship.
अप्पयं, अप्पण, अप्पग, अप्पभूय अप्प	(1.2) soul, living being, consciousness.
अप्प	(4.13) little.
अपग्घ	(7.46) cheap.
अप्पगमप्पएणं	(9.3.11) knowing self by self.
अप्पतेय	(chu 1) with little glow, dim.
अप्पत्तिय, अप्पत्ति	(5.2.12) displease, hurt. अप्पसन्न (9.1.5).
अपमत्त	(8.16) careful.
अप्परय	(9.4.7) with little (*karma*) dirt.
अप्पसुय	(9.1.2) not profound in *Śruta* knowledge.
अप्पहिट्ठ	(5.1.13) not elated; हिट्ठ, हट्ठ pleased, elated.
अप्पिच्छया, अपिच्छा	(8.25) with little desire, one with little desire.

अप्पियकारिण	(9.3.9.) unpleasant.
अप्पावहि	(chu 2.5) one who keeps few objects.
अप्पासुय	(8.23) with living objects.
अबंभचरिय	(6.1) non-celibacy.
अबोहियं, अबोहि	(4.20) ignorance.
अब्भमुक्क	(9.1.15) free from clouds; अब्भ (8.63) sky.
अब्भापुडावगम	(8.63) when the clouds are removed.
अब्भिंतर	(4.17) inside.
अभिकंखमाण, अभिकंख	(9.3.1), wishing.
अभिक्कंत	(4.9) to come to the fore.
अभिक्खणं	(5.1.10) again and again.
अभिगच्छ	(4.21) get, acquire.
अभिगम	9.315) conduct, humility; (9.4.6) knowing.
अभिगिज्झ	(7.17) on discussing.
अभिधाय	(9.3.8) beat.
अभितोस	(9.3.8) please, satisfy.
अभिधार	(5.2.25.) proceed, go.
अभिनिवेस	(8.26) place, establishment.
अभिभूय	(6.59) overpower, (I0.14) defeat.
अभिमुह	9.1.10) alert, ready.
अभिराम	(4.3.1) immerse, engage.
अभिवायण	(chu 2.9) salute.
अभिसित्त	(9.1.11) propitiate.
अभिहड	(3.2) brought to the fore.
अभूइभाव	(9.1.1) causing ruin.
अमच्छरीया, अमच्छति	(chu 2.7) free from external show/display.
अमज्जमंसासि	(chu 2.7) one who takes not liquor and meat.
अ-मम	(6.68) 'not-mine', free from attachment.
अमरोवम	(chu 1) like heaven; अमर—god, death-less.
अमाइ	(9.3.10) without deceit.
अमाणिम	(chu 1) unworthy of honour.
अमुग	(7.6), अमुय (7.50) so and so.
अमुच्छिय	(5.1.1) without attachment; मुच्छा attachment, bondage.
अमूढ	(19.7) one with right faith.
अमोघ	(8.33.) non-failing, not missing target.
अमोहदंसि	(6.67) one who sees virtue in non-attachment.

अयंपिर (5.1.23.) silent, without word/exaggeration.

अयमायहिट्ठए (9.4.7.5) keen to attain liberation.

अयावयट्ठा (5.2.2) inadequate.

अरइ, अरई (8.27) mental distress.

अरक्खिय (chu 2.16) unprotected.

अरिह (8.20) to be able.

अलद्धुयं (9.3.4) on not getting.

अलाय (4.1.20) haf-burnt log.

अलोग (4.22) non-space

अलोलुअ, अलोल (9.3.10) free from greed.

अल्लीणपलीणगुत्त (8.40) restrained in organs of senses and mind; अल्लीणगुत्त (8.44) restrained in mind and speech.

अ-वंदिम (chu 1) not worthy of honour.

अवक्कमित्ता, अवक्कम (5.1.81) go, on going, cross.

अवक्कियम् (7.43) not salable.

अवण्णवाद (9.3.9) speaking ill in one's absence.

अवपंगुर, अवपंगुण (5.1.18) open.

अवरज्झइ, अवरज्झ (6.7) violate, indulge in, transgress.

अवररत्त (chu 2.13) last quarter of the night.

अवाउड (I) (3.12) uncovered, unclad.

अविस्सइ, अवेस्सइ (chu 1) end.

अविहेडअ (10.10) one who abuses not another (des-(pite provocation).

अवे (chu 1) remove.

अवेयवित्ता (chu 1) without suffering.

अव्वक्खित्त (5.1.2) unperturbed, undisturbed.

अव्वहिय (8.27) not feeling pain/regret.

असइ (10.13) again and again.

असंकिलिट्ठ (chu 2.9) not attached to house-holders.

असंजम, असंजय (5.1.29) lacking restraint.

असंथड (7.33) not fit to bear fruit.

असंदिद्ध (7.3) doubt-free.

असंबद्ध (8.24) uninvolved, free.

असंभंत (5.1.1) unconcerned, free from anxiety; संभंत afraid, anxious.

असंविभागि (9.2.22) one who shares not, selfish.

असंसट्ठ	(5.1.34) not besmeared, clean.
असंसत्त	(5.1.23) without attachment.
असच्चमोसा	(7.3) speech whose authenticity is not certain.
असज्जमाण	(chu 2.10) unattached.
असत्थपरिणय	(5.2.23) असत्थ—not deprived of ripeness; परिणाय, परिणामिश्र—change, transform.
असब्भवयण	(9.2.8) uncivil words.
असावज्ज	(5.1.92) sin-free.
असिणाण	(6.62) non-ablution.
असुइ	(10.21) impure.
असुइय	(5.1.98) unspiced.
अस्सिय	(5.1.11) sheltered.
अहण	(10.6) poor, without wealth.
अहम्म	(6.16) sacrilege. अहम्मसेवि (chu 1) one who indulges in acts of sacrilege.
अहरगइ	(chu 1) movement down.
अहागड	(1.4) made for householder's own use.
अहिंसा	(1.1) non-violence in comprehensive sense, including five Great Vows.
अहिगरण	(8.50) violence.
अहिज्जग	(8.49) experienced, knower.
अहिज्जिउं	(4.1) for studing; अहिज्जित्ता (9.4.5.3) after studing.
अहिट्ठ, अहिट्ठग	(8.61) behave, one who behaves.
अहियाय, अहिय	(9.1.4) evil; (chu 2.10) much.
अहयगामिणी	(8.47) doing harm, putting one out of form.
अहियास (य)	(5.2.6) bear·
अधुणा-धोय	(5.1.75) just now washed: अहुणोवलित्त (5.1.21) just now besmeared.
अहे	(6.33) downward.
आइच्च	(8.28) the sun.
आइण्ण	(chu 2.6) feast that attracts a crowd.
आइन्नअ	(chu 2.14) pedigree, of good breed.
आउ	(4.5) water; (8.34) life-span; काय (4.3) water-bodies.
आउरस्सरण	(3.6) remembering previous affluence.
आखव	(chu 2.3) self-control

आगमसम्पन्न	(6.1) master of the *Agamas*.
आगाह-इत्ता, आगाह	(5.1.31) after bath, bath.
आजीववित्तिया, आजीवगा, आजीव	(3.6) one who accepts offer (food) on the basis of status of the donor. 'Status' includes caste, sect, industry, profession and sex.
आणव	(chu 2.11) permit, order; आणा (10.1) words of the *tīrthaṅkaras*.
आणुपुव्वी	(8.1) order, one after another, one by one.
आणुलोमिया	(7.56) favourable words.
आभिओग	(9.2.5) service.
आभोएत्ताण	(5.1.89) knowing, recollecting.
आमग, आमए, आम	(3.7) unripe, green.
आमुसंत, आमुस	(4.19) touch a little, touch once.
आय	(chu 1) benefit; आयइ (chu 1) future.
आयय	(9.4.7.5) spread, extent; आययण (4.15) area.
आययट्ठि (य)	(5.2.34) covetous of liberation.
आयरिय-पाया, आयरिय	(5.2.40) *acarya*, preceptor; सामए (8.60) as prescribed by the preceptor.
आयाण	(5.1.26) come, path.
आयार-गोयर, आयार	(6.2) activities, conduct; पणिहि (8.1) eighth chapter of *Daśavaikālika*; पन्नत्तिधर (8.49) well-versed in syntax and mode of expression. परक्कम (chu 2.3) exertion about conduct; भावत्तेण (5.2.46) theft of behaviour and subjective sense; भाव-दोसन्नु (7.13) one who is conscious of lapse, both internal and external; मंत (9.1.3) those who obey rules of conduct; मट्ठा (9.3.2) desirous of right conduct; समाहि (9.4.3) concentration on conduct.
आयाव (य)	(2.5) expose one-self to weather; आयावंत (4.19) dried.
आयावयट्ठ	(5.2.2) not adequate.
आरक्खिय	(5.1.16) guard, policeman.
आरहंत	(9.4.7) concerning an *arhat*. *Arhat* is one who is worshipped five-times in his life, from embryo stage till liberation.

आलव, आलवेज्ज-लवेज्ज (7.16. 17), आलवंते-लवंते (9.2.20) chatting/discussing again and again.

आलोइय, आलोअ (5.1.90, 91) submit before the preceptor; आलोइय (9.3.1) see, notice.

आलोय (5.1.15) opening, window; (5.1.96) a big pot.

आवगा (7.36) river.

आवण (5.1.71) shop.

आवेउं, आविअ (1.2.) drink.

आवीलंत, आवील (4.19) press.

आस, आसण, आसंदी, आसमाण, आसइत्तु (4.3.,7) sit, seat, seated, sitting.

आसय (5.1.85) mouth.

आसव (3.11) causes which lead to the influx of good and bad *karma*, fetters that tie the soul, *āsrava*.

आसायणा, आसाअ (9.1.4) neglect, overlook.

आसाइत्ताण, आसाइत्त, आसायण (5.1.77, 78) taste, tasting.

आसालय (6.53) easy-chair.

आहरंत, आहड, आहर (5.1.27, 28, 55) bring.

आहारमइय (8.28) concerning food intake.

आहियग्गि (9.1.11) fire-worshipper.

इंगाल (4.20) burn charcoal.

इड्ढि (4.10) fortune.

इत्तरिय (I) (chu 1) short span, transcient.

इत्थंय (9.4.7) state of infernal life, etc.

इत्थी-विग्गह (8.53) body/limbs of a woman.

इरियावहिया (5.1.88) restrictions on movement.

इहलोग-पारत्त-हिय (8.43) bliss in this life and in the next.

उईरंति, उईर, उईरण, उदीरण (6.38) premature bringing up of karma for throwing it out.

उउप्पसन्न (6.68) on the arrival of autumn.

उंछ (8.23) remnant, begging.

उंजंत, उंज (4.20) watering.

उंडग (4.23) a vessel for the use of a monk.

उंड्डय (5.1.87) spot, place.

उक्कट्ठ (5.1.34) pieces of fruits.

उक्का	(4.20) heavenly fire, meteor.
उच्चारभूमि	(8.17) lonely or unfrequented place, suitable for depositing excreta.
उच्चावय	(5.1.14) high and low, pure and impure.
उच्छोलणा-पहोइ	(4.26) one who washes with profuse quantity of water.
उज्जु-दंसि	(3.11) one rooted in equanimity; पन्न (3.11) wise; मइ (4.27) with straight mind (directed to liberation).
उत्तिग	(5.1.59) concentration of ants; उत्तिग-पणग (8.11) vegetation that comes up in rainy season.
उद-उल्ल (ओल्ल)	(4.19), wet, drenched, with water dropping.
उदग-दोणी	(7.27) water-pot.
उदगम्मि	(8.11) a kind of flora with multiplying souls, a kind of moss growing in water.
उदाहर	(8.1) narrate.
उद्देसिय (I)	(3.2) with a purpose (which is to make an offer to the monk);—हडं (6.48) brought with a purpose.
अप्पिलोदगा	(7.39) with water fed by other rivers.
उब्भिंदिया	(5.1.46) raise, remove.
उब्भिय (I)	(4.9) flora, plant.
उब्भेइम, उब्भेइय	(6.17) sea salt.
उवगरण	(4.23) objects of use.
उवघाइणी	(7.11) causing injury/slaughter.
उवचिट्ठ	(9.1.11) serve, obey.
उवचिय	(7.23) well-developed.
उवज्झाय	(9.2.12) teacher.
उवन्नत्थ	(5.1.39) placed (on the table for eating.)
उववज्झ	(9.2.5) conveyance for monarch or men of high status, transport for all occasions.
उववाइय (I)	(4.9) sudden-born, celestial and infernal beings, who are born without parents, and who attain youth in a moment after their birth
उववाय	(8.33) obey, carry out.

उववेय	(9.1.3) equipped.
उवसंकमंत, उवसंकम	(5.2.10) go in, enter.
उवसंत	(6.64) tranquilise, control thoroughly.
उवसंपज्जित्ताणं, उवसंपज्ज	(4.17) come near, embrace, resolve.
उपसंपया	(chu i) court, attain.
उवसम	(8.38), forgiveness.
उवस्सग्र, उवस्सए, उवस्सय	(7.29) residence of a Jaina monk.
उवहण	(1/4) destroy.
उवहिम्म, उवहिण, उवहि	(6.21) objects (used by a monk).
उवेंत, उवे	(6.68) attain, come near; उवेंत-वाया (chu i) gust of hurricane.
उव्वट्टण	(3.5) removing dirt from the body.
उस्सकिया, उस्सक्किया, उस्सक्का	(5.1.63) ignite, add log to oven fire.
उस्सवित्ताणं उस्सवित्त	(5.1.67) raise, place, erect.
उस्सिंचिया, उस्सिंच	(5.1.63) pour, remove.
ऊसढ	(5.2.25) high family; (7.35) steady (trunks of the trees).
एगंत	(4.23) lonely, wholly; —मस्सिए (5.1.11) wholly sheltered.
एगग्गचित्त	(9.4.5) with concentration of mind.
एक (ग) भत्त	(6.22) one full meal.
एलग-मुयया,-मुयग	(5.2.48) foolish/dumb like a ram.
एस, एसणा, एषणा	(1.3) search.
एस-काल	(7-7) future period.
एष (स) णिए	(5.1.36) acceptable, pure, free from objectionable things or associations.
एसोवम	(9.1.6) comparable, like this.
एहंत	(9.25) increasing.
ओगास	(5.1.) place.
ओग्गहंसि, ओग्गह	(5.1.18) take, accept.
ओघ, ओह	(9.2.23) flow, worldly ocean.
ओमजण	(chu 1) inferior, undeserving.
ओमाण	(chu 2.6) feast where so many people have come that there is a shortage of food.
ओयारिया	(5.1.63) take down (from the oven).
ओवघाइया	(8.21) words causing hurt/rousing feeling
ओवत्तिय (।)	(5.1.63) putting food from one pot into another on the oven, turn.

ओववाइय	(4.9) infernal and celestial beings. See उववाइय
ओवाय	(5.1.4) ditch.
ओवायव	(9.3.3) one who lives near the master.
ओसक्किया, ओसक्क	(5.1.63) reduce the flame, take out a log from the oven.
ओसन्न	(chu 1) sunk;-दिट्ठाहड (chu 2.6) brought after due precaution.
ओहाणुप्पेही	(chu 1) one desirous to return to household order.
ओहाविअ	(chu 1) one fallen from the holy order.
ओहारिणी	(7.24) firm speech, words based on facts.
कण्णंगया	(9.3.8) gone into the ear.
कण्णसोक्खेहिं	(8.26) pleasing to the ear.
कण्णसर	(9.3.6) pricking thorn-like in the ear.
कब्बड	(chu 1) small village.
कमाही, कमिय, कम	(2.5) overpower, reduce.
कमयोगेणं, कम	((5.1.1) with proper caution/care; कम (5.1.4) path.
कम्म-घण	(8.63) clouds of *karma*;—रय (4.2.20) *karma* dust; : हेउम (7.42) done with knowledge, expertise.
करग	(4.19) hail-stone.
करण	(6.26) inclinations of mind, speech and body; vitality in action.
कलह-विवज्जण	(chu 2.5) free from quarrel.
कल्लाण-भागि	(9.1.13) covetous of bliss.
कसिण (ा)	(8.39) full.
काउस्सग्गकारि	(chu 2.7) one in standing posture of meditation; काउसग्ग : standing posture of meditation, peculiar to the Jainas.
काम	(2.1) attachment.
काय-छक्कं	(6.7) six types of living beings. They are : earth-bodies, water-bodies, air-bodies, wind-bodies, flora-bodies and mobile beings.
काय-तिज्ज	(7.38) fit to be crossed by swimming.
काल-मासिणी	(5.1.40) woman who is to deliver shortly.

किच्च (।) (7.36) deed; : सेसं (chu 2.12) duties not done.

किच्चाण (8.45) revered people.

कित्तइस्सं, कित्तकिट्ट (5.2.43) describable.

कित्ति-वण्ण-सद्दसिलोगट्ठायाए (9.4.6) praise, fame world-wide renown or local reputation.

किमंग (chu 1) what length.

किलिंच (4.18) bamboo stick, wedge.

किलेसवत्तिणो (chu 1) full of misery.

किविण (5.2.10) poor, miser.

कीय (स्स) (9.1.1) bamboo.

कीय (6.48) bought; : गड (3.2) bought for a monk.

कुंडमोय (6.50) an earthen pot of the shape of an elephant's leg.

कुंथु (4.9) name of an insect without organs of senses.

कुकुडंब (chu 1) kinsmen.

कुक्कुस (5.1.34) husk.

कुतत्ति (chu 1) worry, anxiety.

कुम्मास (5.1.98) sweet made from barley.

कुसग्ग-जलबिंदु (chu 1) a drop of water on the blade of *kusa*.

कुसील (6.58) misconduct; -लिंग (10.20) external mark of a heretic.

केवलि (4.22) omniscient, possessor of supreme knowledge.

कोमुई-जोग जुत्तो (9.1.15) clean and cloud-free firmament.

कोल (4.22) weevil, insects sheltered in the wood.

—चूण्ण (5.1.71) berry-powder; कोल : berry.

कोविय (।) (9.2.23) equipped.

खंध-बीय (4.8) where trunk serves as seed to give birth to a new plant.

खलिय (chu 2.13) lapse.

(क) खलीण (chu 2.14) bridle.

खवित्ताणं; खवित्तु, खवित्त, खव (3.15) exhaust, destroy.

खाइम (4.16) sweets, dainties

खाणु (5.1.4) a heap of logs or hay.

खुड्डुग (6.6) young, not ripe.

खुड्डिया-यार-कहा Chapter three of *Daśavaikālika*, a precise treatise on conduct.

खेम-मप्पणे (9.4.7) good to self.

गंभीर (5.1.66) lonely, dark, a place where sound rebounds/echoes; विजय (6.55) hole, division.

गजांकुस (chu 1) hook for an elephant.

गणि (6.1) *ācārya*, preceptor.

गब्भिय (ओ) (7.35) fully grown.

गरहंति, गरहिय, गरिह, गरहा (4.10) censure.

गहियं, गह (5.1.90) accept.

गल (chu 1) hook (to catch fish).

गामकंटअ (10.11) sense objects pricking like thorns.

गायाभंग (3.9) decorating one's person with cosmetics.

गिहिवइ (इं) (5.1.16) head of the family, rich merchant.

गिद्ध (8.23) attracted.

गिम्ह (3-12) summer.

गिहंतर निसेज्जा (3.5) sit in a (householder's) abode.

गिहत्थ, गिहि (5.2.40) house-holder; गिहवास (chu 1) life of a house-holder; गिहि-जोग (8.21) activities of a house-holder; -भायण (6.52) house-holder's utensils; -मत्त (य) (3.3) house-holder's utensils; -संथव (8.52) acquaintance with a house-holder.

गुज्झग (ा) (9.2.10) denizens of *bhavanas* of celestial abodes.

गुज्झाणुचरिअ (7.53) done in confidence, (here) sky.

गुणओ, गुणव, गुण (4.27) virtue, merit; -प्पेहि (5.2.44) one who admires merit.

गुरुप्पसाय (9.1.10) preceptor's favour or grace.

गुरुभुओवघाइणी (7.11) something causing deep wound.

गुव्विणी (ए) (5.1.39) pregnant woman.

गेण्हमाण, गेण्हाण, गेण्ह (6.14) accept, take; गेण्हावए (6.13) induce one to accept.

गोच्छग (4.23) a piece of cloth used by monks to clean their pots.

गोण (5.1.12) ox.

गो-यर	(5.1.14) pasture, graze, beg; गोयरग्ग (5.1.19) (5.1.19) begging principal meal; -गग्रो (5.1.2) monk gone out for begging.
गोरहग	(7.24) ox.
घट्टियाण, घट्टंत, घट्ट	(4.18) shake, move.
घय	(5.1.97) *ghee*, clarified butter.
घसा	(6.61) loose earth.
चइत्ताणं, चइत्त, चु	(5.2.48) slip, be reborn.
चउत्थ, चउ	(4.24) fourth, four; क्कसायावगए (7.57) free from four passions viz., anger, pride, attachment and greed; रिंदिय (4.9) four organs of senses -व्विह (9.4.4) of four types.
चरंबेर	(7.28) small wooden pot.
चरित्त	(chu 2.9) restraint, conduct.
चरिया	(chu 2.4) (observing) rules of conduct.
चाइ	(2.2) renouncer, donor, large-hearted.
चारुल्लवियपेहियं	(8.57) sweet voice and glance.
चिट्ठित्ताण, चिट्ठमाण, चिट्ठंत, चिट्ठण	(4.22) stay, stand, sit.
चित्त-समाहि	(10.1) concentration of mind; भित्ति (8.54) fresco; -मंत (4/4) with living objects.
चियत्त	(5.1.17) pleasant.
चिराधोयं	(5.1.17) water filtered long ago/already filtered.
चेल-कण्णोण	(4-21) with a corner of cloth.
छंदोवयारं, छंद	(5.1.37) desire, wish; छंदिय (10/9) invite.
छज्जीवणिया	(4/1) six types of living beings. They are earth-bodies, water-bodies, air-bodies, fire-bodies, flora-bodies and moving beings.
छन्नंति, छण	(6.51) kill, injure. (cf. क्ष्णु हिंसायाम् ।)
छमा	(chu 1) earth.
छवि (वी) इय	(7.34) with peas on.
छ-सु	(3.11) six types of living beings. See छज्जीवणिया ।
छाय	(9.2.7) hungry, wounded with lashes.
छिवाडी	(5.2.20) peas.
छुढ	(chu 1) discarded, confined.
छेय, छेग्र	(4·10) pure, good.
जग्र	(7.50) victory.
जइ	(2.9) if; (chu 2.6) monk.

जंत-लट्ठि (7.28) wooden handle.

जक्ख (9.2.10) a category of vyantara god, *yaksa.*

जगा, जग (5.1.68) living beings; (8.12) world ;—निस्सिय (8.24) restricted to city precincts.

जन्नग्गि (chu 1) sacrificial fire; जन्न-sacrifice.

जय (4.8) care, precaution.

जराउय (4.9) born from mother's womb.

जलिय, जलइत्तए, जलण, जलाव (2.6) burn.

जल्लिय (8.15) body dirt.

जवणट्ठथा (9.3.4) for the sake of life.

जस, जसंसि, जसोकामि (2.7) fame, covetous of fame.

जहक्कम (5.1.89) one after the other, in proper order.

जहाभाग (5.1.13) from one's rightful object, e.g., the rightful object of the eye is vision.

जहारिहमभिगिज्भ (7.17) keeping in view what is proper.

जहावइट्ठ (9.3.2) as advised.

जाइ (7.21) species;-पह (9.1.4.) inferior births; -पहाम्रो (10.14) the worldly way, birth and death;-मंत (7.31) high species, noble birth.

जाएसु, जाय (4.22) tree with a firm root, tree about to sprout.

जाणित्ता, जाणित्तु, जाणिय (I), जाण (4.11) know; जाणिऊण (5.1.69) on knowing; जाणम जाणं (8.31)with or without knowledge.

जाय-तेय (6.32) born with a glow; -संसट्ठ (chu 2.6) get besmeared.

जिइंदिय (3.13) one who has conquered his senses.

जिण (4.22) victor; -देसिय (chu 1) as ordained by a victor;-मय Jaina precepts-मयनिउण (9.3.15) well-versed in the Agamas;-वयण (9.4.7.) victor's words;-संथव (5.1.93) hymns dedicated to the 24 *tīrthaṅkaras*; -सासण (8.25) Jaina order.

जीविउं, जीव (6.10) live; (4.4)living being;-नास (9.1.5) killing a living being; जीविय (2.7) worldly

	life; जीविय-पज्जवेण (chu 1) at the termination of life, till life.
जुगमायाए महि	(5.1·3) earth of the length of a human being; जुगमाया about 4 cubits.
जोइणो, जोइ	(2.6) flame, glow of fire.
जोग, जोय	(4.23) activities of body, mind and speech; (संजम, सुज्झाय) जोग (8.61) concentration in (restraint, study); जोग (8.50) mysmerism.
झुसिर	(5.1.66) safe/vacant place.
झोसइत्ता	(chu 1) exhausting.
टालाइं, टाल	(7.32) soft fruit which has not yet taken seed.
ठियप्पाणो	(6.49) one with self control.
णाणा-पिंड-रया	(1.5) collect/beg morsels of food from many sources.
तत्त-निव्वुड	(5.2.22) not duly boiled, become cold after boiling ;-भोइत्त (3.6) taking food not duly boiled—a lapse on the part of a monk ;-फासुय (8.6) without living object in consequence of boiling.
तन्निस्सिय (ा)	(5.1.68), तयस्सिग्र (य) (6.27) one sheltered by another.
तरुणग	(5.2.19) sprout; तरुणिया (5.2.20) fresh.
तवण, तवो, तव	(1.1) penance;-कम्म (6.22) act of penance; -तेण (5.2.46) theft of penance;-समाहि (9.4.3) concentration in penance; तवसि-बुद्धिए (8.31) monkhood and wit; तवस्सि (5.2.42)
तस, तस-काय (काइय)	(4.3.9) living beings with movement.
ताइग, ताइ	(3.1) saviour, monk.
तिक्खमन्नयरं	(6.32) sharper than any other.
तिगुत्त, तिगुत्ति-गुत्त	(3.11) restrained in three, mind, speech and body.
तिण्ह-मन्नय-रागस्स	(6.59) none out of the three (namely, the aged, the infirm and the monk).
तित्थ	(7.37) bank of a river.
तिरिक्ख, तिरिक्खजोणिय, तिरिय	(4.9) animals, non-humans.
तिरिच्छ संपाइम	(5.1.8) infested with flying insects.

तिल-पप्पडग	(5.2.21) sweet made from sesamum;-पिट्ठ (5.2.22) sesamum cake.
तिविहं तिविहेण	(4.10) doing, approving, ordering, by body, mind and speech.
तिव्वलज्ज	(5.2.50) highly cautious and careful.
तुंबाग	(5.1.70) gourd.
तुयट्टेज्जा, तुयट्टंत, तुयट्ट	(4.22) moving on sides while lying.
तेउकाइअ, तेउ-काय, तेउम्मि, तेउ	(4.3) fire bodies, fire.
तेइच्छ (ा), तेगिच्छ	(3.4.) treatment, cure.
तेणग, तेण	(5.2.37) thief.
थंभ(ा)	(9.1.1) pride, haughtiness.
थणग	(5.1.42) breasts.
थद्ध	(9.2.3) stagment, haughty.
थावर	(4.11) static beings, without movement.
थिग्गल	(5.1.15) door set afresh, door supported by bricks.
थिरा	(7.35) come to stay, taken root.
थेर, थेरअ	(9.4.1) senior monk, *gaṇadhara*.
थोवसासायणट्ठाए	(5.1.78) : थोव a little; आसायण taste.
दंडग, दंड	(4.10) stick, kill, punish, chastise; सत्थ (9.2.8) canes and weapons.
दंत	(1.5) one who has conquered senses, restrained.
दंत-पहोयणा	(3.3) cleaning teeth;-वण (3.9);-सोहण (6.13) tooth stick.
दंसण	(4.21) faith, vision.
दग	(5.1.45) water;-भवण (5.1.15) water store; -मट्टिया (5.1.3) water and earth;-वारय (5.1.45) small jar, pitcher.
दमअ	(7.14) poor.
दम्म	(7.24) fully grown-up bull.
दयाहिगारि (ो)	(8.13) embodiment of compassion.
दलय	(5.1.78) give.
दवदव	(5.1.14) go fast.
दव्वी	(5.1.32) laddle.
दस-अट्ठाण	(6.7) 18 items. They are : five great vows, not eating at night, care of, and restraint

	against six types of life, restraint against prohibited objects, another's vessel, bed and garments, taking bath and decorating the body.
दाढुढ्ढियं	(chu 1) with teeth uprooted.
दाणट्ठा	(5.1.47) for making an offer; दाण-भत्त (I.1) donor; भत्त food, rice.
दार	(5.1.15) door; दार (chu 1) wife; दारग (5.1.22) child.
दावए, दाव	(5.1.67) making an offer; दायग (5.2.12) donor.
दिट्ठिवाय	(8.49) *nayavāda*.
दोह-रोम-नहंसिणो	(6.64) one with long hairs and nails.
दीहवट्टा	(7.31) tall.
दुक्ख	(2.5) misery, restlessness, detachment to restraint.
दुग्गअ (ो)	(9.2.19) naughty bull.
दुच्चिण्ण	(chu 1) bad conduct.
दुत्तोसअ	(5.2.32) never satisfied, insatiable.
दुन्नामधेज्ज	(chu 1) ill-reputed.
दुप्पउत्त	(chu 2.14) going wayward/astray.
दुप्पजीवि	(chu 1) hard life.
दुप्पडिक्कंत	(chu 1) evil effort.
दुप्पडिलेहग	(5.1.20) difficult to observe.
दुमपुप्फिया	(1) title of chapter one of *Daśavaikālika*.
दुम्मणिय	(9.3.8) restless.
दुरहिट्ठिय	(6.4) difficult to bear/practise; (6.15) generating hatred; दुरहियास distaste generating.
दुरासय	(2.6) bad shelter.
दुरुत्त	(9.3.7) harsh words.
दुरुत्तर	(6.65) difficult to cross.
दुरुद्धर	(9.3.7) difficult to remove.
दुरुहमाण (ो), दुरुह	(5.1.68) difficult to climb.
दुव्वाइ	(9.2.3) one who uses harsh words, sharp-tongued.
दुब्विहिय	(chu 1) improper.
दुस्समा	(chu 1) unbracing/hard phase of the time-cycle.

दुहम	(7.14) unfortunate; दुहओ (9.2.21) in two ways.
दुह-मह्हेता	(9.2.5) great pain.
दुह्होवणीयस्स	(chu 1) with pain arrived.
वेंतिय	(5.1.28) while giving; वेंत donor.
देव-किब्बिस	(5.2.46) a god of the low order.
देस	(chu 2.8) country, kingdom;-देसिय (5.1.92) advised.
देह-पलोयणा	(3.3) viewing one's body/limbs;-वास (10.21) body as a cage.
दोस	(2.5) malice; (5.1.11) wrong, crime; दोसन्न (7.13) one who knows the wrong.
धम्मो, धम्म	(1.1) religion, spirituality;-कामी (9.1.16) covetous of religion;-जीवि (6.49) living on religion, or as per rules of spirituality;-ज्झाण (10.19) spiritual meditation;-ट्ठकहा (6) title of chapter 6 of *Daśavaikālika*;-त्थ-काम (6.3) seeker of virtue and bliss; पण्णत्ति (4) title of chapter 4 of *Daśavaikālika*;-पय (9.1.12) spiritual words;-सासण (chu 1) spiritual prescriptions.
धाय	(7.51) easy begging, affluent.
धारण, धारंति, धार, धारि, धर	(3.4) hold.
धिइमश्र	(chu 2.15) one with patience.
धिरत्थु	(2.7) fie !
धुणिय, धुण	(4.20) wipe, move.
धुन्न-मल	(7.57) one whose dirt of sin is wiped out; धुन्न sin.
धुय-मोह	(3.13) one whose affection is wiped out.
धुव	(8.17) steadfast;-योग (10.10) restraint of body, mind and speech;-योगी (10. 6) steadfast is *yoga*. The word 'yoga' is used here not in the usual Jaina sense, to signify the sinful activities of mind, speech and body, but to signify concentration and

enlightenment;-सीलया (8.40) rules of conduct, 18000 *silāṅga*.

धूमकेउ	(2.6) comet, fire.
धूया	(7.15) daughter.
धूवणेत्ति	(3.9) smoking pipe.
न+अवणए	(5.1.13) not turning low/earthward.
नमोक्कार	(5.1.93) obeisance, *namokara mantra*.
ना, नाणहिइ, णाण	(4.10) knowledge.
नाणा-पिंड	(1.5) sundry food;-हुई (9.1.11) sundry offerings.
नाभि	(7.28) navel, centre of a wheel.
नायपुत्त	(5.2.49) name of Mahāvīra.
नालीय, नाली	(3.4) dice.
निक्खंत, निक्खम्ममाण, निक्खम	(5.2.4) give up home, court mendicancy.
निक्खि-वित्ताण,-वित्ता -विअ,-त्त	(5.1.19) hurl, throw.
निगनसाई	(4.26) sleeping too much; णिगम too much.
निग्गंथ, निग्गंथत्त	(3.1) monk, monkhood.
निग्गहण	(3.11) suppressing organs of senses and mind.
निच्च+उव्विगो	(5.2.39) ever restless.
निज्जर-ट्ठाए,-ट्ठिय, निज्जरा	(9.4.6) exhausting accumulated *karma*.
निज्जाय-रूव-रयअ	(10.6) without gold and silver.
निट्ठाण	(8.22) fresh and tasteful food.
निण्हव	(8.32) deny.
निद्दिस, निद्देसवत्ति	(7.10) guidance, follower of.
निद्धणे	(7.57) wipe, clean.
निप्पुलाअ	(10.6) innocent.
निमित्त	(8.50) astrology.
नियट्ट	(5.1.23) desist, return.
नियडि	(5.2.37) deceptive, hypocritical.
नियत्तण	(9.3.3) polite behaviour.
नियत्तिय	(5.2.13) return, retrace.
नियाग	(3.2) invite one to make an offer.
निरय, निरअ	(chu 1) hell; निरओवम like hell.

निरासय	(9.4.6.4) without attachment, expecting no return.
निरुवक्केस	(chu 1) pain-free.
निव्वाण	(5.2.32) liberation.
निव्वाविया, निव्वावंत, निव्वाव	(4.20) putting out (fire).
निव्विंद	(4.sl.16) satiated.
निव्विगइ	(chu 2.7) not spoiled by transformation.
निसंत	(9.1.14) morning.
निसन्ना, निसीएज्जा, निसीज, निसीयंत, णिसीश्रा	(5.1.40) sit.
निस्सिंचिय	(5.1.63) pouring drops of water, spray, sprinkle.
निसीहिया (ए)	(5.2.2) place of study.
निसेज्जा	(6.7) cloth, garment.
निस्सेणि	(5.1.67) staircase.
निस्सेस	(9.2.2) liberation.
निहा, निहाव	(10.8) accumulate, cause accumulation.
निहुग्र	(2.8) undisturbed, restrained;-ग्रप्प (6.2) with steady soul;-इंदिय (10.10) with organs of senses restrained.
नीय-दुवार	(5.1.20) low door, small passage.
नी-रय	(3.14) free from (*karma*) dust.
नीसा	(5.1.45) grinding stone.
नेरइय	(4.9) infernal.
नो	(2.4) partial prohibition.
पइरिक्कया	(chu 2.5) loneliness.
पईव-पयावट्ठा	(6.34) पईव lamp; पयांव heat.
पउत्त, पउंज	(5,1.97) apply.
पउम, पउमग	(5.2.14) lotus, lotus pollen.
पग्रोग्र	(9.2.19) whip.
पग्रोय	(7.52) cloud.
पंकोसन्न	(chu 1) caught in the mud.
पंचासव	(3.11) five fetters. They are slaughter, falsehood, theft, sex and possession.
पंत	(5.2.34) end-portion, devoid of substance.
पक्कम, पक्क	(3.13) progress, improve.
पक्खग्रो	(8.45) on the sides, at the same level.

पक्खंद (2.6) rush into.
पक्खलंत, पक्खल (5.1.5) slip.
पक्खोडंत, पक्खोड (4.19) hurl.
पगइ (9.1.3) nature.
पगड (5.1.47) prepared.
पच्चग (8.57) smaller limbs.
पच्चक्ख (ओ) (5.2.28) visible, within sight.
पच्चक्ख (4.10) give up, renounce.
पच्चुपन्न (7.8) present time.
पच्छा-कम्म (5.1.35) posterior acts.
पज्जय (7.18) great-grand-father; पज्जिया (7.15) great-grand-mother.
पज्जव (chu 1) state, condition.
पज्जालिया, पज्जाल (5.1.63) ignite, brighten.
पज्जुवास (8.43) worship.
पट्ठवेत्ताणं (5.1.63) commence.
पडिआय (10.1) drink/take back.
पडिकुट्ठ (5.1.17) prohibited.
पडिकुट्ठ-कुलं (5.1.17) forbidden house.
पडिकोह (6.57) anger.
पडिक्कंत (4.9) return.
पडिक्कम (4.10) desist, withdraw.
पडिगाह (5.1.27) take.
पडिग्गह (4.23) pot.
पडिग्घाअ (6.58) obstruction.
पडिच्छ (5.1.36) take.
पडिच्छन्न (5.1.83) covered from above.
पडिच्छिन्न (8.55) cut.
पडिच्छिय (5.1.80) accepted.
पडिजागर (9.1.3) remain awake.
पडिण (6.33) about western direction.
पडिणीय (9.3.9) sharp/objectionable words.
पडिनिस्सिअ (4.22) infested with, sheltering.
पडिन्नव (chu 2.8) to make one promise.
पडिपुच्छिऊण, पडिपुच्छ (5.1.76) ask.
पडिपुण्णाययं (9.4.7.5) full of scriptures; पडिपुण्ण (8.48) correct in sound, import and expression.
पडिबंध (chu 2.13) tie, share.

पडिबुद्धजीवि	(chu 2.15) living a life of enlightenment.
पडिबोह	(9.1.8) rouse, awake.
पडिमा	(10.12) resolve, promise.
पडिय	(chu 1) fall.
पडियरिय	(9.3.15) serve.
पडियाइक्ख	(5.2.28) forsake, give up.
पडियाइयण	(chu 1) take/drink back.
पडि-लेहित्ता (ण),-लेहिय (ा),-लेह, (लेहगा, लेहय, लेहि)	(4.23) see, observe.
पडि-वज्जिया,-वज्ज(माण)	(4. sl 23) attain.
पडि-संलीण (ा)	(3.12) restraining physical movement, staying at one place.
पडि-समाहर	(8.54), साहर (chu 2.14) withdraw.
पडिसेहिय, पडिसेह	(5.2.13) prohibit.
पडिसोय	(chu 2.2.) against the stream.
पडिहय-पच्चक्खाय-पावकम्म	(4.18) one who has pulled up accumulated *karma* with a view to exhausting them, and checked the influx of new *karma*.
पणग	(5.1.59) moss.
पणास	(8.37) destroy.
पणिय	(7.45) merchandise, wares.
पणियट्ठ	(7.37) one who risks his life for the sake of wealth, trading.
पणिहाय	(8.44) restraining; पणिहा meditation.
पणीय	(5.2.42) fatty food, like milk, curd, butter, etc.; रस (8.56) rich and fresh food.
पणुल्ल	(5.1.18) open.
पन्नत्त	(9.4.1) said; पन्नत्ति (8.49) method of discourse.
पन्नव	(7.1) wise, intelligent.
पबंधेज्ज, पबंध	(5.2.8) elaborate, narrate.
पब्भट्ठ	(chu 1) fallen.
पमज्जिया, पमज्जित्तु	(8.5) clean.
पमाण	(chu 2.11) standard.
पमाय	(6.15) carelessness.
पमेइल	(7.23) fatty.
पय	(8.31) deed; (9.1.11) words, sentence; (10.4) cook.

पयअ	(chu 2.7) careful.
पयत्त-च्छिन	(7.42) plucked with effort; पक्क ripened with effort; लट्ठ obtained through effort.
पयल	(chu 1·17) shake.
पयावंत, पयाव	(4.19) heat, dry.
परं पमाणं	(chu 2.11) right proportion, i.e., four months during rainy season, plus one month during the rest of the year.
परक्कम	(5.1.6) alternative route without holes or diches; (8.32) indulge in; (chu 2.4) strength.
परग्घ	(7.43) costly.
पर-घर	(5.2.27) another's (housholder's) house.
परमाहम्मिय	(4.9) covetous of happiness(cf. परमो धम्मो जेसिं ते परमधम्मिता अतः सुख-स्वभाव)
परमग्गसूर	(9. 3.8) leading-most among the heroes.
परम-दुच्चर	(6.5) highly difficult to practise.
परम्मुह	(9·3.9) disinclined.
	(8.19) same as परगार।
परिकिन्न	(chu 1) surrounded.
परिक्ख-भासि	(7.57) one who speaks after due consideration; परिक्खणा—measure, examine.
परिगय	(9.2.8) spread.
परि-गेण्ह,-गेण्हंत, -णिज्झ, ग्गह	(4.15) take.
परिग्गह	(4.15) attachment, superfluous possession.
परिज्जुण्ण	(9.2.8) old, worn out.
परिट्ठप्प	(5.1.81) place.
परिणय	(5.1.77) duly changed/transformed.
परि (ि) णाम	(8.58) transform, change.
परि-निव्वुड,-निव्वाण	(3.15) liberated.
परितप्प	(chu 1/) lament.
परिदेव (एज्जा)	(9.3.4) feel depressed /dejected.
परिन्नाय	(3.11) one who checks/restrains.
परिब्भट्ठ	(chu 1), परिभस्स (6.50) fall.
परिभव	(8.30) disrespect.
परियाय	(cu 1) monk, order; -जेट्ठ (9.3.3) senior; -ट्ठाण (8.60) place of penance.

परियाव	(9.2.14) suffering.
परि-वज्जंत, वज्ज (य)	(5.1.4) give up.
परिवुड	(9.1.15) surrounded.
परिवुड्ढ	(7. 23) strong, advanced in age.
परिव्वयंत	(2.4) roaming.
परिसंखाय	(7.1) knowing.
परि (ी) सह-रिउदंता	(3.13) conqueror of passions, bearing all hardships. The Jainas have named 22 passions, like hunger, thirst, etc.
परिसा	(4.18) assembly.
परिसाड	(5.1.28) drop.
परिहर	(6.19) keeping for use.
परोवधाइणी	(7.54) causing hurt to others.
पलिओवम	(chu 1) measure of a very long period, a fraction of a *sāgaropama*.
पलो-अण,-एज्जा, पलोअ	(5.1.23) observe.
पवक्ख	(chu 2.1) speak.
पवडंते, पवडेज्जा, पवड	(5.1.5) fall.
पवड्ढ (माणा)	(8.39) on the wax, increasing.
पवयण	(5.2.12) Jaina code.
पवियक्खण	(2.11) expert.
पवीलंत, पवील	(4.19) press (again and again).
पवेइ (य) एणं	(4.1) self-enlightened, initiated.
पव्वइए, पव्वाइअ, पव्वइय	(4·sl. 18) monk, initiated.
पसढ, पसज्झ	(5.1.52) display, spread
पसत्थ	(chu 2.5) right, praiseworthy.
पसूय	(7.35) so be fruit-yielding, with peas.
पहार-गाढ	(7.42) deep wound.
पहीण	(3.13) destroy
पहोइ	(4.sl.26) one who washes.
पाइम	(7.22) fit to be cooked.
पाईण	(6.33) regarding eastern direction.
पाण	(4.9) life, (4.16) water.
पाणक (ग)	(5.1.47) drink.
पाणहा	(3.4) shoes.
पाणाइवाय (ओ)	(4.11) causing injury to life.
पाणिपेज्जा	(7.38) (river whose) water is good for drinking.
पामिच्च	(5.1.55) borrowed to make a gift.

पाय — (3.4) leg, (6.19) used while making reference to venerable persons, (6.19) pot ;-खज्ज (7.32) ripened and made edible;-पुंछण (4.23) cloth to clean/dry the leg.

पारत्त — (8.43) the other world.

पारेत्ता — (5.1.93) after ending.

पावग, पावय, पाव — (4.10) sinful, sin; पाव (9.1.17) attain.

पाहन्न — (9.3.5) dominance.

पिंडपाय — (5.1.87) beg.

पिंडेसणा — (5) Chapter 5 of *Daśavaikālika*.

पिज्जेमाण — (5.1.42) पियाव (10.2) while making one to drink; पिब (5.1.8) drink.

पिट्ठमंस — (8.46) पिसुण (9.2.22), speaking ill behind one's back.

पिहियासव — (4. sl. 9) with influx of *karma* checked.

पिहुखज्ज — (7.34) fit to be taken after being parched.

पिहुज्जण — (chu 1) common folks.

पिहुण (हत्थ) — (4.21) peacock feather.

(4.23) wooden stool or seat.

पीण — (1.2) satisfy.

पीणिय — (7.23) healthy.

पील (।), पीड — (5.1.10) torture.

पूइ-पिण्णा(न्ना)ग — (5.2.22) basil and mustard.

पुई-कम्म — (5.1.55) rotten deed. When food is prepared for the monk, it is called 'adha-karma'. When such is mixed with the rest, it becomes as bad as a rotten thing.

पुग्गल, पोग्गल — (4.41) matter, (5.1.73) outcome, result.

पुच्छ, पुट्ठ — (5.1.56) wipe out; पुट्ठ (7.5) touched, obtained.

पुच्छेज्जत्थ-विणिच्छयं — (8.43) ask question to ascertain meaning.

पुढवि-काय, -काइय, -जीव — (4.3) earth bodies.

पुढो-सत्ता — (4.4) separate existence.

पुणब्भव (स्स) — (8.39) rebirth.

पुणुट्ठए — (5.1.40) rise again.

पुण्ण — (4.15), पुन्न (chu 2.1) virtue, merit; पुण (4.9) again. -ट्ठा (5.1.49) for acquiring virtue.

पुर-कम्म, पुरेकम्म — (5.1.32) prior acts.

पुरओ, पुर (5.1.3) fore; -कड (6.67) done before.

पुर-त्थ (8.28) eastern.

पुराण-पावग (9.4.6) old *karma* bondage.

पुरिस (5.2.29) man, male;-गोत्तेण (7.20) by male surname;-कार, कारिया (5.2.6) exertion; -उत्तम (2.11) best among men.

पुलनिप्पुलाए (10.16) free from demerits that stain restraint.

पुव्विं, पुव्व (2.15) fore, previous;-उत्त (5.2.3) aforesaid; -रत्त (chu 2.12) first part of the night.

पूयणट्ठि, पूइअ, पूइम, पूयण, पूअ (5.2.35) covetous of honour, honoured, honour, worship.

पूइ (5.1.78) emitting foul smell;-कम्म (5.1.55) evil deed, like mixing food prepared for the monk with food in general.

पेहा (ए), माण, पेहिय, पेह, पेच्छ (2.4) sight, vision, glance, see.

पोय, पोयज (4.9) offspring, offspring born straight, like that of an elephant, and has no cover;-पडागा (chu 1) flag of a ship.

पोर-बीय (4.8) where twigs serve as seed.

फरुस (5.2.29) harsh.

फलग (4.23) a piece of wood;-फलिह-अग्गल (5.2.9) (7.27) a log to support the door.

फाणिय (5.1.71) jaggery.

फास (4.19) touch;-फासुय (ग, अ), फासु (5.1.19) free from living being.

बलाहय (7.52) cloud.

बहिद्ध (2.4) outward, towards the enjoyment of worldly pleasures.

बहु (4.9) many, much, sundry; -अट्ठिय (5.1.73) with many seeds/bones; -उज्झिय-धम्मिय (5.1. 74) (food) of which much is discarded/not eaten;-कंटय (5.1.73) with many thorns/eyes; -निव्वट्टिमा (7.33) whose capacity to bear fruit is nearing exhaustion;-मन्नोज्जा (8.41)

	think much of, gives much importance to; -वाहड (7.39) near full;-वित्थडोदगा (7.39) with vast expanse of water;-संभूय (7.33) yielding many fruits;-साहारण (10.1) commonplace, well within reach; -स्सुय (8.43) with profound knowledge.
बायर	(4.11) with large body.
बाल	(6.7) fool.
बाही, बोहि	(5.2.48) right understanding.
बीयरुह	(4.8) plant born from seed.
बुद्ध	(1.5) enlightened;-वयण (10.1) words of the enlightened;-वुत्त-महिट्ठगा (6.54) living according to the prescriptions of the enlightened;-बुद्धेहिऽणाइन्ना (7.2) speech not approved by the wise.
बुया-वयावए	(6.11) speaks not, nor asks another to speak.
भंते, भंत	(4.10) revered, venerable;-(4.9) way-laid, puzzled.
भक्खर	(8.54) the sun.
भज्जिम, भज्जिय	(5.2.20) fit to be fried, fried.
भट्ट, भट्टा	(7.19) honoured man;-(7.16) honoured lady; -भट्ट (chu sl. 12) deviated, way-laid.
भत्त	(1.3) food, rice;-भत्तट्ठा (5.2.10) seeking food; -पाण (5.1.I) food and drink.
भद्दग	(5.2.33) best portion.
भय-भेख-सद्द-संपहासे	(1I.11) dreadful laughter.
भायण	(5.1.32) vessel, pot.
भारह	(9.1.14) Bharat-varsa.
भाव,भावए	(9.3.10) think, extol one's own self; -तेण (2.46) thief of another's idea;-संधम्र (9.4.7.5) concentrated, immersed in one's own ideas; भावियप्प (9.3.10) one who loves flattery; (chu 1. sl. 9) enlightened soul.
भासंत, भासमाण, भासिय, भास, (I)	(7.1) speak; भास (9.1.3) ashes.
भासुर	(9.3.15) shining, effulgent.
भिक्ख-काल	(5.1.1) time for begging;-एसण-सीहिं (5.2.50)

purification of behaviour by begging; भिक्खु (4.18) monk.

भित्ति — (8.4) wall; -मूल (5.1.82) base of the wall, elevation between two houses.

भिलुग — (6.61) opening in the earth.

भुग्रोवघाइणि — (7.29) causing hurt to living beings.

भुंजमाण, भुंजंत, भुंजाव, भुंजित, भुत्त, भुंज, भुज्जमाण, भुज्ज — (2.2) eat, take;-भुज्ज (chu 1) again and again, repeatedly;-भुत्तसेस (5.1.39) remnant.

भूय — (4. sl. 1) life, living being;-ग्रहिगरण (8.50) instruments of causing injury; -रूव (7.33) the tree whose fruits have not yet taken seeds.

भेयाययणवज्जि — (6.15) one who avoids lapse;-भेयाययण lapse.

भोच्चा, भोच्चाणं, भोत्तुं — (5.2.2) on eating, for eating.

भोय, भोग — (2.3) enjoy, suffer, undergo;-भोयण (5.1.27) food;-जाय (5.1.74) edible portion.

भोयराय — (2.8) King Bhoja.

मइ — (5.1.76) intellect, knowledge;-इड्दि गौरव (9.2.22) proud of intellect and fortune.

मइग्र — (7.28) an implement used in farming.

मंगल-मुक्किट्ठं — (1.10) highest good/well-being.

मंत — (8.50) *mantra*, enchanted/holy words.

मंथु — (5.1.98) berry powder.

मगदंतिया — (5.1.54) flower of that name.

मज्जग, मज्ज — (5.2.36) intoxication, pride;-प्पमाय-विरग्रो (5.2.42) free from pride and carelessness.

मणुण्ण — (8.58) appealing, pleasing.

मत्त-छोयण छड्डणो — (6.51) carelessly throwing out dirt/impure water.

मत्थयत्थ — (4.25) located at the crest.

मद्दव — (8.38) humility.

मन्न — (6.36) obey, carry out.

ममत्त, ममाइय, ममाय — (6.21) this is mine, mine-ness, selfishness.

मयाणि, मय — (9.4.4.2) pride (of name, race, beauty, penance, knowledge, attainment, wealth and wisdom).

मया	(9.1.1) double-dealing, deceitfulness.
मरणंत	(5.2.39) after death; मरिज्जिउं (6.10) for the sake of dying.
मल	(8.62) dirt of *karma*, dirt.
मल्ल, गन्ध-मल्ल	(3.2) garland, scented garland.
महग्घ	(7.46) costly, dear.
मह-प्प	(8.33) great soul;-ब्भय (9.3.7) great fear; -महल्ल, महल्लगा, महल्लय (5.2.29) elderly, aged; -व्वय (4.11) great vow.
महा-काय	(7.23) huge body;-आगर (9.1.16) with great merit;-निरय-सारिसो (chu 1) like the great hells;-दोस (6.16) great vice; -फल (8.27) highest result, liberation;-यस (9.2.6) highest fame;-आयार-कहा Chapter Six of *Daśavaikālika*; -आलय (7.31) great expanse;-वाय (6.1.8) great wind, storm.
महिड्ढिय	(9.4.7) with great fortune.
महियाए, महिआ, महियं	(4.19) drizzle, light shower.
महेसि	(3.1) great monk.
माण-सम्माण-काम	(5.3.35) covetous of status and respect.
माणरिह, माणिम, माणिय	(9.1.13) venerable, respected.
मामग	(5.1.17) mine, where entry is prohibited, restricted place.
मायण्ण (न्न)	(5.2.3) one who knows measure/prescription of food, drink, etc.
माया-मोस	(5.2.38) deceit and falsehood; सल्ल (5.2.35) nail of deceit, strive to hide one's fault (according to some commentator. Cf. कम्मगरुययाए वा सो लज्जाए वा अणलोएंत मायासल्लमवि कुव्वति।
मालोहड	(5.1.69) upper or lower storey of a building.
माहण	(5.2.10) monk, kill-not, brahmin.
मिय-असण	(1.29) restricted/measured food;-भूमि (5.1.24) permitted sector, where entry is open.
मिहो-कहा	(8.41) talking about sex, funny word.
मीस-जाय	(5.1.55) mixed food, food cooked for the monk mixed with food cooked for the householder.

मुंड	(4.18) tonsure.
मुंचडसाहू	(9.3.11) give up the way of non-monk.
मुम्मुर	(4.20) flame hidden in the husk.
मुसावाय	(4.12) false words.
मुहाजीवि	(5.1.99) one who lives on begging; -दाइ 5.1.100) a donor without attachment/who hankers not after return; -लद्ध (5.1.99) obtained by begging. मुहा is an expression to signify non-attachment.
मूलय	(3.7) raddish; मुलग (5.2.23) raddish bean; मुल-गत्तिया (5.2.23) slice of raddish; -बीय (4.8.) where root serves as seed.
मेरग	(5.2.36) wine.
मेहुण	(4.14) indulging in sex
मोह	(chu 1) *karma* matter whose sticking restrains conduct and faith.
मोह-संताण	(chu 1) progeny of attachment, multifarious attachment.
रइ-वक्का	(chu 1) title of *Chūlikā* One of *Daśavaikālika*.
रक्खियव्व	(2.16) deserving of protection.
रज्जपब्भट्ठो	(chu 1) having lost his kingdom.
रण्ण	(4.13) forest; रन्न (5.1.16) royal.
रएण, रय	(1.3) engaged, immersed; (4.20) particles of dust; -मलं (9.3.15) dust and dirt; -हरण (4.23) duster used by the monk.
रस	(1.2) flower-honey; (5.2.36) intoxicating juice, wine; (5.2.42) milk, etc.; (9.2.1) fruit-juice; -दया (7.25) giving milk; -निज्जुढ (8.22) devoid of juice; रसय (4.9) life born in juice.
रहजोग्ग	(7.24) fit to be yoked.
रहस्स	(5.1.16) secret chamber; (7.25) short.
राओ, राइ	(4.16) night; -णिय (8.40) superior in initiation; -भत्त (3.2) -भोयण (4.16) taking food at night.
राय	(5.1.16) monarch: king; -पिंड (3.3) king's food; -मच्च (6.2) king's minister.
रिद्धिमंत	(7.53) fortunate.

रीअ	(1.4) go.
रुक्ख (ा)	(5.2.19) trees.
रूढ	(4.22) seeds germinating.
रूव	(8.19) shape, appearance; -तेण (5.2.46) theft of form.
रोय, रोइय	(5.1.77) like, fond of.
लज्जा-समा-वित्ती	(6.22) conduct to support restraint.
लद्धे, लद्ध	(2.3) obtain; -मन्नट्ठ-पउत्तं (5.1.97) obtained from the food prepared by the householder for his own use; -लक्खेण (2.2) one who has attained his aim.
लयण	(8.51) home, dwelling.
ललि-इंदिय	(9.2.14) one whose organs of senses are used to comfort.
लविय, लव	(7.17) speak, call, speech.
लहुत्त, लहु	(5.2.12) lightness; light; -भुय-विहारी (3.10) travel light, after unloading objects and worries; -स्सग (chu 1) with little substance.
लाइम	(7.34) fit to be cut.
लूसिए, लूस	(5.1.68) break, cut.
लूह-वित्ती	(5.2.34) restrained.
लेवमाया	(5.2.1) last particles that stick to the pot.
लोग-मत्थयथो	(4.s1.25) at the crest of the sphere.
वइ	(8.49) words, speech; -विक्खलियं (7.49) one who has made mistakes in speech; -मय (9.3.6) full of words/expression.
वंतय, वंत	(2.6) things vomited.
वक्क	(8.3) words; -कर (9.3.3) obedient; -सुद्धि Chapter Seven of *Daśavaikālika*.
वच्छग	(5.1.22) calf.
वज्जंत, वज्जिय, वज्ज	(5.1.3) prohibit.
वज्झ, वह्या	(7.22) kill, fit to be killed.
वट्ट	(7.31) circle, round; (9.3.3) use.
वड्ढण, वड्ढ	(5.1.11) increase.
वणस्सइकाइय	(4.3) flora, flora-bodies.
वणिमय, वणीमग, वणिम	(5.1.51) poor, miser, beggar.
वण्ण	(9.4.6) world-wide fame (cf. लोकव्यापी जसोवण्णो); वण्णिय (6.22) described; वण्णिया (5.1.34) yellow clay.

वत्ति	(chu 1) profession.
वत्थिकम्म	(3.9) inhaling oil.
वय	(4.12) speak (7.47) go; (4.16) vow; -छक्कं (6.7) six vows; -णं-कर (9.2.12) obedient; -णाभिघाया (9.3.8) lashes of words; -तेण (5.2.46) theft of words/expression.
ववेय	(chu 1) without, free of.
वस	(2.1) submit; वसाणुअ (5.1.9) to be under one's control.
वस	(chu 1) live.
वसुल, वसुला	(7.14) ox—an expression of indignation or contempt.
वाउ-काइय	(4.3) air-bodies.
वाया, वाय	(2.9) wind, air; (4.12) speak; वाया-इद्ध (2.9) swept by the wind; -दुरुत्ताणि (9.3.7) words ill-spoken.
वायंत	(5.1.8) moving, floating.
वार-धोयण	(5.1.75) wash-off from a jar; वारय (5.1.45) a small jar.
वासंत, वासा, वास	(5.1.8) rain.
वास	(chu 1) region, 'varsa'.
वाससइ	(8.55) one hundred years old.
वाहि	(8.35) disease; वाहिय (6.6) patient.
वाहिमा, वाह	(7.24) fit to carry, carrier, pack animal.
विउल-ट्ठाणभाइ	(6.5) covetous of highest state liberation; हिय-सुहावहं (9.4.7) giver of great bliss and happiness.
विउहित्ताण	(5.1.22) remove from one place to another. induce one to move away.
विकत्थ	(9.3.4) rejoice.
विक्खलिय	(8.49) slip, fall.
विगप्पिय	(8.55) cut.
विगलितेंदिय	(9.2.7) with organs of senses in disorder.
विग्गहओ	(8.53) with body.
विज्जल	(5.1.4) mud.
विडिम	(7.31) branches.
विणय	(5.1.88) humility, conduct, homage, right use; -समाहि Chapter Nine of *Daśa-vaikālika*.

विणिगूह (5.2.31) hide.

विणिच्छय (8.43) certain, make certain.

विणिज्झा (5.1.15) look, cast a glance.

विणित्तए, विणी (2.4) remove; विणीय-तण्ह (8.59) conquer/subdue thirst.

विणिय (9.2.21) obedient; विणियट्ठ (2.11) desisted.

वितह (7.4) improper.

वित्ति (1.4) profession; -मेसेज्जा (5.2.26) one who knows the standard of profession (here, begging).

विन्नाय (4.9) know, known.

विप्पइण्ण (5.1.21) scattered.

विप्पमुक्क (3.1) liberated duly and in all respects.

विपिट्ठिकुव्व (2.3) turn one's back.

विभूसण विभूषा-वत्तिय (3.9) decoration.

विमणेण, विमण (5.1.80) absent-minded, lacking seriousness, careless.

विमाण (6.68) celestial abode.

वियंजियं (8.48) distinct and familiar.

वियड (5.2.22) water, pure water; -भाव (8.32) frank. (cf. विकटभावः प्रकटभावः)

वियत्त (6.6) ripe.

वियागरे, वियागर (7.37) speak.

वियाणित्ता, वियाणिया, वियाणंत, वियाण (4.13) know.

विरय (4.18) desisted (from sin).

विरस (5.1.98) without juice, not fresh.

विराय (8.63) stay, adorn.

विराह (4.28) injure.

विरुह (9.2.1) grow.

विरेयण (3.9) taking purgative.

विलिहंत, विलिह (4.18) draw.

विवज्जइत्ता विवज्जेत्ता, विवज्जयंत, विवज्ज विवज्जिय, विवज्जण, विवज्जत (5.1.15) give up.

विवड्ढण (8.57) augment.

विवण्ण-छंद (9.2.8) dependent; -विरस (5.2.32) tasteless and colourless.

विवत्ति (ी)	(6.57) danger.
विवित्त	(8.52) solitary; -चरिया Second Chūlikā of *Daśavaikālika*.
विसम	(5.1.4) uneven, rough.
विसय	(8.58) sense objects.
विसीयंत, विसीअ	(2.1) lament, be sad.
विसुज्झ	(8.62) purify.
विसोत्तिया	(5.1.9) deviate, turn.
विसोहिठाण	(9.1.13) purifier.
विहम्म (इ)	(chu 1) be wounded.
विहर, विहार	(4.17) live; -चरिया (chu 2.5) mode of living.
विहि	(5.2.3) sanctions.
विहुयण, वीयण, वीइउ, वीयाव, वीयावेउण	(3.2) fan.
वीसमत, वीसम	(5.1.93) rest.
वुग्गह	(7.50) quarrel; वुग्गहिय (10.10) qurrelsome.
वुच्च, वुत्त	(1.3) speak.
वुज्झ	(9.2.3) float:
वुट्ठ	(7.51) showered.
वेणइय	(9.1.12) humility.
वेयइत्ता, वेय	(9.4.4) knowledge, know.
वेयावच्च, वेयावडिय	(3.6) service, nursing.
वेरमण	(4.11) desist.
वेराणुबंधीणि	(9.3.7) causing/generating enmity.
वेलुय	(5.2.21) a green vegetable.
वेस, वेस्सा	(5.1.9) harlot, prostitute; -सामंत near.
वेहिम	(7.32) fit to be sliced.
वोक्कंत	(6.60) transgress.
वोसट्ठ	(5.1.91) a standing posture for meditation; -चत्त-देह (10.13) one in that posture.
वोसिर	(4.10) give up.
सइ	(5.2.20) once; -काल (5.2.6) right time.
संकट्ठाण	(5.1.15) a gap in looking at which may generate suspicion.
संकण	(6.58) doubt.
संकम	(5.1.4) bridge, link.
संखडि	(7.36) feast, banquet.
संग	(10.16) attachment.

संघट्टइत्ता, संघट्ठिया, संघट्ट — (8.7) touch.

संघाय — (4.23) harm, pain.

संज-इंदिय — (10.15) one with organs of senses restrained.

संजम — (1.1) restraint, state of equanimity; -जीविय (chu 2.15) one with restrained life; -लज्जट्ठा (6.19) for restraint and privacy.

संजय — (2.10) monk; —विरय-परिहय-पच्चक्खाय (4.8) restrained-desisted-protected-renounced.

संठाण — (8.57) structure.

संडिब्भ — (5.1.12) children's play-spot, nursery.

संताण-संतओ — (chu 1) with progeny.

संतुट्ठ, संतोस (ओ) — (5.2.34) contentment, happiness, alike in pleasure and pain -पाहन्न (9.3.5;) with dominance of contentment.

संथर — (5.2.2) stay, live.

संथव — (5.1.93) pray, prayer; (8.52) acquaintance

संथार — (8.17) a cloth to lie on; संथारग (4.23) a small bed, about five feet in length.

संधि — (5.1.15) joint.

संपडिलेहियव्व — (chu 1) worth seeing.

संपडिवज्ज (इ) — (9.4.4) accept.

संपडिवाइय — (2.10) refix.

संपडिवाय — (9.2.20) perform, do.

संपणोल्लिया — (5.1.30) move, moving.

संपत्त — (5.1.1) attainment, arrival.

संपत्ति (ी) — (9.2.21) merit.

संपमज्जित्ता, संपमज्ज — (5.1.83) clean.

संपय — (7.7) current, present; -आईयमट्ठे in confusion about the present and the past.

संपराय — (2.5) life, world.

संपस्सिय — (chu 1) thoroughly observing.

संपहास — (8.41) loud peel of laughter.

संपाविउकाम — (9.1.16) covetous of liberation.

संपिक्ख — (chu 2.12) see.

संपुच्छण — (3.3) wipe, towel.

संफुस — (4.19) touch.

संबाहृण (3.3) rub.
संबुद्ध (2.11) enlightened.
संभिन्नवित्त (chu 1) one who transgresses conduct.
संजाय (7.23) young.
संरक्खण-परिग्गह (6.21) possession to fulfil restraint.
संलिहत्ताण, संलिह (5.2.1) clean.
संलुचिया (5.2.14) cut.
संलोग (5.2.25) sight, observation.
संवर (4.19) checking influx of *karma.*
संवहण (7.25) carrier.
संवुड (5.1.83) covered.
संसग्ग (5.1.10) doubt.
संसग्गि (5.1.10) relation, link.
संसट्ठ (5.1.34) besmeared, unclean; -कप्प (chu 2.6) mode of receiving food with a besmeared laddle.
संसक्त (6.24) connected.
संसार-सायर (6.65) worldly ocean.
संसेइम (4.9) life born in sweat; (5.1.75) unclean water.
सओवसंत (6.68) always calm.
सक्कणिज्ज, सक्क (chu 2.12) able to perform.
सक्करा (5.1.84) sand.
सक्कारण, सक्कारए, सक्कार (9.1.12) treat, adore.
सक्कुलि (5.1.71) a sweetmeat.
स-खुड्ड-वियत्ताण (6.6) खुड्ड young; वियत्ताण old.
सच्च-रय 9.3.13) devoted to truth; -वाइ (9 3.3) truthful; (ा) मोसा- (7.4) truth mixed with falsehood; सच्चा (7.2) truth.
सचित्त, सच्चित्त (3.7) with life/living object.
सजोइय (8.8) with fire.
सज्झाण (8.62) meditation.
सज्झाय (5.1.93) reading of holy texts.
सढ (9.2.3) deceitful, cunning.
सत्त (4.4.) existence.
सत्ति, सत्थ,-परिणय (4.4) a weapon, weapon.
सत्तु चुण्ण (5.1.71) barley powder.

सद्द (8.26) word, sound.

सन्निर (5.1.70) green vegetables with leaves.

सन्निवेस (5.2.5) village.

सन्निहि (श्रो) (3.3) accumulation, collection; -काम (6.18) one who desires accumulation.

सपिंडपाय (5.1.87) with food articles begged.

सप्पि (6.17) *ghee*, clarified butter.

सप्पुरिस (chu 2.15) good man.

सबीयग, सबीय (4.8) a flora with ten states starting with seed. For details, see note.

सभितर-बाहिर (4.sl.17) within and without.

स-भिक्खु Chapter 10 of *Daśavaikālika*.

समइक्कंत जोव्वण (chu 1) youth having passed.

समण (1.3) monk; -भट्ठाण (5.1.40) for the sake of a monk; -धम्म (8.42) ways of a monk.

समणुजाण (4.10) approve.

समत्तमाउहे (8.61) one properly armed.

समाउत्त (7.49) adorned with (traits).

समाए पेहाए (2.4) with equanimity.

समागय (5.2.7) come.

समायर (4.11) behave.

समारंभ (3.4) begin: -जोइणे Ignite fire; दंडं समारंभेज्जा (4.10) cause injury.

समावन्न (5.2.2) obtain, attain.

समावयंत (9.3.8) forthcoming.

समासेज्ज (8.45) touching.

समाहिय, समाहि (5.1.26) one with concentration, concentration.

समीरिय (8.62) purified.

समुक्कस (5.2.30) pride.

समुद्धर (10.14) rescue.

समुपेहिया, समुप्पेह (7.3) consider.

समुप्पन्न (7.46) be born, originate.

समुयाण, समुदाण (5.2.25) begging, wandering for begging.

समुवे (9.2.1) grow.

समुस्सय (6.16) height, heap.

समोसढ (6.1) come, entered.

सम्मं	(4.sl.9) rightly, properly.
सम्मदिया, सम्मद्दमाण	(5.1.29) being trampled.
सम्मद्दिट्ठे	(4.28) one with equanimity.
सम्मय	(8.60) agree.
सम्मुच्छिम	(4.8) plant born without seed, life that grows anywhere.
सय	(5.1.6) good people : (4.sl.7) lie, सयं (4.10) self; सयण (2.2) bed; सयमाण (4.sl.4) lying.
सयल	(6.4) all, full.
सरीसिव	(7.22) snake.
सविज्जविज्जा	(6.69) knowledge of self. Cf. स्वइति अप्पा विज्जा विन्नाणं आत्मनि विद्या सविज्जा.
स-वक्क-सुद्धि	(7.55) purifying speech.
सव्वत्तग	(4.21) going/moving everywhere, unrestricted.
सव्वत्थ	(6.21) everywhere, at all places.
सव्वभाव	(8.16) in all respects.
सव्वभुय-सुहावह	(6.3) giving happiness to all living beings.
सव्वसंगावगये	(10.16) with all attachments gone out.
सव्व-संजय	(4.sl.10) all-restrained, monk.
स-सक्ख	(5.2.36) in one's own presence.
ससरक्ख	(4.18) covered with dust.
ससार	(7.35) with stalks full of corn.
ससेइम	(5.1.75) unclean water.
ससिणिद्ध	(4.19) wet.
साइ	(chu 1) crook.
साइम	(4.16) dry fruits.
सागर	(9.3.14) sea, ocean; सागरोवम (chu 1) measure of a very long period of time.
साणी-पावार-पिहियं	(5.1.18) screen made from hemp or fur.
सामणिय, सामण्णमि, सामण्ण	(2.1) monkhood; -पुव्वय Chapter 2 of *Daśavaikālika*.
सामिणी	(7.16) mistress of the household; सामिय (7.19) master.
सायग, साय	(4.sl.26) one who tastes happiness, happiness, सायाउलग (4.26) keen after pleasure.

सारक्ख	(5.2.36) protect, preserve.
साला	(7.31), साहा (4.21) branch.
सावज्ज	(6.36) sin; -बहुलं full of mighty sins; -अणुमोयणी (7.54) words supporting sin.
सासय	(4.sl.25) fixed, permanent; (7.4) inclination.
साहण	(5.1.92) spiritual practice.
साहम्मिय	(10.9) brother-in-faith.
साहस	(9.2.22) discourteous, inconsiderate. Cf. साहसिकः अकृत्यकरणपरः ।
सिअ	(4.21) white *camara* (hair).
सीइभूएण	(8.59) being indifferent.
सिंगबेर	(3.7) ginger.
सिंघाण	(8.18) nose dirt.
सिज्झ, सिद्ध, सिद्धि	(3.14) be perfected, perfection, perfect; -मग्ग (3.15) road to liberation.
सिणायंत, सिणाय, सिणाण	(3.2) bathe, bath; (6.63) face powder.
सिणेह	(8.15) minute water particles, dews.
सिप्प (I)	(9.2.13) craft.
सिरी	(9.2.4) goddess Shri, goddess of wealth and fortune; सिरिओ, सिरि (chu 1) grace, beauty, conduct.
सिला	(4.18) slab, stone; (8.6) hail-stone.
सिलेस	(5.1.45) sticky substance, shellac.
सिव	(7.51) free from all troubles.
सिहि	(9.1.3) flame.
सीईभूय	(8.59) being indifferent.
सुउद्धर	(9.3.7) easily removable.
सुएणजुत्ते	(8.63) versed in the *Śrutas*.
सुट्ठिअप्प	(3.1) with soul properly tranquilised.
सुतित्था	(7.36) with good banks.
सुतोसअ	(5.2.34) one who is easy to please.
सुत्त	(4.18) sleeping; (10.15) *Sūtra*; सुत्तत्थ, सुत्तस्स अत्थो (chu 2.11) meaning of the *Sūtra*; -मग्ग (chu 2.11) way depicted by the *Sūtra*.
सुदंसण	(chu 1) Mount Meru.
सुनिसिय	(10.2) sharp (weapon).
सुप्पणिहिंदिअ	(5.2.50) with organs of senses under control.

सुय	(4.1) (already) heard; (8.30) *Śruta*, *Āgamas*, -ग्गाहि (9.2.16) desirous of acquiring *Śruta* knowledge; -त्थधम्म (9.2.23) one who has heard the import of *Śruta*; and likewise सुयलाभ, सुयबुद्धोववेया, सुय-समाहि ।
सुरुट्ठ	(9.1.5) highly displeased.
सुलट्ठ	(7.41) exceedingly nice.
सुसंवुड	(10.7) well-protected against the influx of *karma*.
सुसमाउत्त	(6.3) devoted.
सुसमाहि-इंदिय	(7.57) with organs of senses fully controlled.
सुसमाहिय	(3.12) well concentrated.
सुस्सूसमाण, सुस्सूस (ा)	(9.1.17) desirous to listen; -वयणंकरा (9.2.12) careful to listen and obey.
सुहड	(7.41) well removed/stolen.
सुहर	(8.25) satisfied with small quantity.
सुहुम	(4.11) minute beings.
सूइय	(5.1.98) spiced
सूइया	(5.1.12) delivered, given birth.
सेज्जायर पिंड	(3.5) food with lodging.
सेय	(2.7) bliss.
सेलेसी	(4.23) rock-like, fixed in equanimity.
सोउमल्ल, सोअमल्ल	(2.5) attachment for comfort.
सोअ	(5.2.6) think.
सोंडिया	(5.2.38) state of intoxication, typsy.
सोग्गइ	(5.1.100) good state.
सोच्चाण, सोच्चा	(2.10) on hearing, hear.
सोय	(9.2.3) flow, current.
सोवक्केस	(chu 1) with pain.
सोवच्चल	(3.8) name of a mountain in the north with salt quarry.
सोह-वज्जण, सोह	(6.7) augmenting beauty, beauty, decoration.
सोहि	(5.2.50) purification.
हड	(2.9) flora growing in water.
हत्थग, हत्थ	(4.18) hand; हत्थग (5.1.83) a piece of cloth to cover mouth; हत्थगम्मि (5.1.78) hollow of the palm.

हरतणुग — (4.19) water drops coming up from the earth. Cf. हरतणुओ भूमिं भेत्तूण उट्ठेइ । Also हरतनुः भूमिमुद्भिद्य तृणाग्रादिषु भवति ।

हरिय — (4.22) grass, greenery.

हव्ववाह — (6.34) fire.

हस्सकुहअ — (10.20) make others laugh.

हाअ — (8.35) to be reduced.

हिय — (4.17) bliss; -अणुसासणं (4.4) good prescription; -माणुलोमिया (7.56) words that are good and favourable.

हीण-पेसण — (9.2.23) one who obeys not the words of the superiors.

हीलयंत, हीलणा, हीलिय, हील — (9.1.2) neglect, disrespect.

हेट्ठ — (chu 1) low, downward.

हेमंत — (3.12) season of dew drop, winter.

होउकाम — (chu 2.2) with desires tranquilised.

होयव्वय — (8.3) future.